BUILDING BRITANNIA

Life Experience With Britain

edited by
Roxy Harris and Sarah White

New Beacon Books

George Padmore Institute

First published 2009 by New Beacon Books Ltd., 76 Stroud
Green Road, London N4 3EN, for the George Padmore Institute,
76 Stroud Green Road, London N4 3EN

All portrait photographs taken at the GPI sessions
courtesy Roxy Harris

Photos of Althea McNish's work courtesy John Weiss pp. 61-75

ISBN 978 1 873201 16 9

Printed by Imprint Digital, Exeter, England

Contents

GEORGE PADMORE INSTITUTE

The George Padmore Institute (GPI) is an archive, educational research and information centre housing materials relating mainly to the black community of Caribbean, African, Asian descent in Britain and continental Europe. It was founded in 1991. Its aims are to organise and sustain:

- an archive, library, educational resource, research and information centre, to allow the materials in its care to be available for use by interested individuals and groups, both in person at the GPI and through the use of modern storage, retrieval and communication methods;
- educational and cultural activities including conferences, courses, seminars, study programmes, talks and readings;
- the publication and dissemination of relevant materials.

For further information please see our website
www.georgepadmoreinstitute.org

Introduction

This book is the second volume of a series subtitled *Life Experience with Britain*, the first volume being *Changing Britannia*, published in 1999. The subtitle was carefully chosen by the late John La Rose, chairman of the George Padmore Institute, who sadly died on 28 February 2006. John's selection of the words ***with Britain*** rather than simply ***in Britain*** was deliberate. He wanted to emphasise that the people describing their lives in the series were people who had a significant part of their formation outside Britain – in the Caribbean, to be precise.

In another of John's memorable phrases, for these people and indeed for John himself, it was important to note that, 'We did not come alive in Britain'. This phrase reflects two complementary strands. Firstly, the impact on, and contribution of, the African Caribbean diaspora, in British society; and secondly, the way in which this influence has been developed on the basis of the historical continuities and traditions of resistance emanating from the Caribbean. In John's view this perception was important for both white British people and black British people of Caribbean descent to apprehend.

It is to be regretted that although the talks on which this volume is based took place in 1999, we were unable to produce this book in time for John to see it. The spirit of his infectious enthusiasm and participation in the talks permeates the texts. He would have understood very well our failure to publish the book more quickly. The George Padmore Institute is an institution run by volunteers and, in the period since 1999, we have staged a very wide range of events and activities and also published *A Meeting of the Continents: The International Book Fair of Radical Black and Third World Books – Revisited* in 2005. John's view, though, was very clear – in order to build solid and lasting institutions black people in Britain had to get used to doing what we could with what we have. As far as he was concerned, we in the George Padmore Institute had to see ourselves as 'slow builders and consolidators, not flash and dash'.

As will be evident from this introduction, John La Rose's leadership and guidance is irreplaceable and will be sorely missed. Throughout 2006 and early 2007 many tribute events to John were staged in different parts of Britain. The centrepiece of many of these events was the film *Dream to Change the World* directed by Horace Ové. This covers John's background in Trinidad, his ideas on the relationship between culture and politics, and some of his work in Britain.

Building Britannia emerged from a series of talks and conversations in front of an audience at the George Padmore Institute during 1999. Each of the speakers described the relationship between their childhood experiences in the Caribbean and their subsequent 'Life Experience with Britain'. Dennis Bovell (Barbados) describes his development into a pioneering musician and producer in reggae and popular music. Althea McNish (Trinidad) explains how her early artistic talent flowered into a career in fabric and textile design. Gus John (Grenada) outlines his unexpected trajectory from trainee catholic priest to campaigner for racial equality and social justice and later chief education officer. Wilfred Wood (Barbados) traces his journey to the top of the Church of England as the first black bishop in that institution. Aggrey Burke (Jamaica) explores the links between his youth in the Caribbean, his student years in the UK and his eventual career as a psychiatrist. Yvonne Brewster (Jamaica) gives a vivid account of the roots of her training and later career in drama both as an actor and producer in theatre and television. Finally, Alexis Rennie (Grenada) gives an enlightening insight into his life as a black engineer in Britain in the rarely noted arena of civil engineering and construction.

Apart from the assertion 'We did not come alive in Britain' the talks in the *Life Experience With Britain* series were informed by an additional phrase which John La Rose often deployed. He frequently referred to what he described as 'The Heroic Generation'. What he had in mind was that group of Caribbean men and women whose principal characteristics were a pioneering courage, collective endeavour, self-sacrifice and staying power. From the end of the 1940s until the end of the 1960s they set sail optimistically for Britain in regular waves. Initially surprised by the tide of hostility which greeted them on arrival, they met it head on, dug in against it, laughed at it, but above all survived, and built strong foundations of relative success and prosperity for their children and grandchildren.

The *Life Experience With Britain* talks on which this book series is based, attempt to give a detailed account of how these achievements were constructed.

Roxy Harris – 2009

Dennis Bovell
in Conversation with Linton Kwesi Johnson (25.01.1999)

Roxy Harris: Welcome to the second series of talks of the George Padmore Institute's 'Life Experience With Britain'. My name is Roxy Harris. I'm a trustee of the George Padmore Institute and I'm very excited this evening. We're going to have a conversation between Linton Kwesi Johnson and Dennis Bovell. Dennis Bovell doesn't know this but I'm one of his great admirers, in fact I'm going to tap him later to see if I can get a copy of a record called *Blue Beat and Ska*, the 12 inch version. Nobody ever mentions that record but I thought it was a great record when it came out.

In the course of the evening, as John said in the first series, I hope we're going to find out a lot of things about Dennis, his music and the things that have influenced the rest of us in music that we didn't know before. Of course one of the questions we all want to know is how come a Bajan took reggae and ran away with it? So I hope everybody enjoys the evening and I will now hand over to Linton Kwesi Johnson.

Linton Kwesi Johnson: Before we get into the conversation I would like to say a few words about Dennis and myself because we go back a long way and we've been friends for a very long time.

Dennis and I belong to the generation of young blacks who came to Britain during the early to the mid 1960s and went through secondary education in this country. We belong to the rebel generation, that generation that was **the** problem generation for the British state. We had ambition, we had drive, but we weren't prepared to put up with some of the things that our parents put up with. We weren't prepared to tolerate what they had tolerated and to endure what they had endured. Some of us even went as far as rejecting what we saw as 'shit work'. We embraced black power. Our heroes were Huey P Newton, Malcolm X, Angela Davis, Muhammed Ali, the Soledad brothers. We had our own identity, a distinctive sub-culture based around sound systems, the blues

1

dance and reggae music. We expressed our rebellion in the language of Rastafari and through reggae music.

And it was because of music that I got to know Dennis. We first met nearly 25 years ago. In those days I was a serious student of reggae music whilst studying sociology at Goldsmiths College. I was also an apprentice freelance journalist doing the occasional reggae interview for 'Caribbean Magazine', which was a programme of the BBC World Service broadcast to the Caribbean. I went to interview Dennis's band, Matumbi. At the time they were well on their way to becoming the top reggae band in this country. I think it was at the Four Aces Club in Dalston –

Dennis Bovell: That's correct, yeah.

Linton Kwesi Johnson: – and, so that's how we met. A few years later we began a musical collaboration which has lasted so far over 20 years. I have no doubt in my own mind that I would not have been able to achieve the modest success, that I've been able to achieve as a reggae recording artist over the last 20 years, without Dennis's invaluable creative genius.

I would be hard pressed, I think, to think of any black musician in this country who has had the range and depth of involvement in, and impact on, popular music in Britain and abroad, that Dennis Bovell has achieved. Over the last 25 years he has earned for himself an international reputation, not only as a talented multi-instrumentalist, but also as a composer, vocalist, producer, arranger, recording engineer, dub master, film music scorer and band leader. He's a pioneer of British reggae and the form Lover's Rock. He's toured all over the world playing reggae music and sometimes rock music too. He was a presenter of the BBC television programme *Rock School* which taught people how to play rock music. He composed and arranged television theme music. He's mixed for various artists including Wet Wet Wet, Marvin Gaye. He's recorded Fela Kuti, Ryuichi Sakamoto, Pamberi Steel Orchestra among others. He's produced the Slits, Bananarama, Louisa Mark, Janet Kay, I-Roy, Errol Dunkley and many others. For me, ladies and gentlemen, Dennis Bovell is the Quincy Jones of reggae music. Welcome, Dennis.

Now, you were born in 1953, in a village called Rose Hill in the parish of St Peter, Barbados. Can you tell us something about your family background and your early childhood memories of your native Barbados?

Dennis Bovell: My grandfather – Good Evening – my grandfather was a minister in the Seventh Day Adventist church and also the choirmaster, as it were. He also taught music to the local young people in our village that were interested in learning music, and therefore there were always people in the house taking music lessons from my grandfather. Also, his sons and the younger brother of my grandmother had a quartet that sang religious music on the radio. They had a show, that was the equivalent of 'Stars on Sunday' on Rediffusion, on the radio and they would sing religious music. That was my early kind of family background and my connection with music and that was what made me want to be involved.

Linton Kwesi Johnson: Well, you've anticipated my next question: how did you become involved?

Dennis Bovell: Well, I actually became involved because of my mother's youngest brother, Samuel R Headley his name is. He was a musician, much against the wishes of my grandfather, because he was playing secular music and my grandfather was dead set against this because he was like 'that's the devil's music,' you know, 'no son of mine,' as it were. But he got away with it because he was the youngest member of the family, the youngest boy in the family and was a bit more wayward than the others. And he was playing with a band called Barbara and the Rhythmeers, which was quite a famous band in Barbados, and he bought a guitar. He had to go to town to school, and we lived in the country, so whilst he was away at school I'd pick up the guitar and try and have a go at it. Not until I broke a few strings did he say, 'All right then, I don't want you

3

breaking any more of my strings, so what I'll do is I'll teach you how to play so that you don't break them, OK?' That suited me fine and I was on the way.

Linton Kwesi Johnson: You came to this country in 1965 to join your parents. You settled in Battersea and you attended Spencer Park School. What were your early experiences of England?

Dennis Bovell: Aside from the mods and rockers and the racial tension that used to be in the playground every day. My first two weeks of school, I remember, the school playground would be black kids this side, white kids this side, fight at 4.30 pm.

And then I met some white boys that had musical instruments but couldn't play and I could play but I didn't have any instruments. So we traded. I said, 'I'll teach you how to play that if you lend it to me occasionally.' Then I convinced my mother she should buy me a guitar and we formed a band in 1965, just about Christmas '65, that was just to play pop music and what was going on at the time. I was just about coming up to 13 years old.

Linton Kwesi Johnson: Who were some of your early musical influences at that time?

Dennis Bovell: Well at that time I would say Nat King Cole, Sammy Davis Junior, then moving on to the Beatles, the Rolling Stones, Lord Kitchener, the Mighty Sparrow for sure. Then there would be like the Skatalites, Desmond Dekker, the Pioneers, that was the kind of – oh, Otis Redding certainly, Booker T and the MGs definitely.

Linton Kwesi Johnson: What was the name of the band that you were involved in at school?

Dennis Bovell: That band was called Road Works Ahead. In fact we helped ourselves to one of Wandsworth Borough Council's – at that time it was Battersea County Council – we helped ourselves to one of their signs, you know, the triangle thing that said 'Road Works Ahead'. That was like, our logo, and one night a council official came and took it back, – 'That belongs to the council, lads, you're lucky not to be charged!'

Linton Kwesi Johnson: Was that the only band you were involved in at school?

Dennis Bovell: No. At that same time I was playing with a band of boys my own age, and that was what we call 'bubble gum music', you know, like Simple Simon; the 1910 Fruit Gum Company, I think, was the name of our favourite band at the time, and there were other boys in the sixth form that were playing soul music. They were playing Otis Redding, Booker T and the MGs. They needed a bass player and I told them, 'I can play the bass,' but I was just believing that I could. Then I borrowed the bass guitar from a friend, went home that night with the record, learned the bass part and then I was back at school with these much bigger boys. And they thought, 'We can't see you,' so they put me to stand on the piano. I was playing with these older boys and I didn't know whether I wanted to be with the bigger boys or with the boys of my own age. Because with the boys of my own age I was more of a teacher and with the bigger boys I was learning something.

Linton Kwesi Johnson: All right. What year did you leave school?

Dennis Bovell: Oh, I tried very hard to forget that. 1970 I think.

Linton Kwesi Johnson: Well, like myself, you got married soon after you left school.

Dennis Bovell: That's right.

Linton Kwesi Johnson: What did you do to earn a living?

Dennis Bovell: Well, I became a contact lens technician because I was the only member of my family that didn't wear glasses and I was, you know, concerned about finding a way to help them. And someone said to me, 'Why don't you make contact lenses?' So I went with the intention of perhaps becoming an optician, that's how I started out. And when I left school the Careers Officer said, 'Right then,' and there I was, along to the contact lens lab, and I did it for about a year, I think.

Linton Kwesi Johnson: And what happened, did you get fired?

Dennis Bovell: Well, yeah, I got the sack because it didn't go along with playing sound system all night long in the club and going home at 5.00 am and getting up to be at work at 8.30 am and then working until 5.30 pm and then going off to another club again at 7.00 pm, another sound system do and so, you know, you get tired. So the work suffered a bit because of it, because instead of getting there at 8.30 am, I'd get there at 10.30 am, but I did all the work. And I was supposed to be doing an apprenticeship and I said, 'Well, this is five years.' 'Yeah,' I thought, 'Slave labour, I'm going to work for a boy's wages for five years,' whereas I'd learned to do the man's job within six months. And I kept saying to them, 'Look, just give me the money, I won't tell anyone... No? Well give me the certificate.' You know how it is and they said, 'I tell you what I'm going to do for you, I'm going to help you to become a really good musician, you're fired!'

Linton Kwesi Johnson: And what did you do then?

Dennis Bovell: Well, I took another job working in a wine merchants. I met this man who said to me, 'You know there are no black wine tasters?' I said, 'Really?' He said, 'I think I could teach you how to taste wine.' I said 'Really?' So I embarked on working for this firm called Morton and Langridge, who were the first firm to tin wine, so you can see what philistines they were. Then, I had to leave that job as well because about that time Matumbi had its first release and that didn't go together, working there and playing gigs as well. After being taken to wine tastings, one day I decided, 'This is nonsense, the spitting it out.' So I drank about 30 or 40 different brands of wine, which made the ceiling spin.

Linton Kwesi Johnson: So it was the end of your wine tasting?

Dennis Bovell: That was the end of my wine tasting career.

Linton Kwesi Johnson: Well, you talked about the conflict between your sound system work and your day jobs. How did you become involved in sound systems? Where did you learn about them? Who were your influences and who were some of the sound systems that you played against?

Dennis Bovell: Right. Well, at school I did typography and I was in charge of printing the school magazine. So I was in charge of the printing press and, as a little bit of extra curricular, I got friendly with a lot of sound system people. They used to print these very pretty cards announcing the blues dances at the weekends. I used to print cards for Duke Reid, for Sir Coxsone, for Jim Daddy, for Rocket 69, quite a lot of sound systems. My father used to dabble in that world because he had a bit of a sound system and knew these people and so, because they knew that I could print these cards cheaper than they could get them in the printers, I was printing them at school in the lunch-break. I had the good fortune to have a recording studio built at school where I would, after hours, go and run off a few dubs and tapes. Some of them were put in sound systems as well.

I met up with an old friend who I hadn't seen for a long time and he said, 'Oh, I'm just building a sound system,' and they had, you know, a need of records. So he came to my house to see what I could offer him and to my surprise he wanted to buy everything I had. So I said, 'Well, instead of you buying all these records, why don't I give you these records and why don't I come in with you on the sound system? Have you got a DJ?' He said, 'No.' So that was it. 'I'll be the DJ, I'll make the records and stuff, you know, for the exclusive dubs that we want to play and say these are exclusive to our sound system. We can get the equipment together and you can be in charge of that.' He was an electrician. He got a job to rewire the Barbados Embassy when they moved to Belgravia. So he took all that money and bought amplifiers and speakers and records with it and we were off. Sufferer Hi-Fi.

Linton Kwesi Johnson: So, what were some of the venues that you played and who were some of the sound systems you played against? What was the sound system scene like in those days?

Dennis Bovell: The sound system scene in those days was murder because there was a lot of in-fighting between sound systems. Our sound system would go to play against another in a different area. If a sound system from Battersea went to play in Brixton they would more than likely end up in a fight, or if a sound system from Battersea went to play in Ladbroke Grove. If you went out of your area, you would end up fighting because the supporters of the other sound would start something, or your supporters would start something. So we thought what we're going to do is, we're going to preach peace and love about the sound system. We're going to involve more, you know, girls in the dance, because the sound system was predominantly boys who would go there and just stand there, not even dancing. They would stand there and go, 'That's not a very good record, put something else on.' It struck me why were they there, it's supposed to be a club, they're supposed to be dancing to it, you know, enjoying it, instead of going, 'Haven't you got any better records than that?' And so we tried to introduce girls and to make records with girls, get them singing and get them involved in the thing, get it to a love scene, you know, as opposed to war.

Linton Kwesi Johnson: What was your most memorable clash?

Dennis Bovell: Well, probably I've got two memorable clashes.

The first one was with Fat Man, who was from this part of town. We were just down the road there where there was a record shop called Bamboo on this street, at number 88 Stroud Green Road. We were standing in there one Friday evening buying records and we were going to play against each other that same night and the guy put this record on. I thought, 'I'm not buying that,' and he bought it. And that night in the clash he put this record on and said, 'If you play this record, I'll smash my sound system' and he knew that I didn't buy it because we were buying records that day! I'm going, 'It's crap, it's crap' and he said, 'Well, I'm the only one who can play it and you can't play it,' and I'm going 'It's crap.' And it taught me a lesson – you must buy everything and please the crowd. It's not what you want, it's what they want, right?

And then the other clash was one night in the Carib Club, in Cricklewood. The police came in and caused a scene.

Linton Kwesi Johnson: We'll go on to that, you're jumping ahead of yourself.

Dennis Bovell: Well, you asked about the memorable bits, so ...

Linton Kwesi Johnson: All right. Earlier on you talked about the influences of your grandfather and your uncles and that was significant. Why haven't you said anything about your parents? Were your parents not involved in music?

Dennis Bovell: Well, actually, I thought the reason I became a musician was because I was the first production of my mum and dad. My dad was supposed to have been a student of my grandad, but whilst he was there I don't think he learned much about music! I think he learned more about my mum. And being the first production I thought, well, it was music that made me, it brought them together and I was the first product.

Linton Kwesi Johnson: But your dad used to study music and put on blues dances and all that.

Dennis Bovell: That's right, yeah. My dad used to have a party in the house every couple of weeks or so, you know, against mum's wishes – 'What's all this noise, noise, noise, noise, turn it off!' And he was also a student of the Royal College of Music.

Linton Kwesi Johnson: And your mother can read music as well?

Dennis Bovell: Oh yeah, to this day my mother's the choir mistress at the Brixton Seventh Day Adventist Church.

Linton Kwesi Johnson: Before we get on to Matumbi, you were talking about Cricklewood. You were one of the famous Cricklewood Twelve. Can you tell us who the Cricklewood Twelve were and what was your relationship to them?

Dennis Bovell: The Cricklewood – the other eleven were no friends of mine. I had never met them until we were sat in the dock at the Old Bailey, and this was supposed to be my gang and we were supposed to have beaten up police officers and I was supposed to have egged them on and orchestrated the whole thing, but yet I didn't know any of my soldiers!

Linton Kwesi Johnson: How were you have supposed to have egged them on? Tell us what happened.

Dennis Bovell: This is Friday the 13th of October and we're playing in Cricklewood above Burton's the tailor – and it's a big clash because I've got in my corner Lee 'Scratch' Perry, the Upsetter –

Linton Kwesi Johnson: The famous reggae producer from Jamaica.

Dennis Bovell: Very famous. Yes, if you've ever heard the Cadbury's chocolate advert [Tune sung by DB] ... that's the man, amongst other things, right? And he produced lots of Bob Marley tunes as well. He'd just arrived from Jamaica and I'd gone to meet him at the airport and he brought me a whole bag of exclusive records that were fresh, fresh off the press. And Bunny Lee who was his old enemy from Jamaica. I mean, the sound system clash was born in Jamaica where two sound systems would play off against each other and try and play as much new music, exclusive music as they could against each other, 'Yeah, I've got this by so-and-so,' 'Yeah but I've got this by so-and-so,' and it would be like that all night and the crowd reaction would judge how much the crowd enjoyed it and who won the clash. And this clash, this night, it was a strange clash, because instead of normally one on one, it was one on two. I was playing against two different sound systems.

Linton Kwesi Johnson: Who were?

Dennis Bovell: Who were Lord Koos and another sound system called Count Nick's. Now, Count Nick's was the resident sound system and Lord Koos was the bad boy of Harlesden. I'd promised to give him a thrashing because my band, Matumbi, were involved with backing, playing the music for a singer called Johnny Clarke, who was the flavour of the time and was in London for his first concert tour. And my band were the musicians. So his producer had given me all the exclusives that they had also given to Lord Koos but they didn't know that we were going to meet in the clash. He'd given them to him quite innocently and he'd given them to me quite innocently and then we were going to meet. So I had him snookered. I knew that that was like his top records, and I had the whole lot of them, right, and I had new ones that Lee 'Scratch' Perry had just brought me that day and there was no chance that he was going to get them because Koos and Bunny Lee were friends but Lee 'Scratch' Perry was a friend of no-one.

Linton Kwesi Johnson: The Upsetter!

Dennis Bovell: The Upsetter is his name, the Upsetter! So, I was waiting for Koos to play the first Johnny Clarke record or the first

Bunny Lee production, just to zap him back with it and go, 'You've played that.' And the trick was, I mean these records are called acetates and they're just one-off cuts, right, one-off cuts, and you'd play it, then I'd take an old record and go, 'This is what you played' and smash it and say, 'Well, I'll never play that again,' or I'd just play a bit and go smash that and not play that again, right, and ridicule him, as it were. And so all the way I was on him, on him, on him waiting for the moment to play my top record because I'd played before that at a place called the Metro, from 7.00 pm to 11.00 pm, so I had had a chance to sort out my records and air them for the first time. And the public would follow me from Ladbroke Grove to Cricklewood and then we would begin that session at midnight and end about 6.00 am.

So there I was waiting for him to come out with all his stuff, right, and he knew that I had them as well, right, and the time was getting on and the crowd was like, 'Go on get him now, get him now, do him, do him, do him!' So I put on this record called 'Vix' by Don Drummond Junior – what's his name again? – Vin Gordon, Vin Gordon. Now this tune started off like a real ragtime tune and then went into some serious heavy dub. On the first touch of the heavy dub from the ragtime beginning, the crowd went ape. But it coincided with some policemen coming out of the toilets with a prisoner that they had taken. And when the crowd went ape, my opinion is that the prisoner's friends saw their chance to snatch their friend from this policeman, which they did, right?

Linton Kwesi Johnson: Just to mention, some guy had done something and run inside.

Dennis Bovell: That's what they said. They said that they'd stopped a guy outside driving a car suspiciously and that, upon trying to question him, he had run into the nightclub. The doorman had said no one had run into the club because you couldn't run into that club. You'd be beaten to smithereens if you tried that. You see the size of bouncers at the door you would know not to try that, right? Especially if you were coming from somewhere else and you weren't one of the sons of the doormen or the son of the owner of the club, there's no way you'd get in. And the crowd – the queue to get in there, the people in the queue – would have had you for jumping the queue, right? So anyway they gone into the club and they'd gone into the toilets and arrested someone in the toilet and were taking him out. Then, because my sound system was the nearest to the toilets, the commotion upset my sound and it wouldn't work after that, the amplifiers and stuff like that, wires out, plugs out. Then the other sound, Lord Koos, on the other side of the room, started playing anti-police songs, you know 'Beat down Babylon', right. All that was attributed to me in the trial. But because I didn't want to be a grass, when I was in the police station they'd go, 'Well, if you didn't do it, who did do it? Go on, tell me.' I was going, 'Well, I don't know.' They were going, 'Don't give me that, you were there. Tell me. All you got to do is give me the names.' So I made the mistake of saying to this Detective Chief Inspector, 'Why don't you find out for yourself, Sherlock?' And that was my undoing! Because he then said to me, 'I tell you what, right, I don't have to do anything, right, if you don't tell me who it was I'm just going to say it was you. And that's it.' And he called some guy in who I'd never seen before and he said, 'You saw him?' 'Yes, sir, that was him.'

Linton Kwesi Johnson: And what were you charged with?

Dennis Bovell: I was charged with inciting a riot and causing an affray because what had happened was this police officer said he came into the club, asked the owner to switch all the lights on, the owner switched the lights on, the place was fully lit and I stood on the stage with a microphone in my hand saying, 'Get the boys in blue.' I don't know how I'd be saying that to a bunch of black people, 'Get the boys in blue,' right, and I was inciting this crowd. I wanted to ask him, 'Why didn't you arrest me then, if I was doing that?' Right? And then all the other police officers that were supposed to have been in the room came in and said it was too dark, we couldn't see a damn thing, right? But they believed this one guy.

He said 'I've had 19 years' experience, they're just a bunch of rookies. The lights were full on. Right? OK? And I saw him with the microphone in his hand.'... Complete fabrication.

Linton Kwesi Johnson: So what happened at the trial? And with the other eleven?

Dennis Bovell: Well, in about a week or so the client of Rudy Narayan was excused because he was causing so much trouble in the defence. This was the first time there was going to be 12 black people and 12 black lawyers in the Old Bailey, and Narayan's client was excused earlier on. At the end of the trial nine of the 12 were acquitted. Three, of which I was one, had a hung jury and, British justice being what it is – and me thinking a person's innocent until you are proved guilty, if the jury hasn't found you guilty it hasn't been proved, they should have let me go – but the judge said, 'Well, this is more than my job's worth and it's going to have to be a retrial.' Then there was three of us back in the dock of Court Number One in the Old Bailey where they send IRA murderers and people that kill people and abductors of little children and that sort of stuff. There I was defending myself. And that second trial lasted three months. The first trial lasted nine months. So I was at the Old Bailey every day from 10.00 am till 4.00 pm for nine months. And then to be told 'retrial' and that lasted three months every day 10.00 am till 4.00 pm, nearly losing my bail several times. One morning I got there late and the judge said, 'Why are you late?' 'Because of the traffic.' 'What bus did you get?' 'Number 19.' 'You're a liar, I get the number 19!' 'You're late for this court another day you're going to lose your bail!' Camp outside the door!

Linton Kwesi Johnson: What was the verdict?

Dennis Bovell: They deliberated from about 12 midday. At five minutes to ten the judge called us in and said, 'Look, if they haven't come back with the verdict by 10.00 pm we're going to have to throw the whole thing out. Right?' At five to ten or two minutes to ten, verdict. All right, great, gone in there. 'How do you say?' 'Dennis Bovell guilty.' 'And is that the verdict of you all?' 'No. It's a majority verdict. Ten to two.' 'I'll accept that,' he said. Next guy same thing. Next guy acquitted. Now, the third guy that was acquitted, his story was that he was with me when the whole thing happened, right? In fact, when I was charged he came to the police station and bailed me. Then, two weeks or three weeks later he was nicked as having done something so that I could lose my surety when I went to court but, luckily that day I had my Mum with me, otherwise I'd have gone inside. If your surety is charged with a crime, then you got no surety so – inside. And I said 'Oh, my Mum's here. Mum!' And, yeah, I got bail.

Linton Kwesi Johnson: What was the sentence?

Dennis Bovell: Well, they sentenced me to three years in prison.

Linton Kwesi Johnson: And where did you serve your time?

Dennis Bovell: In Wormwood Scrubs. I went to Wormwood Scrubs. I was in 'A' Wing for about a month then I was put in 'C' Wing where I met up with loads of people that I had tried to stay away from all my life because I knew they were going there. I remember the first morning I woke up in jail, I was relieved that I didn't have to go to court that day, right? Well, they can't do anything more to me now, I'm in here, that's it. I lie in bed and I got out and I walked down the corridor and I see a fella, 'Argh! Expletive – expletive. Ha ha ha ha ha.' He's going, 'What are you doing? I thought you were in Jamaica?' 'Well, I brought something back with me and they decided to keep me.' So, it was off to a reasonable start and then I found ways of amusing myself in there by getting literature –

Linton Kwesi Johnson: Pornographic literature –

Dennis Bovell: Pornographic literature, yes! And leasing it to other prisoners, you know, just alleviating their spell inside.

15

Linton Kwesi Johnson: Anyway, you were a bit of a celebrity in Wormwood Scrubs and after six months you won your appeal.

Dennis Bovell: That's right.

Linton Kwesi Johnson: And you were out. Can you tell us something about your band Matumbi who at one time were the top reggae band in this country? Tell us the history of Matumbi because in those days it was very difficult for British reggae bands, the British reggae public saw them as being second-rate to the real Jamaica thing.

Dennis Bovell: Very much so.

Linton Kwesi Johnson: And often when a reggae band would be playing at a night club they would be the support act for the sound system. Matumbi was able to break through that prejudice. How did you do it?

Dennis Bovell: Because I had lots of friends in the sound system world and I was in the sound system world as well, I kind of knew what the latest things were. So we just learned them. All the new records that hadn't been released yet. So when we were playing on stage we wouldn't be playing stuff that had been released, we were playing stuff that the sound systems were playing and that was something that no band had ever done before. Bands were playing old Nat Cole songs, old Ben E King songs reggaefied – and we were playing the latest Burning Spear song – no one had ever seen Burning Spear but they'd heard the record, or the latest Bob Marley lick, you know. In fact one time, in a place called Huddersfield, when Burning Spear released his record called 'Old Slavery Days', some guy came up to me and went, 'There's a guy called Burning Spear released your record!' I was going, 'Well, actually it's his, but it's just you've never heard him sing it!' They think it's us. And we also were the backing for people like I-Roy, Pat Kelly, Ken Boothe and those were the artists of the day that were coming from

Jamaica. We were playing their latest stuff and we'd play that on stage and we'd sort of invented a way to play dub on stage as well with all the echo parts instead of using echo machines from the desk. We would do the echo part, we'd play in echo. And, you know, people seemed to like that.

Linton Kwesi Johnson: Who were the members of Matumbi? How did the band start?

Dennis Bovell: Well, one day at school we were singing in the woodwork shop, banging things and that. This teacher, we used to call him Iron Arse – Mr Williams – came in and said, 'Right you lot, you better sing for me' – what was it we had to sing? 'My Girl', or we'd all get the cane. Right? So we started out in a three-part harmony. It was like, 'You lot can do that? You should form a band.' By then my pop influences had gone astray, by this time I was hanging around more with Jamaican kids. That seemed to be the hip thing to do because every other band was playing soul music. Every other band was a soul band and there weren't any reggae bands in England apart from Greyhound, this group that had a hit with 'Black and White', you know that song, and then 'The Pied Piper' and they'd done reggae versions of them. There were Freddie Notes and the Rudies as well, but they were so big that they didn't play in England any more, they were on the continent a lot.

So there was an opening for a band to come through. And we decided, and people called it professional suicide, we decided to play ONLY reggae because there were bands that would play a few reggae tunes, a few soca tunes, a few funk tunes, a few soul ones, but we decided ONLY reggae. And we decided to speak on stage as though we'd never been to England before, but with the rawest and the streetest of Jamaican accents. It was considered disrespectful to do this in front of the elders. We went to this club called the Georgian in Croydon, where there's all the elders there dressed up in their evening gear, you know, Mr So-and-so, Mrs So-and-so out for the evening trying to get into the middle classes, long evening gowns and stuff. Then suddenly we would come on saying things, instead of 'Good Evening Ladies and Gentlemen,' it would be 'Wha happen?' 'It's all right, love man, reggae, 'ow dreadful to be 'ere, everyting dread,' you know! And you'd hear people go, 'Cheeky little fellow!' So, then we decided, yeah, only reggae, only reggae, and one-drop reggae, not the kind of Bob and Marcia style of reggae where it would be 'Young, Gifted and Black', that was too poppy for us, right? We were roots, we were writing songs about how much we hated Enoch Powell and stuff like that, and what we were, how we were going to take Africa and take it back and stuff like that.

Linton Kwesi Johnson: What were some of the early recordings that you made? Perhaps we can hear a bit of some of the early recordings that Matumbi made.

Dennis Bovell: Actually, the first Matumbi album has never been released to this day because we didn't pay the studio bill. Well, not us, our management didn't pay the studio bill and so the studio kept the record. The studio was closing down about five years ago and he called me up and said, 'You know, I've had this tape of yours for 25 years. You might as well have it back now!' So I said, 'No, I've paid you for all the stuff I've ever done in your studio.' He's going, 'No, there's one, there's one.' I'm going, 'All right then' and I sent my son to collect it because I thought he was having me on and he came back with the first original Matumbi recording. And I remembered thinking, when I listened to it that it wasn't all that good because we'd done a reggae version of 'Ten Green Bottles' and it was a sing and toast so the singer was singing and then I would toast a bit. Then at the end of the song it goes, 'So there's no green bottles left standing on the wall', right, and then the singer comes in 'One green bottle'! We then went to RG Jones Studio in Wimbledon where Brian Jones, who was the guitar player of the Rolling Stones, had a mellotron. We'd recorded all these songs that we wrote ourselves. At the end of the session I fancied doing a reggae version, completely against the band's wishes, because we'd sworn not to do any covers, I fancied doing a reggae version of Hot

Chocolate's 'Brother Louie', which is the story of a black and white liaison – it was a kind of Romeo and Juliet, the families were against it – and we decided to just do a little spoof up of it.

And we went proudly along to Trojan Records and said, 'We're budding new composers, we're the new Beatles of reggae. Listen to our work, isn't it great? Listen to that song about Enoch Powell.' They're like, 'Well, I don't know about that man, a bit racial there.' We'd go, 'Listen to that song there about how they treated us and stuff and what we're going to do.' They're going, 'Oh, no, no, no, we don't like them, sorry lads. But we like that cover version of the Hot Chocolate song.' We're going, 'No, no, no, no we don't want to put that out. We don't want to put that out!' 'Well, either you put that out or it's no deal.' And the band were not happy because I was not the singer and I was the one who was singing. We said, 'We can't have our first record out with the guitar player singing, what's the singer going to do, stand there doing backing vocals?'

Perhaps I should play you first a bit of the one that we wanted them to put out, this is because Enoch Powell had just made this speech about rivers of blood – and we were replying to it on record. This intro's the same as 'Everything I Own', by Ken Boothe. They took that from us!

[Plays excerpt of beginning of 'Enoch Powell' song:]

> Enoch Powell noh want we ya
> so we've got to go back to Africa
> they're making a bill, dat ah go pressure we 'til
> we go away to where we know we can stay
> he say : "Black man go back weh yuh come from"
> Black man go back weh yuh come from
> Black Man go back weh yuh come from
> Go back home
> Go back home
> go back home
>
> They took our gold and silver too
> but they don't want us cos we're Black and feeling Blue
> at their invitation we came to help England re-build

now Enoch's predicting that blood will be spilled
Black man go back weh yuh come from
black man go back weh yuh come from
Black man go back weh yuh come from
Go back home
Go back home
Go back home

Dennis Bovell: So they chose this one instead.
[Excerpt from beginning of 'Brother Louie' song:]
She was Black as the night
Louie was whiter than white
Danger danger when you taste brown sugar
Louie fell in love at first sight
nothing bad, it was good
Louie had the best girl he could
he brought her home to meet his mamma and papa
Louie knew just where he stood

Louie, louie, louie
louie, louie, louah
louie, louie, louie
louie you're gonna cry

Dennis Bovell: So we ran away and we paid for our own recordings again and made the song that was very popular. For two years we didn't release the song because the sound system played it everywhere, and that was the only way to ensure that the sound system played it, by not releasing it. Two years later we put it out in the same week that I was sentenced to three years in jail.

Linton Kwesi Johnson: What's that, 'After Tonight'? This is the song that really established Matumbi as the top reggae band in England at the time.
[Excerpt from the beginning of 'After Tonight' song:]

I'm your key
To set you free
You can come to me anytime for cover
Don't play shy
Let me try
It's you I really want and not another
Baby don't you fight
or get your little self get uptight, you know
Baby after tonight
Baby after tonight.

Linton Kwesi Johnson: And another big hit of the time was also a cover you did of a Bob Dylan tune.

Dennis Bovell: Well, I was writing a tune which had nothing to do with the Bob Dylan tune. Then I heard on the radio a group called the Persuasions, which was an American a cappella group. Their album was called *Street Corner Symphony* and on it they had done a version of one of Bob Dylan's songs like you never heard before. I mean, I had the Bob Dylan version and it was very wuh-wuh-wuh-wuh-wuh, and they had actually made it sound as though there was a melody there, right. They had! And I thought oh, brilliant. And that made me like that song because I hated the Bob Dylan version. And then I was doing this other song, I was trying to introduce a kind of, I don't know, Hank Marvin style into reggae –

Linton Kwesi Johnson: Tell them who Hank Marvin is.

Dennis Bovell: Well, Hank Marvin was the guitar player with the Shadows, Cliff Richard and the Shadows. Hank Marvin was the guitar player, and for a long time one of my idols as a guitar player until Jimi Hendrix came along and then he just blew him out of it. And I tried to do that kind of tone with the front of this tune. Then I couldn't think of anything to write and it struck me one day that the Bob Dylan melody, if I shuffled it around a bit, I could fit it on to this song. And I've regretted doing that ever since, because he's

21

taken all the publishing. This is the song. In fact, incidentally whilst I was in prison – we'd recorded these two songs together, and hadn't put them out. What's that guy, 'Little Help From My Friends'? Joe Cocker – Joe Cocker had gone to Jamaica and recorded a version of this same song with Sly Dunbar, Robbie Shakespeare and them lot, right? And I heard it on the radio and I thought he's trying to pip us to the post, we've got to put ours out. So we formed the Matumbi label and this was the first song on the Matumbi label.

[Excerpt from 'The Man in Me' song:]

> The man in me will do almost any time
> And as for compensation, there's little that he would ask
> It takes a woman like you to get through
> To the man in me
> It takes a woman like your kind to find
> The man in me

Linton Kwesi Johnson: Now, together with John Kpiaye, you were one of the pioneers of that British style of romantic reggae that we now know as Lover's Rock. In those days you were based at DIP Studios and Gooseberry Studios in Soho and you produced a lot of British reggae around that time. Can you tell us something about that period?

Dennis Bovell: Dennis Harris had just been successful with a Susan Cadogan tune 'Hurts So Good' and that had gone to number one in the charts. He'd also sold his supermarket and had a bit of money and wanted to open a recording studio. And the drummer of a group called Los Bravos, whose big hit was 'Black Is Black', was fed up with sitting at the back of the band while all the front members were getting all the adulation. He was also a very good electronics engineer, so he built an eight-track recording machine which Dennis sponsored. Dennis opened his own studio, and called the studio Eve Studios, and he was looking for a sound engineer, so he called me up. He said, 'Deal with it.' So we launched off into a record company putting out records and our aim was to put out an album every month. He also wanted another person involved and that was John Kpiaye. Now, I was a guitar player and John Kpiaye was a guitar player, and Dennis said to me one day, quite tactfully, 'You should start to play bass because you're crap at the guitar!' And he said, 'You're a good bass player but you're a crap guitarist. I've got someone who can play the guitar much better than you, right, so I don't want you to play guitar on my tunes.' I was like, 'Oh, thanks,' and he was, 'No, you're the sound engineer and bass player if you want but you're not the guitarist.' So I said, 'Well, bring this guy I want to see him.' And he brought the guy and when he sat the guy down, the guy started to play guitar. The first thing I said to him was, 'Do you want to join a group with me?' Because I thought I'm never going to be as good as that on the guitar. He just blew me away. So I thought I'd better learn how to play the bass and you're never going to play the bass as good as me. 'That's all right Dennis, I don't want to play bass, you can.'

Linton Kwesi Johnson: John Kpiaye, incidentally, had had a group called the Cats and in 1968 they were in the top 20 national charts with a reggae version of 'Swan Lake'. I don't know if people remember that.

Dennis Bovell: He was also a guitar player in the band that backed Dandy Livingstone, if you remember 'Susan Beware of the Devil' and all that. The group was called In Brackets. He is a formidable guitar player. He also wrote a lot of songs by Cassandra and ...

Linton Kwesi Johnson: Brown Sugar.

Dennis Bovell: Brown Sugar. On Sundays we used to hold auditions for young artists to come along to the studio and show what they could do. And one Sunday these three young girls turned up and the thing that struck me was how closely knitted their vocals were, how close the texture of their voices seemed to resemble each other. One of them was Caron Wheeler, that girl who sang for Soul To Soul 'Keep On Moving Don't Stop', that song, and there was

Pauline, and the other one was a girl called Kofi, who'd just had some success on a reworking of John's song. He'd written this song called 'I'm in Love with a Dreadlocks' and we were looking for the best way to out it and we went through, you know, a few bottles of cognac and a few ideas and then came the idea to call the label Lover's Rock. This was after a song by Augustus Pablo called 'Lover's Rock', an instrumental song. We thought let's call the record label Lover's Rock and while we're at it let's say that this is a new style of music. Soppy lyrics and soft tempo, slow tempo and Dennis was like 'Yeah! That's it!' He even drew a Cupid arrow through the heart, right, so we had a pink heart and it was born. The first song on that label was 'I'm in Love with a Dreadlocks' by Brown Sugar. Lover's Rock was out.

Linton Kwesi Johnson: That's how Lover's Rock was born. But you didn't only produce Lover's Rock.

Dennis Bovell: Oh no. I was producing roots music at the time. My favourite writer of roots things was a guy from Birmingham called Tabby Cat Kelly. Now he had a song and this song's called 'Don't Call Us Immigrants'. He was saying, you know, we're West Indians and we're not immigrants, right, it's not about immigrants, we're not immigrating. Quite truly, when I came from Barbados to England I wasn't emigrating I was just relocating within Britain as a British citizen. So to be referred to as an immigrant, it was not correct. So we come up with this song.
[Excerpt from beginning of 'Don't Call Us Immigrants' song:]
>Oh yeah
>Freedom and justice is what we want
>Equality and love throughout the land
>Respect my colour and Ill respect yours
>Yours could never be superior to mine
>Remember how we cleaned your mess
>Dont you think we did our best?
>The job that we're doing for a small wage packet
>can't get no promotion

They're calling us immigrants
Don't call us no immigrants
Don't call us no immigrants
We are West Indians
Don't call us no immigrants

Dennis Bovell: Tabby Cat, Eddy.

Linton Kwesi Johnson: Right, now over the last 25 years or so you have deservedly earned a reputation as one of the best recording engineers in the business, not only in reggae but in rock and in other forms of music. You've worked with people like Bob Geldof, Sir Bob Geldof, Fela Kuti, Amazulu, the Irish singer Sharon Shannon –

Dennis Bovell: She's an accordion player.

Linton Kwesi Johnson: Yeah. Can you tell us something about some of the people you've recorded?

Dennis Bovell: Well, I was once approached by a fella from Phonogram who said to me, 'I want you to do me a favour. I'm sending these three young girls over to you. Can you do something for them?' And I was in the studio the night before and I thought I'd better not go home because I won't make it back in time and I fell asleep on the old settee there. Then I was woken up in the morning with these three girls called Bananarama and I said, 'All right, where's your material?' They said, 'We ain't got none.' 'What do you mean, you ain't got none?' 'Well, you've got to do it all.' And it was just me in the studio. So I quickly put the drums together, because I played the drums, and the keyboards and the bass and the guitar and then they sang it. Then the record come out: 'Produced by Bananarama, remixed by Dennis Bovell!' I was very annoyed because I'd been working before that with these girls called the Slits ...

Linton Kwesi Johnson: We won't listen to the Slits.

Dennis Bovell: We won't listen to the Slits? Oh, please. OK. Now, these are the original female punks of this country and they had written this song called 'Typical Girls' that said 'Typical girls get upset too quickly, typical girls buy magazines' and when I heard that lyric I thought, I'll work with you, you're radical!
  And then I did some work with a group called The Thompson Twins and Tom was on a parallel to me because – this is the lead singer of the Thompson Twins – his father was a minister in the church and he was desperately trying to write some songs that would be all right with his Dad but, you know, he was trying to break away from the old religious part of the family and stuff and so I did the first Thompson Twins album called *Product Of.*

Linton Kwesi Johnson: Tell us about working with Fela Kuti. What was he like? What was it like working with him?

Dennis Bovell: Incredible. In fact, Fela Kuti had discovered that EMI had short-changed him on the old royalty statements and he'd come over bearing an obeah man, the Professor Hindu! He'd come to inflict X amount of magic on EMI, right? And, you know, he was going to work the old ju-ju and he looked me in the eye and he said, 'I've been told that you're going to record me' –

Linton Kwesi Johnson: He didn't say it like that.

Dennis Bovell: No, well he said, 'Na you go do am!' So I said, 'Yeah.' We went to Holland. It was Amsterdam, trying to record this *Live in Amsterdam* and the lights were giving a problem because lights quite often do, as Linton knows. When we're on stage sometimes they go. I told the lighting engineer, 'No lights, just put the lights full on and leave it there because we're recording this.' He's like, 'It's more than my job's worth mate.' Lights, lights. He's looking at his mates and going, 'Do you hear that?' So the head of A & R, who was this Italian American who'd just come into London to pull EMI London into shape, was ready to take his head off.

Anyway, we got the tapes back to London. I must say that normally you would get at least five or six songs on a reel of tape at 15 ips, which is 15 inches per second. Fela managed to get just one song on. You'd have to put two reels on in case the tape ran out before one song had finished, because he'd compose music for 45 minutes, each song 45 minutes. That was to rid him of piracy. The pirates in Nigeria only had C60s and he had done a deal with someone and armed himself with C90s so that if the pirates tried to pirate his thing their tapes would run out, and he wouldn't start singing until the first 30 minutes had gone by. So we got back to London and were doing the mixing. I managed to filter out all the noises of the lights using gadgets, using noise gauges, compressors, expanders, you name it, the kitchen sink was in there. But on the bass track I couldn't get it out because right where the bass sound needed to be was a big 'mmmmmmmm'. Well, Fela was ready to kill a few people. So, to prevent this murder I said, 'Look, I'll play the bass for you. I'll do the bass again.' 'Can you do that?' 'No problem, I'll do that for you.' And I put the tape on and I was playing this bass line and 15 minutes in I was like, 'Damn, I'm losing concentration!' because it was so hypnotic. What I had to play wasn't particularly difficult but I found myself drifting off, you know. I was trancing.

So, he then decided 'I like you, I want to record my album in your studio but, is it your studio? Is it YOUR studio? YOUR studio?' 'Yeah, it's my studio.' 'OK.' And this was all said on the doorstep before he said to the troops, 'OK, in we go.' So in he went with wives and children and family. In fact one day the wives made an open fire in my kitchen on the floor – 'Have to cook de food, cook de food, cook de food!' I was going, 'There's a stove over there, it works by gas, cooks just as good!' 'No, no, no we need wood for de fire!' And we were working and it comes up to Christmas Eve and he says, 'What time do we start tomorrow?' 'Hey, Fela, tomorrow is Christmas.' 'Christmas, what is it? What is it?' It suddenly struck me that he was so flippant that he didn't give a damn about Christmas or he was Muslim. And we did a song called 'Army Arrangement' and he was, you know, incarcerated. Yeah, just afterwards he got put in jail.

Linton Kwesi Johnson: And the ju-ju man couldn't get him out?

Dennis Bovell: No. You see, the thing was that Fela had taken it upon himself to take all the money for the whole troupe with him on leaving the country and the rule of Nigeria was, the law was, you're not allowed to take more than X amount and that used to happen over here. I remember going on school journeys in the 1960s. You had to take your passport to the bank to get it stamped to see how much money you're taking out of the country. That was one of the reasons why the Conservatives won the election, yeah, because Labour did that before. Anyway, so he'd taken all the money with him so the army had him then. 'How much money you got? You're leaving the country with more than the specified amount.' And so they did him for that and he said, 'But this is my ...' 'Ah, no, you should give everybody their money.' Yeah, but if he did that some of them wouldn't come back!

So, they put him in jail and whilst he was in jail his manager came to me and said, 'Look, we've got to finish the Fela project.' And I had to be the one to try and convince Fela that he had to use this new instrument called a synthesiser and he was going, 'No! Get me a piano!' 'Get me an organ! But no synthesiser! I don't want that, it's not African, no.' So, also he wasn't keen on electric drums or anything that sounded remotely modern. He didn't want to know and in 'Army Arrangement' he had this really sinister kind of Doctor Vibes organ. You could feel your hair standing up on your skin because he was talking about how the army had arranged everything, that's what the army arrangers were. 'One answer you go get, army arrangement, put am together, mathematician put am together, army arrangement, paddy paddy put am together, army arrangement ...'. I mean, you know his never-ending onslaught on the army. In fact, they murdered his mother and he'd gone to jail. His management came to me and said, 'Look, we've got to update the sounds, make it more new.' So I said, 'When I get back from tour with Linton I'll see what I can do.' They said, 'No, no, no you've got to do it now.' So they went off and did it without me. When they did it they came back and played it to me I said, 'Have you played it to Fela?' They said, 'No. What do you think?' I said 'He's gonna curse you.'

Linton Kwesi Johnson: Who had done it?

Dennis Bovell: Pascal had done it with Bill Laswell, the American producer Bill Laswell. He'd taken some very intricate Afro-beat that only Fela could do, this Afro-beat, and transformed it to just boof-geesh boof-geesh like a robot, and the beat was du-du-para-pa, du-da-pata-ta, – intricate – and they'd transformed that, rubbed that off. And they were going, 'This is America, man, this is America!' And Fela said, 'You can put America up your anus! I don't want am!' Because a tape recorder had been sneaked into the jail to get Fela's reaction. He thought Fela was going to be ecstatic and it was completely the opposite. I mean four bars in it was like, 'Aaahhh! modda! Who did dat! Ah, which bastard? Who do dat!' And then, when it came to Fela's organ solo, this sacred piece of organ, they'd rubbed that off and put some kind of green onions. I heard the sound of someone going like that on the record player and on the tape because he was so pissed off. When he came out of jail in fact he re-released it, and he told all the public, 'Don't buy that record. Don't buy that one, this is the real one.' And also he made one called 'You Give Me Shit, I Give You Shit', and the lyric was 'Anybody wey give me shit, him go get he shit, him go get he shit' and the next line was 'Like Abiola him go get, him go get him shit, plenty plenty shit' –

Linton Kwesi Johnson: Abiola?

Dennis Bovell: Abiola. He said, 'Dennis, when it come to Abiola put the voice louder!' to make sure that that word wasn't lost!

Linton Kwesi Johnson: OK. So Fela was one of the people that you recorded at your studio, Studio 80. How did that studio start and who were some of the other people that you recorded down there?

Dennis Bovell: Well, the studio started when I'd done the music for *Babylon* the film.

Linton Kwesi Johnson: Say a bit about that.

Dennis Bovell: Well Franco Rosso was introduced to me because he'd just done a film with Linton, on Linton's first album *Dread Beat An Blood*, and he came to me. In fact he came to Linton and said, 'I want you to write the music for this film' and Linton said, 'You better go and see Dennis.' So then he came to me and we got it together, to do the music for this film. Now I had lots of money that the taxman was going to take away unless I did something with it all so I thought I'll spend it, open a recording studio. And also I needed then to be not just an engineer working in the studio, because I found that I couldn't keep quiet. If I sat in the studio and saw and heard something that wasn't right I'd have to speak and quite often people just used me like a producer but were only paying me like an engineer. So I thought well I'm going to open my own studio. Then at least, if I'm being used, at least the studio price is coming back into my coffers, as it were. So I decided I'm going to build this studio.

Then I got a telephone call from someone going, 'Hello, I'm calling from Japan.' I thought 'Yeah?' It was one of my friends winding me up, right? 'Ah, you're building studio?' And he said 'I have some equipment in Germany, I'm going to send it to you. I want to use your studio.' I was like, 'Yeah, all right then, when do you want to book it for?' And I just took the booking but I thought one of my friends was going to come and say, 'It was me winding you up.' Then one day before we'd finished a big truck pulled up outside. 'Dennis Bovell, we're looking for.' 'Yeah, that's me.' 'Sign here.' 25 million yen worth of equipment. 'Whose is it?' Ryuichi Sakamoto from Japan. Oh boy, it wasn't a spoof, he's going to come! So I had to quickly go to see George Martin to borrow some equipment off him to make my studio up for it and then Ryuichi Sakamoto came over and he was kind of the Paul McCartney of Japan. He was very very well-respected. If you've ever seen the film *Merry Christmas, Mr Lawrence*, he was the one that played the Japanese officer with David Bowie. And that was the first time I was seeing all this new Japanese technology first-hand because he brought his own stuff over and we made an album called *B2 Unit*. He was the first person to use the studio. Then shortly afterwards I did Errol Dunkley's 'A Little Way Different', and Linton brought a friend of his from Jamaica called Mikey Smith –

Linton Kwesi Johnson: The poet.

Dennis Bovell: The poet Mikey Smith, and we did the album there with Mikey Smith – *Mi Cyaan Believe It*.

Linton Kwesi Johnson: What were your impressions of Mikey Smith?

Dennis Bovell: Well, I thought he was an immensely intelligent person but miserable with it, you know. He was the kind of person who could put the cat amongst the pigeons, as it were. He'd give you all a scenario and give you a chain of events and say, 'What do you think? What do you think?' And then when you tell him what you think he'll go, 'Nah, that's not it.' He would give you these two-pronged, you could take it like this or take it like that, 'What do you think?' 'I'll take it like this.' 'No, no, no you should take it like that.'

Linton Kwesi Johnson: You're talking about the time when he said, 'If I had £10,000 hidden underneath my bed, which one of the two percussionists would I send to get it?'

Dennis Bovell: Exactly! Exactly!

Linton Kwesi Johnson: Anyway, you worked with Mikey Smith, on his album yeah?

31

Dennis Bovell: Well, Leroy Smart, he was another character. He came to the studio. He had taken a plane, come over to London and wounded a pirate. Now, a pirate had released his record from Jamaica without permission and, instead of getting a lawyer to do anything about it, Leroy bought a plane ticket and a knife, arrived at Heathrow. From the airport he went straight to the pirate's office and gave him the knife and was arrested, put in jail for that. He got bail and the first night he got bail he came to see me. He said, 'I want to make a record with you.' I said, 'Fine, whenever you're ready.' 'I want to make a record with you tonight.' I goes, 'All right, once we've finished this session we'll take you on, right?' So we finished that session, the session we were doing, at about 2.00 am. 'Right, Leroy, right. What do you want? Right, what shall we play?' 'Play anything you like. Just play what you like, you're a musician aren't you? I'm a singer. I'm going to sing.' And it was an interesting challenge. So then I quickly made up a few chords here, a bridge thrown in there, you know, and he would take his notebook out and write something. 'Right, I'm going to call that one whatever. Right, next!' And by the time we'd made it to nine songs I thought, no, no, no you're using me, I'm writing songs for you. He's going, 'Yeah, but I'm going to pay you. Look, I want ten songs.' I goes, 'No, no, no, no, I'm not doing any more.' And he was really really livid. So I says to him, 'Look, you see this track here? You could sing two different songs on the same piece of music, right?' And he went, 'Yeah, good idea.' So, we composed, recorded and mixed in one night the album *Propaganda*. And the next day we were cutting the album in John Hassall. So that was Leroy Smart. Let me see now ...

Linton Kwesi Johnson: Who was that tall English woman I saw you with, saw down the studio one time? You did a record which was a hit.

Dennis Bovell: That's right. She was a singer of a group called The Flying Lizards and they'd just done a talking version of the song 'Money', yeah – 'That's what I want' – with a kind of Maggie

Thatcher voice, right? 'You can give it to the birds and bees, I want money, that's what I want, that's what I want, that's what I want, that's what I want' – and that was at number one for ages. And they called me in to do the follow up to this and we did a version of Otis Redding's 'Respect'. Well, in the middle of it she said 'R-E-S-P-E-C-T, find out what it means for me'. I went, 'Who me? I'm the producer! And you'd better have some respect for me.' Quite flippant, you know. That was Deborah Evans.

Then in came Bob Geldof to say to me, he wanted me to mash up one of his tracks that he'd done, I think it was 'Tonight' by the Boomtown Rats. And then I did a whole album with them called *VD* with Tony Visconti, and then they did a reggae song called 'House on Fire' which got to about number five in the charts and made me popular in Ireland.

Linton Kwesi Johnson: I'm just going to ask you two more questions and then we'll take some questions from the audience. Can you say a little bit more about your involvement in film music? Apart from *Babylon*, what else were you involved in?

Dennis Bovell: Well, for TV I did the *Rock School* series. In fact the first *Rock School* series was me playing all the instruments, right? I explain the drums and then play a bit of drums, I explain the guitar then play a bit of guitar, explain the keyboards ... and when we cut it all back together it looked awfully like showing off. One of the guys said, 'It's you doing that and you doing that and you doing that and you doing that.' And there was a poster on the street of me, and I was on the bus with my young daughter, because I'd left the lights on in my car and the battery was flat so I needed to get somewhere really quickly, so we were going on the bus. The bus stopped right outside the poster, a huge full-size poster of me. She said 'Daddy.' 'What?' 'Daddy! That's you!' So I started to go into music at that time where people wouldn't see me. I'd just sit in the studio. I did the music for a TV series. ITV started the first straight half hour. Programmes on ITV used to be 15 minutes, adverts, 15 minutes, adverts. And they did the first straight half hour and they did a show called *The Boy who Won the Pools*. It was about a boy who won the pools and spent the money on a girl, to make her into a singer and they contacted me and said, 'How long will it take you to write this music?' And I said, 'Give me two weeks.' They gave me the two weeks anyway to see if I could do it or not and then they could call it their loss and I wrote 17 songs in these two weeks. 'Right, OK, you've got the job.' And then Linton approached me to write some music for Darcus Howe and Tariq Ali, for *The Bandung File*. And the other thing I did was for the Malibu advert. They couldn't afford to buy the Bob Marley tune that they wanted, it cost too much money. So they came along to me and said, 'Can you somehow make a spoof of it?' So I thought it was a challenge. It took me the whole night to programme a drum machine, just to play the drums – but for 20 seconds, which is what the advert was, I had to make people believe it was the Wailers so I copied every note, every piece of the thing, every link, every tone from the record and reproduced it for them and then Family Man called me up and said, 'If someone calls up and asks you to do that again, tell them you can't.'

Linton Kwesi Johnson: But before that you'd done some music for television, hadn't you? When you were in Matumbi.

Dennis Bovell: Yeah. *Empire Road.*

Linton Kwesi Johnson: That's where that song 'Blue Beat and Ska' comes from, the one that you were being asked about earlier.

Dennis Bovell: That's right. Well, with 'Blue Beat and Ska', we were ridiculing the song called 'Elizabethan Reggae'. There was a line in it that said 'There was a song there called 'Elizabethan Reggae', what a disgrace I thought, cause what did she know about reggae?' They made us take that line out. Also in another song there was a line that said 'these are the days and times when every nigger is a star, that means in South Africa it's not just war, it's star war'.

Linton Kwesi Johnson: Now, right now you're working on another movie. Can you tell us something about that?

Dennis Bovell: Yes. There's a musical called *South Side Story* which is a rewrite of Shakespeare's *Romeo and Juliet* with a twist to it, that Romeo is now called Tony Julietto and he's Sicilian and Juliet is called Romara and she's Nigerian and –

Linton Kwesi Johnson: This is in Italy, right?

Dennis Bovell: This is in Italy. I had to brush up on my Italian to get the part, to write the music and to sing in the studio, which I did quite well. Then the producer came along and said, 'We've got to try and get a voice and a face to fit your voice on the tape.' They interviewed lots of people but they couldn't get anyone and she said to me, 'How would you like to be in the film?' So I thought, 'Hollywood, here I come!'

Linton Kwesi Johnson: What part are you playing in the film?

Dennis Bovell: A bad man!

Linton Kwesi Johnson: What kind of a bad man?

Dennis Bovell: Well, the leading lady is a Nigerian and a prostitute, and I'm her manager!

Linton Kwesi Johnson: OK. Tell us something briefly about the Dub Band, how it got started and all that. You'd left Matumbi by then.

Dennis Bovell: That's right, I'd left Matumbi and I had to put together a band of just session musicians. The problem was that Matumbi were anxious that I was, you know, engineering for other people and playing on other people's records and whether or not I was giving too much of myself to other people as opposed to giving it to the band. So I left Matumbi and I just decided right, we won't have any of the players from the band in this new band, the Dub Band. I'll be the only one from Matumbi. And I teamed up with Angus Gaye – Drummie Zeb from Aswad, the drummer – and Tony Gad the bass player from Aswad and he became the keyboard player and John Kpiaye, who's a guitar player. So John Kpiaye, Drummie Zeb, myself and Tony Gad were the first Dub Band. But we were only supposed to be the studio Dub Band. Then I made an album called *Brain Damage* and needed to play it on stage and they got me a gig at Richard Branson's club, the Venue. And I said right, I'm gonna preview this album so I pulled out all my old friends like the horn section that were in Matumbi with me, the two Tenyue brothers, who were the only ones I took out of Matumbi to be in the Dub Band because I needed a horn section.

Then Linton said, 'I can't go on with this tape recorder and tapes anymore on stage.'

Linton Kwesi Johnson: In those days, when I used to perform live with music, I used to have my music pre-recorded on a revox tape machine and I had three dancers and I would just recite my poems to this pre-recorded music and people used to come up to me afterwards and say, 'Great gig but where was the band?' That's how I started to work with him.

Dennis Bovell: Right, so he said, 'Let's form a band and go out and tour.' And by this time I was fed up with sitting behind a desk all day, or all 24 hours a day I was in the studio, I'd put on a lot of weight, so I thought get out and do some exercise, get on stage and jump around a bit. I think Sweden was our first performance and from there on the Dub Band was born.

Linton Kwesi Johnson: OK, I think this is a good point to take some questions from the audience. Right at the back there.

Member of the audience: What's the meaning of Matumbi?

Dennis Bovell: Oh, Matumbi means 'reborn'.

Member of the audience: What language?

Dennis Bovell: Yoruba.

Additional points made by Dennis Bovell in response to questions from the audience.

On recording steel bands

That was a challenge. A friend called up and said, 'I've got this whole steel band in the studio and I want to record it.' I said 'Right. You got enough microphones?' That was the first thing. It was a challenge to try to record three bass players playing six pans each, that was 18 pans to get the whole bass sound, and one note would be here, the next note would be over there, so to catch it all you have to have microphones all around the 18 pans. There was this studio the size of a football pitch and there was two other studios attached to it. So I went round to the other two studios and took all the microphones from them, all the microphones from three studios. The people who were working in the other two studios were looking through the window going, 'Hey, what's he doing?' I was lying on the floor trying to get the right sound, because in my earlier experience of steel band records there was no bass, they were all very trebley. That was one of the reasons why I never used to listen to my steel band collection, because you couldn't hear the bass, and I really loved that bass. So I tried to apply the reggae recording technique to the steel band, because when you go and listen to a steel band live the bass shakes your trousers, you know. But the thing is because it's so spread over such a wide space it's hard to capture unless you've got a lot of expensive microphones. So we were in the Abbey Road studios of Paris, called Davout.

On recording in Jamaica and America

In Jamaica I recorded Chalice, Pablo Moses. In America there were some young lads – what's that saxophone player? – Junior Walker.

Yeah. Junior Walker's sons had a band in Washington DC and I went over to record them. I did some stuff as well in New York with a couple of rappers in 1986. Also, I recorded Herbie Hancock and Foday Musa Suso, an African-American liaison between this kora player, playing the kora and Herbie Hancock playing the piano.

On working with Linton
Well, I just have to listen to what he's saying, do what he tells me, do what he wants. One time I did say to him, 'Don't put my name on that record' because he's going 'The SPG dem a murderer, murderer', so I said, 'I'll help you make this record but don't put my name on it!'

On Eddy Grant
Eddy Grant and me were two of the few black musicians who had 24 track recording facilities in London. It wasn't big enough for us both so he had to go to Barbados. He was a friend of mine, still is in a kind of way because, you know, music and that, and him living in Barbados. He released a song of mine called 'Silly Games' on an album called *The Best of British* in Barbados, but he didn't make the contract with me, he made the contract with someone else, so we fell out, but apart from that. I was the first person to use Eddy Grant's studio when it was relocated to Barbados. I took the members of a group called Orange Juice down there and we did a project called *Ape the Scientific*. It was the first recording in Eddy Grant's studio when it had been relocated to Barbados.

On the record business
I see it as a hassle because there's been so many people who've ripped off so many people in this business. That was the reason why, when my eldest daughter was seven or eight and she said, 'Daddy, what shall I be?' I said, 'You should be a lawyer, because one day I'm going to use you to sue a few of these people who've been ripping me off.' And she's now 27 and a lawyer, so beware record companies!

This record here says *The Best of Matumbi*, which it is far from, because it was at the beginning of our career, right? And that photo in the front was in fact taken in black and white for a magazine called *Black Music and Jazz Review*, and then it was bought by this company and doctored. My mum used to have photos that were taken back home in the fifties that they doctored. Some geezer would paint black and white pictures and turn them into colour, right? And that was exactly what was done there on this one. They had reportedly lost some of this material and they didn't know where it was. So when we finished the relationship, suddenly, the album was on the street *The Best of Matumbi* with a lot of unfinished material on there as well. And add to that all those people there, us, who ought to receive three per cent of 90% of the wholesale selling price of this record to share between us, and the record company is still marketing it. In fact, the other day when I screamed at them down the phone they sent me a mint copy of it as you can see. And it's since 1973 they've been doing that, I mean, all over the world. This is *Marie Pierre* the first Lover's Rock album of my time in this country – another record, same company, Trojan. I went to Japan and found this on CD two years ago. When it was made the CD hadn't been invented. My contract says to make vinyl or cassette. This is a new format, so legally they should have renegotiated with me before they put this out but they put it out in Japan because they think, 'He's never going to go there, he's never going to find out.' How wrong they were! Also, I've seen an album called *The Dub Master* in Tower Records in Tokyo with a full biography of me and tracks of mine on there. When I traced it, it was a company in New York who'd sold it to a company in Holland who'd made the sleeve in Yugoslavia and were pressing the record in Germany and it was being distributed from London.

On other artists who didn't get their just rewards
Dennis Bovell: I would say, Dandy Livingstone. I would say Toots Hibbert, Derrick Morgan. Jackie Opel who died early, Nicky Thomas, you know. The Pioneers, right? I would say most of the old school because of Trojan Records. You're talking about a record company who didn't enlighten the artists to the fact that there was

such a thing called publishing and that there was such a thing called copyright because when they bought your record, that was it, you didn't see any more, that was it, you just got a few hundred quid and then bye-bye, you know. And they've still got all that back catalogue. You go through Italy, you go through Spain, France, Germany and you'll see it in the bargain bins for two or three quid but there's millions of them all over the world so that's still three million quid, you know?

I had a good laugh recently when I'd taken a taxi and the driver said to me, 'My uncle-in-law used to be involved with reggae.' I said, 'Oh, yeah, what was his name?' And he said, 'Lee Gopthal. You know that guy? He died two days ago.' And I was like, 'Take me to the nearest pub, I'm gonna have a drink.' Because he was the architect of robbing so many artists, by not paying any royalties. The royalties were very slim and then they didn't pay the copyright at all. Or, in fact, on a lot of records, you would see that the producer or the person who paid the studio fees claimed the publishing. Desmond Dekker's 'Israelites' is a classic example. You look on the small print of that you'll see that the producer Leslie Kong is credited as the composer. Now Leslie Kong is dead and has been for over 20 years so he's not going to say to the record company, 'Look, where's my statements, I'm sure that's not right.' And I'm sure that they didn't pay any money to anyone else around, they just kept it.

On dub

Linton Kwesi Johnson: One thing we didn't really touch on, Dennis, was finally, maybe you could say something about dub because you earned the reputation of being the King of Dub in Britain, with five or six big-selling different dub albums including *I Wah Dub, Higher Ranking Scientific Dub, Who Seh Go Deh, Yu Learn* and so on. Could you say something about your involvement in dub? Explain what dub is first.

Dennis Bovell: Well, dub is the stripping down of the musical tape whereby you would put extra effects that people would consider disturbs the vocal ordinarily. Or you would remove things that they would consider supported the vocal. Or you would remove the vocal itself and strip the track down to just its drum and bass form and occasionally injecting rhythm instruments, a bit of voice here and then lots and lots of effects, you know. Delay echoes, chorus, spins, all that. And King Tubby was the man and Errol Thompson, Joe Gibbs Studio, King Tubby's Studio. They were the ones who were making it and Lee 'Scratch' Perry. His were mostly popular on sound systems because they hadn't yet become the form that people would put on the 'B' side of a record. Because before that, they'd just have the vocal and then the instrumental just minus the vocal. But then dub had gone a step further to mash it up, as it were, just submerged everything in echo and lots and lots of reverb, huge rooms and stuff like that and it's more of the engineer having fun with what he recorded. Usually you'd sit there and everything would be neat in place and it'd be like, I don't know, stacking a lot of cards up and then just blowing them over.

Linton Kwesi Johnson: The art of deconstruction.

Dennis Bovell: That's right. So I then had to make exclusive dubs for my own sound system, as well as dubs to sell, to earn a living, to other sound systems. So, you know, it stretches the old imagination a bit and the more things that you could come up with that were really alien to reggae.

Linton Kwesi Johnson: Not conventional.

Dennis Bovell: Yeah, unconventional stuff. The more of that you could think of putting in there to make it more crazy, and the better the dub would be received. So we started out to make these albums, and it was also to underline my opinion that reggae could be made in this country. And if it was made well enough, and the listener didn't have any idea about who had made it, then it would be just, 'Do you like it or don't you' and not be prejudiced by if they look at the label and go, 'Ah, made in England, can't be any good.'

People get a deaf ear, see? So, I came up with this idea to make records and make them as though they were coming from Jamaica. But it wouldn't be as neat as that, it wouldn't have a label, it would be just, you know, as though someone had thrown it together in your front room and was on the street selling it the next day, kind of thing. And so we decided to do that and –

Linton Kwesi Johnson: White labels with no information.

Dennis Bovell: No information at all, who's doing what, right? Just either you like the record or you don't. As soon as they saw Dennis Bovell or Matumbi on the label, they'd go, 'Ah, English boys' and it would go to the back of the pile. But if a record comes, 'Ah this is hot from Jamaica, I don't even know who's doing it' right? And I'd stand there and go, 'Look at them, look at them!'

On Distribution for records
Dennis Bovell: Well, I'm not a distributor but I've helped a few people along the way. We bought a Volkswagen van and inside we kitted it out – a friend of mine's a carpenter – with compartments to put the records in and then that van would drive from London to Leeds every day to distribute the records and on Saturdays to collect the money. Then we could buy more materials to make more records and just go and press some more. The major record companies would not distribute us, so we had to get our own distribution system together and that's how we did it.

On hit songs
Linton Kwesi Johnson: Apart from 'Silly Games', Janet Kay's 'Silly Games' which went to number two in the top ten and sold I don't know how many hundreds of thousands of copies abroad, Matumbi had another top ten or top twenty hit. What was that? And when was that?

Dennis Bovell: We had 'Point of View'. This angered me because I was in Barbados on holiday, paid for my own ticket, sitting there at my grandmother's house, telephone rings. 'Hello, EMI.' 'What?' 'We've changed your ticket, you're on the night flight tonight back to London, you got *Top of the Pops* tomorrow.' I said, 'I'm not coming.' They said, 'Well, I'll tell you what I'll do. If you come we'll send you straight back again when you've done *Top of the Pops*.' Great, I thought, I'm going to London for a night, I'll be back tomorrow! Didn't materialise, so I'm standing on *Top of the Pops* going [makes face].

Linton Kwesi Johnson: Say a little bit about the arrangement before you play 'Point of View' because it's one of the most interesting brass arrangements and vocal arrangements I've heard in reggae for a long time.

Dennis Bovell: Our singer Bevin Fagan, and me, we sat next to each other in school from the second year, third year, fourth year, fifth year, sixth year, right through to second year sixth. We decided to pay a visit back to our old school one day. We were walking along this road called Windmill Drive and he goes, 'Eh, I've got a song coming on.' I said, 'Yeah, let me hear it.' He's going, 'I've got to squeeze a little loving out of you.' I was going, 'Yeah, yeah.' So I started going 'Boo-ba-boo-ba' [brass instrument sound]. Yeah, Glenn Miller reggae, Glenn Miller reggae! And we were walking along and singing. And one day we got in to the demo studio and said right, let's do it. And we actually did it to be an encore song, after we'd done the show we'd do this Glenn Miller kind of reggae thing. And the record company said, 'You should do that, it should be the title of your next album.'

So we went along with it, we did it and we got *Top of the Pops* out of it. We were the first ones to do a video under the flyover in Ladbroke Grove, with this video of 'Point of View'. And also it was the first reggae video to be played on MTV America. MTV when it first opened didn't play reggae at all. Stevie Wonder, on his radio station – it was Kiss FM in Los Angeles – played this song to death, right, he loved it. What happened is while we were recording it, the guitar player in Stevie Wonder's band was in EMI and he heard us playing and he came down saying, 'Hey, you guys playing that old reggae thing. You all from the islands, huh? You all some island boys playing the reggae.' And it was like, yeah, Stevie Wonder's guitar player, I'd better hide, there was a real guitar player in the room! And then it came to the solo part, I said to him, 'Hey man, how about guesting with us? You know, playing solo.' So he said, 'You sure?' I was going, 'Yeah man.' 'OK' and he played this incredible piece of guitar and it was the demo. And when we went to the real studio to make the real record I thought I want that guitar. The band goes, 'No way, if you want that on there you have to learn to play it.' So I learned what he'd played and then replayed it on this record but whilst I was doing it I thought, I'm going the whole way. I had all of my amplifiers outside the studio out on the grass, mike and all that, you know, I did it like Jimi Hendrix, a column of amplifiers as wide as that fireplace there, yeah! But the studio was outside of Gatwick Airport and every time we went to do a take, 'Wait, wait. Stop, aeroplane! Aeroplane!' Until when I was doing the solo one aeroplane went over and I said, 'Leave it like that.' So in the back there's an aeroplane going over!

[Record played: 'Point Of View':]

Take a look at it from my point of view
And when you'll really find out
love you too
The love I've got inside is so warm and kind
It's a cool gentle touch, and yet it hurts me so much
I need to squeeze a little loving out of you
I said I need to squeeze a little more loving out of you
Now we've been together for such a long time
Gee It makes me feel so good to know you are mine, ah baby
Now love is a secret not to be told
You'll never find out until the day you grow old
That I could squeeze a little loving out of you
I said I need to squeeze a little more loving I need you baby
I ain't gonna reason the question why
I'll just follow my heart 'til the day that I die
I need to squeeze a little loving out of you....

Linton Kwesi Johnson: Thank you very much, Dennis Bovell!

Roxy Harris: Thank you very much Dennis and Linton. Great evening, fantastic talk. Hope everybody enjoyed it.

Dennis Bovell has earned himself the reputation of being Britain's reggae maestro, from pioneering early developments in the genre over 20 years ago to producing classic hits. He is renowned as an accomplished multi-instrumentalist (playing guitar, bass and keyboards), sound engineer, composer, band leader and producer and continues to lead the UK scene with innovative and adventurous music.

Born in Barbados in 1953, Dennis Bovell joined his parents in London when he was twelve. Whilst still at school Bovell joined his first band, Road Works Ahead, before forming the group Stonehenge. Influenced by rock steady, this band gave birth to the three-part harmony section that was later to become the trademark of Bovell's next group, Matumbi, formed in 1970.

Matumbi (meaning 'reborn' in Yoruba) were to become Britain's premier reggae band at a time when the genre was spreading from Jamaica to a wider international audience. After a period backing visiting Jamaican artists such as Pat Kelly and Ken Booth, the band enhanced their reputation further with a string of successful singles. 'After Tonight', the band's first hit, is to this day played on continuous rewind in the Revival Hall of Fame and another single, 'The Man In Me' is regarded as a British reggae classic. In 1979 Matumbi reached the UK Top Ten charts with 'Point of View'. Altogether the band made four albums for EMI.

At the same time Bovell was building his formidable reputation as a musician, producer and sound engineer, collaborating with great artists including I Roy, Steel Pulse and Errol Dunkley and Johnny Clarke. After leaving Matumbi, Bovell continued to diversify his musical talents He produced Janet Kay's huge hit 'Silly Games', which reached number two in the UK charts in 1979 and opened his own recording facility, Studio 80.

Bovell also formed the Dub Band, beginning an enduring partnership with reggae poet Linton Kwesi Johnson which has resulted in classic albums including *Forces of Victory* (1979), *Bass Culture* (1980), *Tings An' Times* (1991) and *LKJ in Dub: Volumes One and Two* (1981, 1992). It has also meant tours around the world playing to audiences from South Africa to Sweden, from Japan to Germany.

The 1980s saw Bovell in great demand as a producer, working with bands as diverse as The Slits, Chalice, The Thompson Twins and Bananarama. He re-mixed albums for the great Marvin Gaye as well as Wet Wet Wet and The Boomtown Rats and worked closely with Nigerian Fela Anikulapo Kuti. Other great artists that Bovell has worked with include Alpha Blondy, Ryuichi

Dennis Bovell

Sakamoto, Dexy's Midnight Runners, Edwin Collins and Pablo Moses.

Bovell has also carved a niche out for himself in the world of television and film. He was the musical director for the film Babylon and for the TV series *The Boy Who Won the Pools* (ITV). He wrote the theme music for the Channel 4 documentary series *The Bandung File* and for the BBC 2 programme *Rhythms of the World*.

Throughout this period Bovell continued his career as a solo artist, releasing a number of albums: *A Who Seh Go Deh*; *Leggo A Fl We Dis*; *I Wah Dub*; *Higher Ranking Scientific Dub*; *Yu Learn*; *Strictly Dubwise*; *Brain Damage* and *Audio Active*. His 1993 release *Tactics* was lauded as 'assured, polished reggae from a master producer and musician' (*Elle* magazine) and featured a wealth of great musicians such as Rico Rodriquez (trombone), Eddie Thornton (trumpet) and Steve Gregory (flute and saxophone).

Bovell's latest album *Dub ofAges* (1997) contains ten inventive and inspired tracks, the latest in a series of dub excursions which began over 25 years ago when Bovell began making exclusive cuts for his sound system Sufferers Hi-Fi. It also heralds Bovell's 25th, year in the music business, and promises another great quarter century ahead from the man who is justly dubbed 'Britain's reggae maestro'.

Althea McNish

in conversation with John Weiss (22.02.1999)
with John La Rose in the chair

[Numbers in bold indicate illustrations in text]

John La Rose: Welcome on this wild and windy night. What I want to say about Althea is that I have known her for quite some time. I never met her father but I did meet her mother and she was as welcoming as Althea has always been. Easy and welcoming, in spite of the enormous achievement which has been her career, very outstanding and world wide in its implications and acceptance, from Japan to the United States and different parts of Europe. Althea's career has spanned a long time and it's very significant that a young artist becomes famous just as she leaves the Royal College of Art. It must have indicated a very outstanding talent at the moment of her having finished her work at the RCA. I saw her exhibition at the Hockney Gallery which was held in September 1997. It was one of the most stunning exhibitions I've seen in London.

I want also to welcome John, her partner, husband, an architect and a designer, and I also want to thank them both for the extent of their assistance to us at the George Padmore Institute in helping us with the choice of our lighting for this room in which you are now sitting here tonight. They gave a lot of their time and patience to moving around with us, talking to the lighting experts whom John had taught in his career and they helped us devise the lighting we have. We hope, if we can manage it in the future, to have small exhibitions in this room.

So tonight I welcome both John Weiss, John McNish Weiss, and Althea McNish Weiss to this important event. Welcome to you John. Welcome to you Althea.

Althea McNish: Thank you very much.

John Weiss: Those of you who know Althea well know that she is not at a loss for words. But we agreed that we might do this a little bit in partnership, inspired partly by Linton Kwesi Johnson's interviewing last time though I wouldn't match myself with him.

47

We do quite often lecture together and I interrupt Althea and so on, though that didn't seem quite appropriate for here so I will interview her. I will be the feed man. I will see how much she will talk. Normally she is talking to designers, design students, an audience who are already tuned in to visual matters. Now some of you are and some of you aren't. But in the spirit of the sequence of these talks, these lectures, 'Life Experience With Britain', I will be trying to excite Althea into talking about things she doesn't normally talk about to designers – how she has coped with Britain, the weather, the people, Europe and so on. Anyway, we'll see how we go on. The middle of the sandwich will be illustrated and that is why our hosts have invested in this screen above us.

Althea, when I first met you at a party on Thursday 11th February 1967, and that date by the way is crucial for another bit of the story, it took about two hours before I actually found out your full name and then I was able to blurt out in my rather naïve way, 'Not **the** Althea McNish!' As an architect who hated wallpapers and preferred white walls, I had fallen in love with this fantastic collection of wallpapers in Althea's contribution to the Palladio range that was put out by the wallpaper manufacturers to try and seduce architects who liked white walls into using wallpapers. And the only wallpapers that I really liked were by this little old Scottish lady called Althea McNish. I wasn't the only one to fall into that trap and there had been plenty of new clients calling at the door and being slightly surprised when they saw how Althea McNish faced them. I had fallen in love with these designs. You had already made a big name in textile design and this new connection through wallpapers with architecture took you back to your earlier aspirations in Trinidad. Now, you had been a painter since you were a child. Can you tell us about this painter who had planned to be an architect and what sort of problems you faced? This was in Trinidad before you came here.

Althea McNish: Yes, well I started painting and drawing very young and of course my parents were slightly worried. They didn't quite know what this was all about but they thought, 'Well she's having fun', so this painting went on throughout my childhood. And I remember at school everybody said, 'Let Althea set the still life.' I hated still life in any case, so I used to set the still life up for them and before you could start I'd say, 'Shall we change?' and I'd turn around and switch the whole still life. It was supposed to be a still life but I'd briskly change things around because I was bored after the first five minutes of all this. Anyway this went on throughout my school years and of course drawing and painting was so essentially my life that I went out and joined associations like the Junior Art Society which was then the only such organisation in Trinidad, when I was a child.

But it all started, I think, when I won the Tiny Mites competition which was run by *The Guardian*, I believe, at the time. My mother took me down to collect my prize, and they had a beautiful doll which they were going to give me as the first prize. My mother found me looking to the side where there was an enormous painting set. So I kept looking at this thing, but the doll was being handed to me, and I said, 'But I would like those paints instead of the doll.' I think my mother must have been rather embarrassed but the person who was giving out the prizes decided, 'Well Althea you've won the first prize of a doll so you can have whatever you want.' Well that settled it, I took the paints. But she added, 'You also have the doll' to my mother, who was even more embarrassed because I didn't even go away with the doll but went away with the paint set. I think this was the beginning of my great urge and desire to paint. At that time I was only using crayons so I graduated into water-colours. This was the beginning of my water-colour life as a painter.

John Weiss: Althea, it's quite clear that very early on you decided that being a painter was going to be your life's work, your life's career, now at what point did you switch into architecture? How did you decide that you wanted to be an architect?

Althea McNish: I decided this more or less before I finished school. I was studying to take my GCEs or whatever you called it at the time. I was 16 and my mother decided that she had to find somebody to teach me. I told her I wanted to do architecture and she listened to this and thought she will see how it goes. So by the time I finished and I had the year off, she had found a tutor for me. We had no schools in Trinidad at the time that were run as architectural schools or anything like this, but there was the town planner who ran classes for architects and I was one of the first girls to go into this. So on my 16th birthday my mother gave me this; as a gift I presume. I started to take tuition from the architect. Well this was the beginning of it all, I think, because my desire to put buildings up was very, very strong then, and the painting went along with it. I was so keen and interested in the architecture that some of my friends saw this and decided, 'Mmm she's good,' so I went on doing it. I finished my school and the results came out. I don't know if you remember the Red House in Trinidad – after school I would go down on my bicycle and go to the Red House. I picked up some of these forms which you had to sign, fill out, if you wanted to work for the government, and it was, I think, just a big joke or whatever. Anyway I filled it out and sent it in. In the meantime I was given my first exhibition at the Junior Art Society. I put it on and among the people who came to see it there was the government entomologist at the Agricultural Department, and he saw my work. I was still a junior just finishing school, and he said, 'Well if that girl wants a job at any time, I'd like her to work for me.' He spotted something which must have been there. And I got a call, a letter came in asking me to come for an interview and I was very, very worried about this. I said, 'Why are they sending for me?' I went and he interviewed me. I wasn't yet 18 so I couldn't be taken on.

John Weiss: You weren't at the proper age to be a civil servant?

Althea McNish: No, so I went on probation for the next 18 months.

John Weiss: In other words it was as a result of being a painter that you became a colonial civil servant, which is an unusual sequence.

Althea McNish: This was for me, you know, a lot of fun and interesting and I went into it with both feet.

John Weiss: As part of that job you were doing your illustrations but you were also involved in cartography.

Althea McNish: Yes, I became a cartographer because that was the job really.

John Weiss: For people who are familiar with Althea's freedom in her painting and her textiles, the idea of her doing minutely correct entomological illustrations and doing surveying with land chains and so on and drawing maps meticulously is interesting. She does her maps more meticulously than me.

Althea McNish: I had to.

John Weiss: While you were doing that you got involved in actually designing houses and doing drawings for septic tanks and so on.

Althea McNish: Oh yes, yes. I made my name in septic tanks. I had a lovely time. I cottoned on to this septic tanks thing and it went to my head. I think I must have been very good at it and I used to develop the blueprints in the back yard under my two sheets of glass in the sun. Who knew about all the technology at the time? But that was enough and I would tell my mother, 'Mum when they come …' I would have the invoice made out, put it in the envelope and the septic tank would be rolled up, 'Mummy when you hand them that they must hand you back the money.' I think it must have been something like ten dollars, I don't know. Anyway my mother could not understand where did she get this daughter from, you know, who had her mind on septic tanks and money.

John Weiss: One of the interesting things about this artist is that she is very businesslike. Now you worked as a civil servant. You were also doing your septic tanks and your houses and it was quite clear to your parents that you couldn't really progress as an architect unless you had an education in England.

Althea McNish: I had to be educated.

John Weiss: So in the end they moved house, but before then you had got slightly disenchanted with the fact that people didn't see why they should pay a woman for work even when that woman actually built the house.

Althea McNish: They were living in the house.

John Weiss: And your second setback to studying architecture was your sight of the British weather when you arrived in England. You and I both had places at the Architectural Association for the same year and you decided not to study architecture and I decided to study elsewhere so it took us 16 years to make up for not meeting on that occasion. So you had your cartography in your portfolio instead of the architecture. You switched to graphic design at the London School of Printing but it was partly aided by government, the colonial government; a secondment so you could do cartography at the same time. Now you did very well in graphic design, illustration. It was called commercial design, commercial art at that time. But having switched once from being an artist to an architect and then having to side-step the architecture, then going into graphic design, how did the textiles arise?

Althea McNish: Well, the textiles came about while I was studying graphics. I used to go to exhibitions – half the time when my tutors couldn't find me I would be at an exhibition somewhere in the West End. I met a friend, she's still a friend with us now, Heli Poser, and she took me to an exhibition at the Central School where I saw all this glorious textile happening. Miss Batty, I think, was then the head of the textile department. Well I was so enthralled with this whole display of work and textiles, and I said, 'This is what I want to do, textiles. Get rid of all those flower pots off women walking around, you know, on their bodies. I want to do something in textiles.' So I immediately applied to the Central School. I went there in the evenings while I did graphics in the daytime. As I finished my course at graphics school, I had a scholarship which took me off to the Royal College of Art to do graphics. But then I was in quite a dilemma. I didn't know what to do about it. I was interviewed by 20 people sitting around a table and they each fired a question at me, you know, why did I want to do … and in the middle of it all I said, 'Well I don't want to do graphics any more. I want to do textiles.'

So they must have thought they had quite a crazy one there in front of them. They said, 'Are you sure? But you've been recommended and this is what your …' I said, 'No I think I want to do textiles. I've had enough of graphics!' Well I think that must have really … anyway I ended up by getting a place to do textiles and not graphics at all.

John Weiss: Would you say that you were a perfect student?

Althea McNish: I was a terrible student. I think in a way I was very wayward and the painting was still very strong in me. I used to paint on Saturday mornings at a special class. Get rid of all that frustration from the graphics into painting. But they all said I was a very good student but I also warned them that I was one of the first black students to go to the Royal College of Art in this area. I don't think they had another before. So I felt sometimes as though they treated me like a mascot. But then I had freedom. If I had an idea I wanted to use – sandblasting for example – I would get a letter from my professor who said, 'Althea is going to visit you' and I would spend a week sandblasting to get the effect I wanted. I would go to the painting school and sculpture school. Whatever occurred in my brain that I wanted to do, I wanted to experiment with, and as I said I had a great sense of the technology of what I was doing, and I wanted to learn the complete technology of my business. I didn't just want to paint pictures and show you this idea there. It had to go further than that. So much so that my whole time, when I got into college in my first year, I spent in the laboratories and in the print room and showing the technician quite a lot of techniques which I had picked up at the graphics school. I had learned my serigraphy there with the man who designed and produced Letraset. He was called Mackenzie.

John Weiss: You learned all about the techniques of silkscreen printing?

Althea McNish: I did serigraphy in order to produce my own paintings in editions.

John Weiss: Can I project from there into your reception in the textile industry? At the Royal College your knowledge, your pre-knowledge of textile printing, what Mackenzie had taught you, meant that you had absolute freedom. What he hadn't taught you about putting an image onto a screen wasn't worth knowing.

Althea McNish: Yes that's right.

John Weiss: But you found at the Royal College of Art that other people didn't have that same knowledge and, on the other hand, you were doing very much freer designs than them. Now that, I think, continued into your career and I've seen this in operation. I also get the impression that in terms of the textile industry it may have been unusual for them to have a black designer, but then equally it was unusual for them to be dealing with a woman.

Althea McNish: Very much so.

John Weiss: And the technical people you dealt with saw that you knew their business. They looked on this designer with a slightly different air. Instead of being impatient they were much more sympathetic.

Althea McNish: Yes I think this was the whole key to it all.

John Weiss: You made your career in London which is the centre of the textile world. You made a career in Europe really. How was it to find yourself in places where you were a curiosity? In Copenhagen? On the ski slopes?

Althea McNish: It was fun in a way. People used to turn and stare and my dad would say to me, 'Althea they don't see a black girl so attractive going through London, you know. You mustn't get worried about it. They're admiring you.' So having put that in my head, it helped not to be worried or get sensitive about it. When I went to the ski slopes in Switzerland, as John mentioned, the train would stop and there was dead silence and I was on the skis waiting to go off and my tutor, he was very aware that something was happening, so he said, 'Althea, they're looking at you.' I said, 'They're looking to see me take off and break my neck I suppose.' So I started to go down and then clapping went up like this and I thought, 'Look at this, I'm putting on a performance for this lot here.' But I had a lovely time skiing and in the middle of the skiing small children would stand and look because all they could see really outside of the goggles was this change of skin.

But it never occurred to me that I was anything different and I think this was very important for me, especially as I was travelling through Europe at the time when many black faces were not seen. If I was of a sensitive nature about that, it might have been a problem. But it wasn't so for me at all. I just thought it was fun.

John Weiss: When you met the textile industry, which was a very male industry, you went at one point to talk to the Bradford Textile Society ...

Althea McNish: Yes, in Harrogate.

John Weiss: ... and I would like to read the introduction to the report on your presentation to them: 'Trinidad, which is fairly represented amongst the present population of industrial Yorkshire, came and conquered our design conference in the person of Miss Althea McNish'.

It's quite obvious that those industrialists there were quite aware that they had black people in their factories but it rather sounds as if this was the first time they'd had a black person up on the platform lecturing to them. How did they take to it?

Althea McNish: Well the then chairman of the Bradford Printers and Dyers, I think they were called, asked me if I would come and give this talk to them. I said, 'Yes.' I thought it was fun and I went up. Then I was presented to an audience of 200 men, only men! All I could see was these grey suits in front of me and I thought, 'Althea, what are you doing here?' I thought I was completely out of everything. I looked on the platform and a journalist was there. She was a woman. She had come from London. So then I felt a little better and there was that man from Carnaby Street. I can't remember his name. He was there as well and Mr Hopkins, the man who expected me to talk. And I looked again and I thought, 'Hhhhu, you better get on with it.'

John Weiss: But it didn't really trouble you?

Althea McNish: Not really, no.

John Weiss: They had a new experience.

Althea McNish: I didn't know it was a new experience for them, of course, but it was so interesting. Having got over the shock of an audience of only men, I told them what is wrong, you know, 'I think men should show more interest in their clothes. I mean there are only grey suits here.' That was a lot of cheek actually standing in front of an audience of these men and saying, you know, only grey suits here. Then having said it, I looked and it was true. They thought, 'Well this is something.' Again I showed slides and this excited them very much and it was quite overpowering.

John Weiss: You got over it. Now before we start the slides let me just ask you about something I read in *The Trinidad Guardian*, around 1971/72. You were reported as having been asked your views about colour, meaning obviously not textile colour but people colour, and you were reported as having said you only see people in two colours – grey and red. You couldn't stand grey people and you only liked red ones. Could you say a little bit more about that?

Althea McNish: I think there's a catch to this one.

John Weiss: Did you mean by grey, grey suits or grey personalities?

Althea McNish: Yes, you see grey is a colour I would never use on my palette. Black! Because it has the power in it to do for me what I want. I use black in my paint. Whereas grey is a non-colour for me, red is colour. It's vibrant. I mean if you look at my things you can see it is red throughout. I never leave red out of my palette. But I have no use for grey. However, when I have to do a collection, whatever I do, I have to do a collection of another six colourways to the design as a textile designer. The idea is you can't just as a painter produce one idea. You have to have a range of colours for that first idea that you've put there for the producers to do. Coming back to Liberty's, one of the firms that I worked for at the beginning of my career, I was asked to do a collection for the older woman. And I thought, what do they mean by the older woman? What's wrong with the older woman? Why does she have to … And you know the man tells me grey and I say, 'Grey I don't use!' and I presume it must have been with a very determined sound in my voice. He said, 'But Althea, you know, the older woman …,' and I say, 'No! She doesn't need it. She has grey hair already. What does she need with grey and grey and grey?' You see, this was my rather strong feeling about it. And it was strong and it came out. They asked me for a colour range with grey in it for Bézique, my design with textured stripes such as Liberty's had never printed before. I compromised for the first time and I did one colour range that had grey in it. And they couldn't believe that they were actually seeing grey because I used grey in a very clever way. I didn't use it as the grey colour. It was so intermingled and entwined with the rest of the design that they weren't even aware that they were having grey in their collection. You wouldn't see anything with grey in it in my samples around because, as I say, grey is a sort of non-colour for me.

John Weiss: I think, Althea, we would like to see some of your designs. There is a slide show which will show some of Althea's inspirations as well as the designs themselves. I'll give a little bit of commentary and Althea will talk about her designs. This is the entrance to our house. The point of this photograph is that Althea fell in love with the cottage and that's the first of them. [1] [2]

Althea McNish: That's my poppy or the poppy. [3] The poppy is one of the most exciting flowers for me. I don't think we grow them at home so much. When I came first to Germany, at the villa where I stayed with my friends, the poppies were growing in great abundance. The little boy called Markus, he's now quite a big man, said, 'Blümen! Alle diese Blümen. Come and see Blümen!' So he led me by the hand into the garden to see all these beautiful blooming poppies. [4] This is one of the drawings of my poppies. As you see I have very large scale drawing and this is what the producers have to cope with.

John Weiss: This is the real size. As you see it on the screen that's the size of the drawing.

Althea McNish: But it's fun and my work is fun. I enjoy it. Now here is a panel which I did for an exhibition and it was shown in Leicester and other places. [5] It's painted velvet, on cotton velvet.

John Weiss: And that's four feet wide.

Althea McNish: Yes and three metres high or something. Here

I'm putting them up for the exhibition. [6] I like to hang my things myself because I'm very, I don't know, I suppose, sensitive about how things are hung and how the lighting is. I paint on the velvet panels using most of the techniques combined. I am a designer. I can't stick to any one method. I use all the techniques which are there and I just do as I feel.

John Weiss: This just shows that our house is almost all studios. [7] Almost everywhere there's work. Kitchen, living room, everywhere. This is part of Althea's reaction to the European environment. [8] This is a tiny insignificant flower, a blackberry blossom, but she uses it on this scale and she transforms all the tiniest English hedgerow flowers into tropical splendour. She tropicalises the daisies.

Althea McNish: Well, this [9] is from a collection I did for the sheet manufacturers Courtaulds, and it was produced and they did a very big range and it was sold in the big shops like Harrods and so on. It was on a very nice cotton. This [10] is one of my inspirations from Stuttgart botanical gardens – the palm house.

John Weiss: We usually travel around Europe between January and March. Europe at that time is much colder than England and we

3. Poppy
6. Poppies, two textile hangings, dyestuffs on cotton velvet, with Althea in front, working on the exhibit (at Leicester Magazine Workspace 1983)
11. 'Chaconia', printed textile commissioned by Trinidad and Tobago government for furnishing the temporary residence of HM Queen Elizabeth on an official visit to Trinidad
12. Plant of the banana family in the tropical house at Kew Gardens, London
14. 'Fresco' printed furnishing textile, designed by Althea McNish for Cavendish Textiles
15. Hanging banana stem in the tropical house at Kew Gardens, London
17. Fitzwilliam Museum, Cambridge, view looking up at the ceiling of the entrance porch
18. 'Theodoric', printed furnishing textile designed by Althea McNish for Cavendish Textiles

Photographs courtesy John Weiss

3. 6.

11. 12.

14. 15.

17. 18.

always make a bee-line for tropical houses wherever we find them so that I can make Althea feel a little bit more comfortable. We always find palm houses and so on.

Althea McNish: I did this [11] for the ...

John Weiss: The Queen Mother?

Althea McNish: No the Queen herself, Her Royal Highness. She paid a visit to Trinidad and my High Commission requested a design to be used in her rooms and this was done in a great hurry. Chaconia flowers were flown up for me here. They came on one of the flights and I did it and my printers went into production straight away. So everything was done very fast, very quick and sent down to Trinidad to put in the Queen's rooms.

John Weiss: I think it must have been just before independence.

Althea McNish: Yes it must have been.

John Weiss: When I first met Althea I was horrified to find she was a royalist, but a lot of Trinidadians love the royal family. I even found after 1976 that one or two Trinidadians didn't realise that Queen Elizabeth wasn't still their queen. So I mean we're not showing you photographs of her hobnobbing with the Duke and with the Prince. She's been on committees and so on with them. But on the other hand her father travelled a lot in the States and ensured that when Paul Robeson visited Trinidad he came and visited Althea and her mother. Althea met Claudia Jones through her father's contacts. So she was fairly wide in her tastes.

Althea McNish: Inspiration again from the palm house. [12] I did long murals from this.

John Weiss: This is a piece of a sculpture by David Smith. Some of you might know his work. [13]

Althea McNish: Very beautiful.

John Weiss: Althea's inspirations come from a very wide range. Sometimes they are very precisely copied as you saw with the poppy, but in general the visual sources pile one on top of each other. Now this [14] is a design that might have come from either of those two sources but it might also have come from the banana.

Althea McNish: The range was produced by Liberty's. And here are bananas. [15]

John Weiss: We had some metal shavings in a plastic bag. We spun it around and photographed it and that has been the inspiration for more things. [16] This is the Fitzwilliam Library in Cambridge, the ceiling of the porch, looking upwards. [17]

Althea McNish: The fabric that came out from that was called Theodoric. This one. [18] This got copied and I used to see it in caravans and all over the place. What they can do, what the producers can do if they lift a design from any other source, they drop a screen then you can't do anything, you see. They drop a screen and that's it. They say, 'It's not yours anymore.'

John Weiss: So it might have been printed with six or seven colours, each with a separate screen, and claiming copyright protection when somebody only copies some of the colours used to be problematic.

Althea McNish: Yes this is the problem. This is called Summer Madness. [19] That's the original. You might have seen others but that was the original, produced by Cavendish Textiles. This one is called Midsummer, a dress fabric produced on Sirocco cotton by Liberty's. Here it is shown in Brisbane at an exhibition there. [20] The jewellery around the model's neck is John's jewellery.

John Weiss: One should say it's Althea's.

Althea McNish: It is mine, yes.

John Weiss: The transition from my jewellery collection to Althea's isn't always noticeable but is very definite when it happens.

Althea McNish: Usually when I capture it, it remains in my collection. I haven't got a sample of fabric of this one [21] but it was produced and did very well. Sometimes, you know, I don't always get a sample of everything. If I'm not in England I can miss certain things, and by the time I get back it's all finished.

John Weiss: Althea, can you tell us about the origin of this design, Frangipani, that was poduced for Shridath Ramphal when he came to London to take up his post as the Commonwealth Secretary General. Before he actually started his duties he called Althea and said, 'I would like some marvellous things for my official residence.' **[22]**

Althea McNish: Oh he was lovely.

Member of the audience: What period is this?

John Weiss: That was 1975. During the ten days or so before he actually had to sit in his office it was a very interesting time. I used to talk to him a lot and of course suddenly he got busy. He caused quite a revolution in that particular environment. I mean the design environment. Of course he caused quite a stir in his official environment as well.

Althea McNish: This comes from the Mexican. [23]

John Weiss: This is another series of Althea's inspirations mixed in with some of the designs that come out.

Althea McNish: This is the god, a Mexican god, praying for rain and this is a fabric that came out from the Mexican. [24] You get the movement from this sculpture. This is a colourway. [25] Of the same design this is another colourway. [26] This is what I say, for each design I have to have at least five colourways because you know women have a choice, each of us want a different colour. This is the way you can get around it in the fabrics because possibly no two or three of us will go in and choose exactly the same colourway and if you have a range of colourways for any one design it has a much better life, getting sold and spreading around. These are all from the Mexican sculpture.

John Weiss: I helped pick out the slides with Althea and what comes out of this shows that in fact there are many different origins. [27] [28]

Member of the audience: What period would those have been, the Mexican ones?

Althea McNish: They range between the 1960s and 1970s.

John Weiss: But then you did some similar designs also in the 1980s.

Althea McNish: Yes, when I did a big collection for the Italians. This is our jungle, our living room. [29] I haven't got to go anywhere. I stay at home and I have it all there.

John Weiss: It did start reducing the light a little bit too much in the living room so we had to prune it.

Althea McNish: Well, we had a banana tree which was taking over. But on one occasion we were away during the winter and our neighbours killed it with love. They're lovely people and they do take care of the plants and the animals for us when we're not there. But they can get a bit over-zealous at times and each one would water. So when we came back it was over-watered.

This is one of the famous Bézique stripes. [30] This came after

'Terylene' goes mad-about-pri

32

A TOOTAL FABRIC

QUALITY		COMPOSITION		WIDTH		DEPTH		
	CARIMBA	100% HIGH TENACITY TERYLENE		46/3 ins 118 cms		9023	MADE IN ENGLAND	
COLOURS	1		2		3		4	

the original Bézique and this was done on organza and foulard silk. I've put in a bit of the original design. That's how the original was and that's a production. The Queen was supposed to have worn this at one of her garden parties. Not in that style of course! You heard John say I am a royalist. You see the reason why.

John Weiss: You might find in the biographical note that on Althea's first day out of college she went for an interview with Liberty's and Arthur Stewart-Liberty immediately commissioned designs from her instead of taking her on in the studio, which was what she was supposed to be looking for. When he finished with her he put her in a taxi to Ascher who was a Czech textile producer, who got stranded in this country at the beginning of the war and had made a name doing fabulous fabrics and inviting artists from all over the world to design scarves for him – Matisse, Picasso and so on. Ascher bought Althea's designs and this is some of what he produced from her designs for the French fashion houses. [31] A brilliant man but not a marvellous business man.

And this is the beginning of a promotion that Althea was engaged especially for. [32] This is Hollins Thomson, later Tootal Thomson, working in conjunction with ICI, who had finally produced a man-made fibre that would take strong colour. It may not be understood nowadays but in those days if you had a Terylene shirt it could be white or it could be pale pink or pale blue; or it could be even grey, because we didn't have biological washing powders then. And suddenly they invented something that could take strong colour. And who was the best designer to help promote it? The tropical Althea McNish.

31. Designs by Althea McNish for printed fashion textiles produced by Ascher (from Jours de France: garment sketches and front-cover illustration of modelled garment)
32. Terylene Toile: promotional page showing modelled garment using a textile designed by Althea McNish
34. 'Carimba', printed fashion textile designed by Althea McNish for Tootal Thomson as part of their Terylene Toile promotion (headboard with four colourway cuttings and a larger sample)

Althea McNish: They were very happy about it.

John Weiss: This was on Tobago. [33]

Althea McNish: Yes, on Italian toile, and this Italian toile was supposed to be a man-made silk. This is another range from the Italian toile collection. **[34]**

John Weiss: They not only produced the fabric but they engaged with about a dozen fashion houses, British fashion houses and later with Swedish and Swiss ones. They used Althea to design special fabrics for their special collections. It's been written up in an MA dissertation as one of the earliest uses by a textile fibre firm of design as part of their promotion for the new fibre.

Member of the audience: Oh is that yours? [35]

Althea McNish: Yes. Nobody knew the Design Centre at that time. This is the work going on. [36]

John Weiss: Some of our friends say they walked past without realising it was the Design Centre because of the colour.

Althea McNish: This is the work going on. [37] I printed them all at John's college.

John Weiss: You probably understand that when Althea is working as an industrial designer, a designer for industry, she uses the designs on paper but she doesn't engage in the production of the textile. But when she's doing architectural work, hangings or panels then she is very much doing it herself with help.

Althea McNish: Of course. And these are all printed on a vinyl sheeting.

John Weiss: This was a strange quality with very difficult pigments which were very poisonous.

Althea McNish: I'm in Sweden printing in the studios there. [38] [39] There I am experimenting again just as I did for the original Oriana – my murals started from that time.

John Weiss: The first Oriana was launched in 1960 just at the time that P&O amalgamated with Orient Line. They brought out two ships that were meant to be in competition to each other. Orient Line engaged Althea to design fabrics for them but in the end she did laminate panels and that was the beginning of a lot of her mural work.

Althea McNish: That mural [40] was 60 feet long. I worked on canvas with acrylics and used various techniques, spraying, drawing, printing.

John Weiss: This is an intermediate stage. [**41**] [42]

Althea McNish: I was able to use a friend's studio which was very good.

John Weiss: This is called Casino [**43**] and it's in the Nordic Empress next to the casino itself and, once Althea had done the painting, then the architect chose the colour of the furnishings, the leather. [44]

Althea McNish: They're sort of trying to match up things.

John Weiss: Althea was never quite sure that that's the match she would have made. That's me working as an assistant. [45]

Althea McNish: He's a marvellous assistant. Does everything you say.

John Weiss: This was one of two large textile hanging murals for the old British Rail offices in Euston. [**46**] There's one of them called

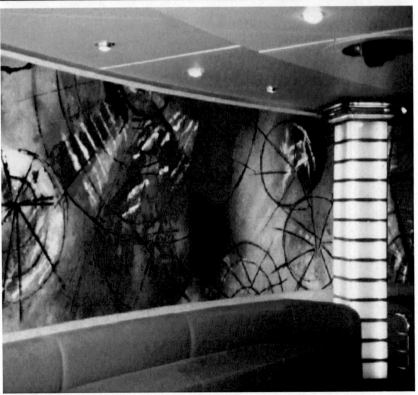

Wheels in the Boardroom. You can't see but the wheels aren't quite round and the engineers who came to meetings got quite disturbed.

Althea McNish: No, they're not supposed to be round.

John Weiss: This is the one we were working on but at a later stage. [47] It looks rather nice with the light coming in but in the final location it was all internal. Althea has always liked playing with light and in the actual location of it there is unfortunately very little.

Althea McNish: All the workmen that were working there stopped, came and had tea and cakes with us.

John Weiss: Althea took me to Trinidad for the first time in 1976 and those of you who are aficionados will recall that was the year of Peter Minshall's great triumph with 'Paradise Lost'. I was thrilled. I didn't quite realise that everybody else or nearly everybody was thrilled as well. He did not use trollies for his kings and queens. His angels looked as if that's how people would be if they had wings. This is the Angel of Fire. [48]

Althea McNish: There's a small bat. [49]

John Weiss: These were the bats, the traditional bats.

Althea McNish: Small ones with lovely …

John La Rose: There's something about the bats, their special dances. The bats and the dragons had special dances.

41. 'Casino', mural by Althea McNish, 1990, commissioned by architects Bidnell Phillips for the casino of the passenger cruise liner 'Nordic Empress' (Royal Caribbean Cruise Line): trial sample, photographed in the artist's studio
43. 'Casino', mural by Althea McNish, 1990, commissioned by architects Bidnell Phillips for the casino of the passenger cruise liner 'Nordic Empress' (Royal Caribbean Cruise Line)

John Weiss: I wasn't aware of that. What became apparent when we got home was that it wasn't just exciting for me, it was a refreshment for Althea and an inspiration.

Althea McNish: This is a serpent of paradise. This is a serpent in 'Paradise Lost'. [50]

John Weiss: Saint George and the Dragon both combined into one. [51]

John La Rose: What should be said is that Peter Minshall had more or less begun his work on 'Paradise Lost' here in London and then he went to Trinidad with it and developed it there beyond what he could have done here.

John Weiss: It was Althea who encouraged Peter to come to London to study.

Althea McNish: Yes. Because his mother was the journalist Jean Minshall and she wrote about me. There I am. Judging. [52]

John Weiss: While I was in the background getting out of the sun, she was in the sun for the whole day.

Althea McNish: You see how I'm protecting myself. [53] I can't cope with that sun anymore. The sun was stinging me. She's having a lovely time. She's on the veranda. This is down Frederick Street. [54]

Member of the audience: It reminds me of New Orleans. [55]

Althea McNish: Yes it is very much.

John Weiss: Don't forget this is 1976. It's slightly bigger business now. It's louder and bigger.

Althea McNish: We went to all the camps. [56]

John Weiss: This is just a fragment to show another aspect of the textile designer's life showing in trade fairs and you take your tent there. [57] You put it up. You sit there. I mean this is me as an architect doing textile designer's work and you hope that people will come and look at you. In fact most of Althea's business, I discovered, was always through people who already knew her or heard about her through word of mouth.

Althea McNish: My clients, yes.

John Weiss: That is all her best business. But it was quite fun going to the exhibitions and meeting old friends.

Althea McNish: It was quite an introduction for you into this world. This is, where is this one? [58]

John Weiss: That was in London. Now this was part of a job for British Rail. [59] The curtains here were something that I did. I got inveigled into learning about weaving. Althea hated weaving. The head of industrial design called in Althea and said, 'Look, I've been saddled with a new train interior.' This was for the Advanced Passenger Train that some of you may remember during its short life. [60] It was charcoal-grey and they were looking around for somebody who could do something about it and Althea McNish was the person who came to mind. But it couldn't be printed textiles, it had to be woven. So I learned a little bit about weaving. Although you can't see it very well here, [61] her colouring, the bright reds and I hope some bright purples, it doesn't show up enough here, but very intense reds, very intense purples set against the grey really made quite a startling effect.

Althea McNish: I wish I could have overcome those greys.

John Weiss: Well the grey had to be included. I recall we were talking earlier about Althea's technical involvement. Althea did some dye samplings to send to the weavers and she used proper dyestuffs to produce a really intense orange and when the fingerings came back, the small yarn samplings, they were a sort of muddy orange. We phoned them up and they said, 'Well, we thought it needed a little bit of grey.' This is part of a series of hangings for another ship. This is Monarch of the Seas and this led Althea into painting again. [62]

Althea McNish: Yes, I had a wonderful time working on these velvets for the ship, complete freedom.

John Weiss: This is a painting, 'Hurricane', [63] which you will find on the face of her catalogue [64] and it was prominent in her exhibition. [65]

Althea McNish: I had a wonderful time doing it.

22. 'Frangipani', printed textile for furnishing, designed by Althea McNish in 1976 to a commission by Sir Shridath Ramphal on his appointment as Secretary General of the Commonwealth, for his official residence in Carlton House Gardens, London Printed by Hull Traders Ltd

46. 'Wheels', textile hanging by Althea McNish, 1979, commissioned by the Architect to the British Railways Board for the Board Room

63. 'Hurricane', painting by Althea McNish: reactive dyestuffs on cotton velvet, 1991, 117x84cm detail

67. Still from animated experimental sequence, Althea McNish and John Weiss, produced on Atari computer 1992-93

70. 'Nicotea', printed fashion textile designed by Althea McNish for Liberty of London: sample printed on Ascot Silk, ref DC1161, Liberty ref G2-8291A

72. 'Marina', printed fashion textile designed by Althea McNish for Liberty of London: one of the earliest of Althea's fabrics to be produced by Liberty's

74. 'Golden Harvest', printed furnishing textile designed by Althea McNish for Hull Traders

78. 'Full House', BBC2 Television Programme, February 1973, studio setting of work by Caribbean artists arranged by Althea McNish
Althea McNish: textile hanging; printed textiles 'Golden Harvest' and 'Van Gogh' produced by Hull Traders; woven textile 'Winnona' produced by Sekers. Other works by Ronald Moody, Colin Barker, George Lynch, Xavier Llewellyn, Roy Cabou, Aubrey Williams, Errol Lloyd.

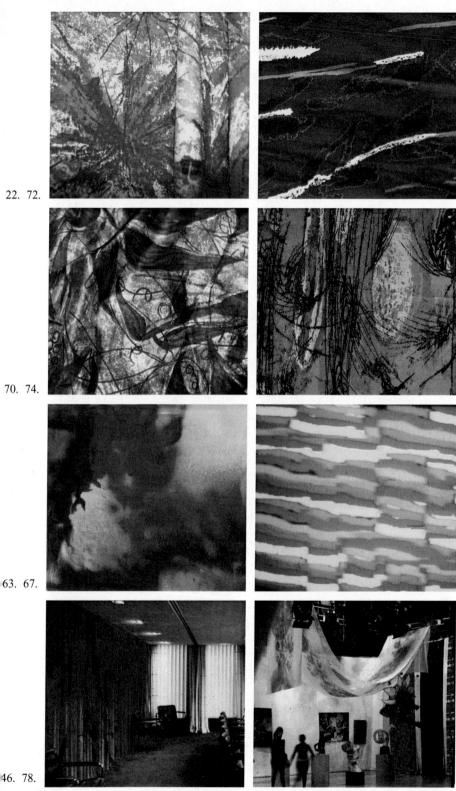

22. 72.

70. 74.

63. 67.

46. 78.

John Weiss: Althea persuaded me with our very first computer to find some programmes that would allow her to play with colour.

Althea McNish: That I don't find very sympatico for me, the computer, but it's fun. I can use it for a day if I want and that's it. It's fun. Oh this is one ... [66] [**67**] [68]

John Weiss: That's not a computer of course. It's a passion flower. [69]

Althea McNish: Passion flower. One of the first we had in the garden. This is a Liberty's print which I did after a visit to Chelsea Flower Show. [**70**]

John Weiss: This is the first of one of half a dozen of Althea's in the early part of her career. This is Liberty's.

Althea McNish: This is on foulard silk. [71]

John Weiss: It's a collection of all her Liberty's archives which we put up in one of the trade exhibitions and a young man started looking at them closely and he started protesting that Althea didn't have the right to show them.

Althea McNish: I think he thought that I had picked up samples from the shop, you see, and put them on the wall. I said, 'Hey mister, I'm the designer of these! Nobody has the right to tell me what and what not to show!' and I just said, 'Look at this little twerp!' That was one of the first dress designs that I did. [**72**]

Member of the audience: It's not silk?

Althea McNish: No, no. It's in cotton, a superfine cotton which Liberty bought out and it's only four pounds or whatever. It was a first design. This one is called Trinidad on an Austrian cloth. It's a furnishing fabric for Heal's. [73]

Althea McNish: Heal's is the shop which is now on Tottenham Court Road. This is a furnishing fabric in the Secretary General's offices in Carlton Gardens. [**74**] [75]

Member of the audience: Did you prefer furnishing to fashion work?

Althea McNish: Well, I started on furnishing. When I was at college my whole collection really was furnishing. I never liked working on a small scale. I did dress fabrics but I didn't have a great love for it because of the scale. I like working big and to come to bring it down to that size was quite a terrible thing for me. But from the time I finished college and Liberty's wanted me to do a collection for them, I began to bring it down. One thing I learned to do was to half-drop it, size it, whatever. Also I brought my mind around to convert my enormous ideas into smaller spaces. I got the first Cotton Board scholarship and that brought me down to scale. I came back with all my big ideas and my big things and I brought them down to scale. It was a marvellous exercise.

John Weiss: If you talk about scale, this shows an exhibit happening in the Swiss Cottage library, which was designed by Basil Spence, some two or three years after it was opened. The person who curated an exhibition of textile hangings was Peter Carey. [76]

Althea McNish: He was lovely.

John Weiss: He commissioned Althea to put something in this giant skylight and there was about 900 yards of three-metre-wide Terylene net and muggins here had the job of joining them together to make nine-metre widths. [77]

Althea McNish: I did the printing. We started at 8.00 am.

John Weiss: If you've ever sewn slippery Terylene net on a sewing machine you might know that it's not easy.

Althea McNish: Oh it was lovely. He never recovered from that. It was beautiful. I enjoyed it.

John Weiss: It was gigantic.

Member of the audience: Where is it now?

John Weiss: It's rolled up in our loft.

Althea McNish: It's been overseas and come back. It went to Canada and came back.

John Weiss: It went to Kilkenny for a big festival there.

Althea McNish: They had just the space for it in the cathedral.

Member of the audience: Nobody bought it?

Althea McNish: No, no. It's my exhibition piece. It's not for sale.

John Weiss: This was 1972 and the following year it formed part of a job that Althea did at John La Rose's request. This was to do with the Caribbean Artists' Movement.

John La Rose: It was *Full House* on BBC 2. I produced this programme in 1973 and I commissioned Althea to do this for the studio. [**78**]

Althea McNish: You can see the fabrics hanging in the background – Golden Harvest and another one, Van Gogh, and my Trinidad.

John Weiss: Althea negotiated with a lot of famous Caribbean painters and sculptors. John, you may remember that at the very last minute they said they didn't want to spend any time looking at the visual work and we all said, 'Well then we'll take it away.'

John La Rose: I was in charge so they had to do it. I was the producer.

Althea McNish: These are Ron Moody's sculptures. [79]

John La Rose: That man you see there is a reggae artist.

Althea McNish: He was quite a character.

John La Rose: Prince Miller. He was a great performer.

Althea McNish: He had everybody in stitches.

John La Rose: It was a 90-minute programme.

Althea McNish: Yes, it was wonderful.

Member of the audience: Althea, when you're working on something like velvet, which dye do you use?

Althea McNish: Well, for my velvet I use cotton velvet because most of the fabric that one finds is a mixture and dyes do not take very happily to mixtures. You might want red and instead of getting red you end up with a pink and things like this. So I did a research on velvet and had samples sent for me from Germany and other places. Listers were the ones that I have used from that beginning up to now. They gave me a range of their velvets, the pile is important.

The dye stuffs are ICI. They must be natural dye. Well Procions are the best. They fix well. All my things that you see on large hangings and murals, I take them down to the factory and they're fired at 240° F or something like this. They go through the machinery.

Member of the audience: Are they painted?

Althea McNish: They are not processed wet. I use dry baking because if I use the wet steaming it could end up with running, which I don't want.

Member of the audience: How do you do it for fabrics which are used for clothes?

Althea McNish: The same. No problems. Using industrial dyes.

Member of the audience: Are they washable?

Althea McNish: Yes, the industrial dyes hold fast. You don't have a problem with that. But I don't print fabrics for use. All my printed things are produced by the manufacturers. So the industrial dyes are the ones that the producers use and you haven't a problem with that. If there is a problem, sometimes you may have a red that may bleed a little, it doesn't really matter. As long as you don't wash certain things together. I tell people, 'You don't put your nice fabric in the washing machine. Forget it. You can't wash it. Your blouse, who wants to put a silk blouse in the washing machine? Forget it!' You see certain things like this but otherwise no problem. The industrial dyes are from ICI. If you ever have any problem you write to them and they're very good.

Member of the audience: So if you're making a design and you're giving it to the producers, are they allowed to enlarge it or shrink it in size?

Althea McNish: No, no.

Member of the audience: Is it just the size that you want?

Althea McNish: Yes, but it all depends. I have complete control up to a certain point with my work. I sell you my collection and if there is anything that needs to be done, I will do it. I don't even agree that the studios do it because sometimes people don't know your handwriting. They're not in sympathy with the way I work, and I have a very distinct handwriting. It's not very easy to copy, or whatever you call it, so I usually say you send it back and I will do colourways or whatever is needed to be done because not everyone can translate. John has got very good. He can translate anything that I do.

John Weiss: I can use a tiny brush and imitate her very big arm movements.

Althea McNish: Yes, he has looked at me and the movement that I do. But normally if I sell a collection or if I have to work on a collection, I just say I'll do the lot. I insist on that.

John Weiss: This is one of the big problems for a printed textile designer, the manufacturers tend to feel that once they've bought the design, and there's a query as to what that means, they don't really want the designer to interfere with the process in general. On the other hand Althea has been in a sense fortunate, in that a lot of her manufacturers have come to her for the full range of what she can do for them. Once they get to know, then they want her to do the alterations because they know she can do it. This comes back to the point we were making much earlier. She absorbed herself in the technology very, very thoroughly. Not many designers do that. The result of it has been that she has complete freedom in her design, which is an unusual thing.

Member of the audience: Althea you've been doing those things, working with the best and most famous shops in town from many years ago. Can they come back after 20 years and say, 'Hey we would like that design that you did for us in 1976?'

John Weiss: Well, you must understand the distinction between the things that Althea does herself by hand, for instance, her textile hangings for architecture and the designs that she produces for industrial production, where her designs are on paper. Now basically once, I mean this is talking very vaguely, once they've bought a design on paper, then it's theirs to use. They don't have to come back to Althea.

Member of the audience: They don't buy the copyright?

John Weiss: Ah well, unfortunately Geoffrey Adams, who was in the audience until about five minutes ago, is the European expert on design copyright. I was hoping that he would join in this discussion, but he obviously had to go. It's a sore point for designers. Copyright legislation has changed anyway. In theory a manufacturer would not have the right to change the designer's design. But if one is talking about the fashion field where a design has a very, very limited life, maybe three months, nobody's got the patience to deal with anything like that. With furnishing designs it's a different matter. If it's on the shelves for less than seven years it's a failure. With a fashion design if it's on the shelves for more than two months it's a failure. You know it works in different ways. It turns out to be very, very difficult in practice for a designer to exercise her rights.

Member of the audience: So if the fabrics that she does are actually used for clothes and given their life capacity, because in relation to fashion it is a matter of six months, somebody can come after 15 years and produce a copy.

Althea McNish: Yes it happens.

Member of the audience: From high fashion to street fashion, how long does it take to get a design out?

Althea McNish: A few hours. It's shown in the collection and by 3.00 pm it's out there.

John Weiss: I have been with Althea at Interstoff, in Frankfurt, which is one of the biggest fairs in Europe for fashion textiles. We happened to meet an old friend of Althea's, who was one of the 12 British manufacturers at the Tootal Thomson viewings in their promotion in the 1960s. Althea indicated to him that a very good silk printer in Corno, Riccardo Mantero, had recently bought some of her designs. 'Oh yes,' he said, 'I must go and have a look' because his fabrics are very expensive, 'I'll buy a metre or two of Althea's designs and copy it.' Now what was so intriguing was that it never occurred to him that he was doing Althea in the eye.

Althea McNish: Doing me out.

John Weiss: Riccardo Mantero, if he'd seen a copy of the design, could easily have imagined that Althea had sold the design again to somebody else.

Member of the audience: That's the problem.

John Weiss: Now, the essence of the problem which we have tried to tackle, with another Italian manufacturer who produced one of Althea's designs, was to license the design and not to sell anything. This is what one really ought to do and it's what industrial designers in the product field do. In the end he agreed to a very complicated licensing arrangement but the Italians are very litigious and the Italian courts are very crowded and it soon became apparent to us that if there was any breach of the agreement, we wouldn't have a chance in hell of actually doing anything about it. So I learned very early on that the textile designer's world is a problem. But Althea's personality brought her to a lot of success with her manufacturers. If you wanted to be technical about the copyright issue it really is, well … I mean we have friends here who struggle with copyright in other fields, in the music field, but at least people know quite precisely what it ought to be even if there are arguments as to who owns a copyright. With the textile field a lot of the industry, including the designers, couldn't care less. I mean this is me as an architect feeling frustrated and I've been doing this with Althea for 30 years.

Althea McNish

John La Rose: Althea, one of the things you didn't talk about and it would be interesting to hear you say something about is daily life with people like Sybil Atteck, M.P. Alladin and those painters from Trinidad.

Althea McNish: Well I met them from childhood because, as I told you, I became a junior member of the Trinidad Art Society, which was where they all were. Mildred Almandoz, Amy Leong Pang. There was a Chinese painter Geoffrey Holder, Carlisle Chang, and many others.

John La Rose: They encouraged you.

Althea McNish: Very much so. Andrew Carr, who was I think the secretary of the Trinidad Art Society, came to my mother and said, 'Mrs McNish I would like Althea to join the society as a junior.' So mummy said, 'Yes, Althea would love to, I'm sure.' So she said, 'Althea?' and I said, 'Oh, yes!' But I was a little apprehensive, I didn't know who was there. It wasn't my school friends or anything like this, you see. Anyway I went to the first meeting and there were all these painters sitting down at easels. Everybody had their boards and I looked around me and there was a model, first time I'd seen a model, in the nude, see. So I caught my breath and I sat back, I mean I didn't want anyone to know this was the first time this was happening to me. So I just looked at what everybody was doing and I just joined in and I sat down. It took me a little while to recover from this nude model sitting there and my charcoal came out and I went to town and I had a marvellous time. Nobody had a clue that it was the first time and when my mother asked, I said, 'Oh Mummy it was lovely and there was a nude model.' She said, 'Really, so you enjoyed it?'

So this is how my life started in the Art Society and I continued to be a member throughout until I left home. I had my first exhibition when I was 16 and they gave me the rooms to show it in and I showed it there and this is where the entomologist saw my work at this exhibition. At Whitehall, I think it was called. So this is where I met them all and I painted with Sybil Atteck.

John La Rose: What did you think of Sybil Atteck?

Althea McNish: She was a mentor. She was very good. She ran the group and things like this and she would call and collect me and I would go. I sat for her. I sat for all of them and they did a lot of paintings of me and I had a marvellous time. I remember she painted me in a white blouse and yellow skirt. My hair was pinned up. I'd come from school and taken my ribbon out, my plaits and pinned it up and she painted me in that. They were very nice, the older painters. They were very, very nice and kind to the young ignorant ones I would say. I had no training and she had been abroad already. M.P. Alladin, he was marvellous. I painted with all of them and I think I learned a tremendous amount but I always went my own way. I was mentally wayward like that. I mean they call me a naïve painter because I may look and see you there but I don't particularly like possibly what I see and I paint from my own head. But I enjoyed it.

When I was still at school, the priest in Boissière must have seen the exhibition, he asked if I would come and do a painting class for the children in the village, Boissière village. I remember very well. I used to come out of school, pin up the plaits again, get on the bicycle and I was off. I brought their work to England with me when I came and I had an exhibition at the Central School showing what the children in Trinidad had done. They were eight-year-olds and they would be waiting at the gate for me, 'Miss, Miss come in,' and I get off my bicycle and come in. In a way I wasn't all that much older than many of them but they all felt that they had to take care of me. If you turned up, everybody would come out and look at you and want to know what it is you want. One wonderful thing in Trinidad was that when my parents' friends knew that Althea was doing things, Salvatori had an art shop and they gave us paints, jars of powdered stuff. They gave us paper because the village school had nothing. My parents and friends gave us a shilling or so and I was able to go in and buy things. People gave us things, mainly as

I say Salvatori, *The Guardian* and friends of my parents and so on. The priest was so happy and he used to come as a sort of guardian and see if the class was alright. It was marvellous and I would take the children out to the gardens to do painting, outdoor painting. My mother would make up a lemon juice drink and I would take bottles of this. You know I was always raiding her larder to take stuff for the children. It was a lovely part of my life and it did something for me. I've always been able to work with children. They've no inhibitions. They're marvellous. You tell them Carnival today, you tell them, 'Do me what you saw yesterday,' and fantastic things would come out. It's wonderful working with them.

Member of the audience: Are you involved in teaching, doing workshops?

Althea McNish: I have been a lecturer where I have gone out on request to lecture at colleges and I was artist-in-residence for one of the local schools.

John Weiss: Most of Althea's educational work has been as a visiting lecturer. She's visited all the textile and fashion courses in the country either as a lecturer or an examiner but she's never done any full-time teaching. Also in the ordinary way she hasn't done any school teaching. Her assignment at the local school two or three years ago was something quite unusual for her.

Althea McNish: I was dead scared of them personally.

John Weiss: It was a tough school.

Althea McNish: Well you know 12-year-olds can be quite a handful. Sometimes I would look at these little devils and think, 'Oh my God, they're going to eat me alive.' But I had a lovely time. I spent three weeks or something like that with them. There was one little boy I remember, he was from Zaire, beautiful child. He came to the door and he was screaming his head off. I looked at him and I thought, 'What's the matter with him?' They told me that he didn't want to come and I said, 'He's alright. Leave him. He will come when he wants. Don't worry. Just leave him.' They left him and he stood at the door, the tears rolling down his face and he was looking at me and I wasn't taking him on. In the middle of it I sort of wandered up and said, 'Hi, you want to come and join me?' And then somebody said, 'He doesn't speak English.' So I said, 'Well what does he speak?' He's from Zaire. So I said, whatever it was I said, my French came to my brain, and he said, 'Oui Madame.' I said, 'Good, come, join us.' I said, 'Paper, pencils, you draw for me?' And that child he settled down and I got my French working. I thought something's going to come out and he isn't going to be sitting there analysing my sentences. And we got on like a house on fire. He came at the end of the session and said, 'J'ai fini' and I said, 'Oui'. And I found out that this child, he was from Zaire, he was brought to school at 6.00 am when his parents went to work. 6.00 am! Who is in the school at 6.00 am? So he was there until the kids turned up at 8.00 am or 9.00 am, whatever time it is and no one tried to get through to him. He spoke French so that was it. He came from Zaire so that was it. For the three weeks that I spent there, at the end of the time he was the most charming little devil you'd ever seen. I said, 'The day you learn to speak English you are going to give them what it takes!' and these little eyes looking up at me and every time he saw me he'd come to the door and smile. Wow! He was in harmony with life and everybody. But this was it. Nothing was wrong with him. It was just that he could not communicate and this was his only problem. I quite enjoyed myself with the children on this occasion. It was the first time and it was fun and they said, 'Miss coming back?' and I said, 'Yes, I'll come back some time.' I was dead scared to do it but I enjoyed it.

Member of the audience: Have you ever collaborated with other artists, dancers, or theatre people or film people?

Althea McNish: Not really. I designed some costumes once. They were for a dance group from Trinidad. They were going back and I did the costume drawings for them, but it's such a long time ago I'd forgotten about that until you asked me.

John Weiss: It's the sort of question Althea would usually answer by saying, 'Well not yet and have you something in mind?'

Member of the audience: What are you doing now?

Althea McNish: I'm getting my retrospective ready.

Member of the audience: When will it be and where?

Althea McNish: I don't know.

John Weiss: It's not next year.

Member of the audience: Where?

Althea McNish: Where is the thing, and I think I need to have sponsorship so I will have to start to work on my manufacturers. Liberty's said, 'Oh it would be a wonderful thing, and I must do such a thing but now the chairman's just died, the past chairman.' My Ascher man, Zik Ascher's son was also for this and he even has my original screens for one of my first designs ever printed. It was during my Monet period because I have Monet drawings, at the time there was a Monet exhibition on at Paris, that I did for both Liberty's and for Ascher. They produced them.

Member of the audience: I'm surprised they don't produce it now.

Althea McNish: Well you see a lot of the new people don't even know. They have to go back to the archives to find out.

Member of the audience: Because that would have been popular with the exhibition in London.

Althea McNish: Yes definitely but that was a very, very good period because I went to France and I saw the exhibition and it was fantastic.

Member of the audience: Do you have a catalogue yourself of all the things you've done?

John Weiss: It's gradually being compiled.

Althea McNish: I have catalogues of several things, yes. That is one, that's the most recent one. [80] That's the most recent thing that I have. This is why I say I'm working on my retrospective so I will have many things there. It's coming. I have to do it. Nobody else can do it. I just look at something and I know when, who produced it and where, things like this. I have to get all this together which I'm in the process of doing. I have hundreds of files which I've been going through. It's a long job but I have to do it. No one else can and once I prepare all this and it's ready, anyone can take it over to produce it. Otherwise it will be chaos if I don't do such a thing. I'm not a person who has time in her brain so sometimes if you say, 'When did you do that? When did you do that?' I say, 'Around such and such a time,' but I can never get the precise time in my head. That is something I don't know. It doesn't bother me because I can look at something and say, 'I did that in the 1960s,' and then somebody will say, 'What date?' and I say, 'It doesn't matter what date.' This is how I feel about it. So this is what I'm working at. I never destroy my diaries, I have all my diaries, so I'm going back to my diaries where I'm finding a lot of the information that I need. It's correct because I have the times. It was 11.30 am when I first met Sir Arthur Stewart-Liberty.

John La Rose: I can see a friend here from the period of the Caribbean Artists Movement. Errol Lloyd. And I remember the very first session we did on visual arts and Errol was there and so were yourself, Aubrey Williams and Ronald Moody and Jerry Craig.

Althea McNish: Jerry, yes I'd forgotten. I saw Jerry in Jamaica when I was there last. He was wonderful. He is a professor at the university. They all came out, they had to, I gave them a talk, they all had to sit down under the trees because the place isn't large enough to hold all the students so it has to be done in sections. It was lovely and hot.

John La Rose: Errol said on that occasion that he couldn't call himself a sculptor or a painter because he was doing his apprenticeship. Now I want to bring to your attention two things: this is a card based on her work which was in an exhibition at the Royal College Art in the Hockney Gallery, and as I told you, it was one of the most stunning exhibitions I've seen. This is another card based on her work and I would recommend both cards to you. They're only 50 pence. Now, this is the catalogue of the Hockney exhibition and it contains more information than you had in your short biography. So if you wish to get some of the information some people were asking for tonight, you will get it from looking at this. [81] Thank you all very much for coming out on this wild and windy night but I'm sure you're glad you came because I think, and I want to say publicly for Althea to hear it, and I've thought so for a long time, that people like Aubrey Williams, like Ronald Moody and Althea McNish are geniuses that we have produced and I think I would like you to give her a round of applause.

Althea McNish, born in Port of Spain, was a painter from early in her Trinidad childhood. In the 1950s she came to London and made a career in textile design; bringing tropical colour to Britain in designs for Liberty's and Ascher, she became Britain's only black textile designer of international repute.

Althea's background to her design career was her life in painting in Trinidad, working with and encouraged by eminent Trinidadian artists, including Sybil Atteck, M.P. Alladin and Boscoe Holder. By the time of her 1958 solo exhibition at London's Woodstock Gallery and the 1961 exhibition of the Trinidad and Tobago Art Society which she mounted at the Commonwealth Institute, she had already made her name as a textile designer, and the work she showed included designs on paper and preliminary drafts of murals. From that time on and until the late 1980s, she exhibited only textile designs and samples of manufactured textiles. Her career has always been international, with frequent journeys around Europe to show new collections of textile designs to her many international clients. Manufacturers come to her London studio from many parts of the world to buy or commission designs for printed textiles.

From the time she started her career. Althea had an impact on the British design world. In 1957, on leaving the Royal College of Art and with her introduction to the commercial world of textiles by way of Liberty's and Ascher, she immediately made her name as one of the leaders of the strong new movement in British printed textile design of the time, largely centred on her circle from the RCA. This movement exhibited a new vigour in pattern and colour and a freedom from inhibition. Arthur Stewart-Liberty said in later years that he saw in Althea's designs exciting colour contrasts for which the British public was then reaching. She brought to London a tropical framework of reference and an invigorating reaction to British attitudes to textile design, recorded in numerous books on modern textiles and recently the subject of a postgraduate dissertation.

Althea's contribution early in her career to that dramatic period in the development of British textiles is a public example of the influence on British culture of artists and writers of the colonial and ex-colonial peoples. With the Caribbean Artists Movement she took part in seminars and exhibitions, and in February 1973 she organised CAM artists' work for the BBC magazine programme *Full House*, proclaiming to the British public the presence of the Caribbean arts. In the context of the unacknowledged contribution and influence of the black artist, Althea McNish had a visible effect on British textiles and thus on, and in, British culture. The vehicles of her influence have been the promotion of her work by notable producers, her participation in official exhibitions of British textile designers' work internationally, and her contact with the many students she has taught, visited or examined in design schools throughout the UK.

Her work has been recognised also in the institutional world of design, presenting a rare black, and female, face on public and professional committees. She became a Fellow of the Society of Industrial Artists and Designers (now the Chartered Society of Designers), was a member of its Council over a period of 22 years, with a term as a Vice-President, and she is currently on the National Council and London Committee of the Design and Industries Association. Her public service has also included the Board of the Design Council, the Governing Body's of Portsmouth College of Art, the Advisory Committee of the London College of Furniture, the Formation Committee of the London Institute of Art and Design. She has a continuing commitment to young people entering the design world through her work for professional and educational bodies,

Althea's attitude to her cultural affinities echo that of Trinidad itself and its own great diversity of cultures. She states a comparable pride in being a citizen of the world whilst manifestly rejoicing in the richness of her Trinidadian upbringing and of her family heritage drawn from Europe, Africa and America,

Althea McNish

native American as well as imported African.

In 1979 a commission for textile hangings for British Railways Board's offices inspired her to experiment with dyestuffs on fine cotton velvet to create effects of vibrant luminosity, which she used to good effect in hangings shown in The Peoples Gallery in 1982 and the Leicester Magazine Workspace in 1983. Murals and hangings for Royal Caribbean Cruise Line ships Nordic Empress and Monarch of the Seas led to works on velvet and silk and to paintings in acrylic on canvas, signalling the return in recent years to her life as a painter.

In September 1997, Professor Christopher Frayling, Rector of the Royal College of Art, said in opening her solo exhibition in the College's Hockney Gallery: 'Althea came to the College with a scholarship in graphics – but decided to practise printed textiles instead, under the inspiration of Eduardo Paolozzi in particular and the colours and sensations of her native Trinidad in general. As she has put it, her tropical ideas certainly stretched her teachers at the College, and after she left in July 1957 she was immediately commissioned by Liberty's to design a new collection – an extraordinary tribute to someone who had graduated only the day before. Althea has recently written: "On the day I saw Liberty, my professional life started. It has been devoted to designing for industry, and my designs are all meant for industrial production – on the day I discovered textiles I stopped painting pictures. It is only in recent years that commissions for murals and textile-hangings for public buildings and cruise liners have inspired me to move towards painting again. I have always" she continues, "seen myself as a citizen of the world, drawing inspiration from the flora and fauna of every country and the art and artefacts of all cultures." The results of these recent developments are the substance of this exhibition: not culture but cultures not one country but the world, a fusion of design and art which is at the heart of the Royal College of Art and what it continues to stand for ...'

In 1976 Althea's work as artist and designer was recognised by the Government of Trinidad and Tobago when she was awarded the Republic's Chaconia Medal (Gold) for 'long and meritorious service to art and design' and in 1988 she received the Scarlet Ibis Award of the London High Commission for Trinidad and Tobago.

For the last 30 years Althea has worked in partnership with her husband, John Weiss, in which they support each other's design projects as well as working together on joint projects. In addition to their design work, they now collaborate on collecting material from archives on both sides of the Atlantic for his work on the settlers of the Company villages of Trinidad (the 'Merikens', part of the 4,000 black Americans who took their freedom in the course of the War of 1812), and they attend conferences together to tell the world about this special Trinidadian community. Althea continues the tradition of these independent, adventurous and hardworking ancestors.

John McNish Weiss, December 1998

Gus John
introduced by John La Rose (15.03.1999)
with Roxy Harris in the chair

Gus John: Colleagues, welcome. It's good to see a number of familiar faces – some of whom have been engaged with me in the struggle over a number of years, others with whom I went through a sojourn in a borough not far from here. Welcome. And others whom I have known from attendance at the International Book Fair and other events which our cultural and other activities have made us all part of over the years. I want to do two things principally this evening. First of all to say something about my early life in Grenada and my early life in England and secondly to relate that to the political activism that I came to be a part of after meeting John in the middle of the 1960s.

I was born on the 11th of March 1945 in the glorious little island of Grenada. In those days, my godparents, or whoever, decided to call me Gregory, because the 12th of March, as I came to realise later, was the feast of St Gregory. I suspect I must have been born round about midnight or something so it's all very logical. The other thing that is logical about it, of course, is that I was born into a very devout Roman Catholic family, my mother more than my father. My father had a certain detestation of priests, he thought they were pretentious, full of humbug, and generally got in the way of people's spirituality. So he did not have too much time for priests and churches. My mother was very different and she brought us up to be God-fearing children. I became an altar boy at the age of five, and I didn't stop, basically. I graduated from being an altar boy to being a seminarian and I'll fill in the gaps between in a moment. Wilfred John, my father, was a very big man, six foot, broad, and I learned an enormous amount from him. In fact, his life enabled me to get a grasp early on of the intersection of class and of the economy in our struggles as people in the Caribbean. When I was born he was in the Dutch West Indian island of Aruba, working with the Lago Oil Refinery. He had migrated there some years earlier and he made visits home regularly and I came to learn that

Gus John

was a pattern that had been established some time earlier. He worked in the oil fields in South Trinidad and also worked in the Panama Canal and did a number of things in between, including picking apples and tomatoes or some produce or other in the United States. So he was one of a whole number of emigré workers, who left the Windward Islands, and I suspect the same must have been true for Jamaica, to go and earn in countries that were larger, more industrialised, particularly in terms of oil, like Trinidad, Aruba and Curacao. And my mother stayed behind, bringing up us children and eking out an existence as a peasant farmer and housewife. As children, there was my sister, my one and only sister, my brother Clement, whom some of you know. He lived and worked in this country as a youth worker and assisted with the Book Fair in successive years. Then me, then a younger brother, Stanley, who is living in West London. And I'll say some more about the West London connection in a moment.

So, with these children, my mother lived in a small two room shack and the twins she had before she married my father, older than us, also lived with us, my bigger brothers. One of them later perished from typhoid fever because some quack was giving him drugs for something completely other than typhoid which hastened his demise, to the shock and horror of the whole village. They slept in a partitioned kitchen which was just above the yard of the house because we couldn't all fit into the little shack. My mother had one room and my sister with her, and my brothers in the other part of the house.

We belonged to a family that was quite unusual in some respects. My maternal grandmother was a member of a large Louison family and my brother, Clement, has constructed a very elaborate family tree. I won't even begin to get into that. Suffice it so say that among the Louisons there were those that were poor, there were those who were middle class and there were those who were relatively rich. My grandmother was a very humble, hard-working soul. I never knew her. I'm told that she was a pillar of the village and did a lot of things in terms of getting the women of the village organised, marketing produce and those sort of things. So we lived in a yard.

It was a yard where different relatives, different elders of this extended Louison family, had their little parcels of land. And I came to realise later on that we were all connected in some way or another, aunts and uncles, grand-aunts and grand-uncles, and all sorts of stuff and that piece of land had been parcelled out and we all lived as one sort of communal family. So the influence of those women in the yard, on all of us, including some wayward sons given to drink and other questionable activities, in their eyes, the influence of those women was phenomenal. The grandfather in the family was a very reputable head teacher, F.J. Louison, one of the stalwarts in Grenada history, a contemporary of T. Albert Marryshow and such people, and reputed because of his political acumen and the fact that he was a brilliant teacher and teacher trainer.

So it was in that village that I grew up. My father finally returned from Aruba when I was aged six, and with his money he built a house to accommodate us in more comfort and with the prospect of more human dignity. That caused a stir in the village of course. Who is Wilfred to go building such a mansion, who does he think he is, the man can't even read or write, and those sorts of things that villagers are notorious for. We lived through all of that and I began to understand it more and more. But the church played a major part in that, too. And I came to realise fairly early on that the Anglican church was effectively the church of the rich, the Church of England, the rich middle class families belonged to the Church of England. The poor and the peasants belonged to the Roman Catholic church. And side by side with the Roman Catholic church in our village was the traditional African religion, the Orisha religion, the Yoruba religion. My elder brother's godmother was what we call a Shango Queen and she used to have the sacrifeast, all of that, just behind our house, in fact behind the kitchen which ironically was just 50 yards away from the Catholic church. So there was a kind of cat and mouse game between her and the Roman Catholic priest and some of the more devout Roman Catholics in the village. There were certain things that you didn't do at certain times of the year because that was the Roman Catholic church's time. The rest of the time the Yoruba people came and had their worship and so on. So I grew up with both those religious tendencies, very much with the priest but at the same time very much with the Orisha people, and the Caribbean derivation of that, the very derivative Spiritual Baptist faith to which I now belong.

My primary school was very formative. I was blessed with some absolutely excellent primary school teachers and they were, in a sense, an extension of our family. You dared not cross any one of them. They saw you as their own child and your parents believed without question whatever the teacher told them on their way from school. So if you wanted a story to go home and have the right resonance you'd better sort it out with your teacher before the teacher got up the hill and told your mother and father what was actually happening. They turned out some very good people. For them education was not just about the pursuit of academic excellence, it was about the building of character, and everything in the school reflected that.

I stayed in the Concord government school. The head teacher was an Anglican and he had a penchant for sucking eggs. He also happened to be my godfather. I well recall regularly being called out of class to be sent up the hill to my mother's home, about half a mile away, to get some more eggs to satisfy his addiction to sucking eggs. How that man lasted so long is anybody's guess. It was a school that did a lot for us because it basically reflected what we were and what we were aspiring to be, and it demonstrated the importance that our parents attached to education. But all kinds of crazy things used to happen in that school too. We sang a hymn every morning and I well remember one particular hymn which puzzled me and in fact as I grew older it angered me. I think it was Hymn 117 in the Westminster hymnal, I remember it well, 'Thy kingdom come O God, Thy rule O Christ begin, Break with thine iron rod, the tyranny of sin'. But the verse which really got my goat was the one which said, 'Over heathen lands afar, thick darkness broodeth yet, arise o morning star, arise and never set'.

It became very clear to me that those heathen lands afar were places where we came from, and yet we sang that hymn with particular gusto in the week that was, I think, Christian Aid week, or some strange thing like that, where we all had to all go round the village doing jobs, ask our mothers for more pocket money and contribute to keeping starving children in Africa alive. Yes, a sort of variation on 'Buy a black baby'. For us it was a bit ironic because we were struggling to stay alive ourselves most of us, and the notion that somehow we were superior and could be assisting these 'heathen lands' was something that I found a bit difficult to take in.

But all of that is important for another reason because throughout that period I studied all kinds of things. We had a Nelson reader, well-thumbed, a very yellow reader and well used, and a whole number of other things besides – the geography of the Caribbean, physical geography, not social geography. But it was only many years later that I got to know that there was any book at all written by a black person, whether the person was from the Caribbean or anywhere else. In all of my 12 years, well eight years, from the age of four when I went to primary school to the age of 12 when I left to go to the Presentation Boys College in Grenada, I had no knowledge whatsoever that black people could write books, or had written anything. Just about everything we dealt with was constructed in a colonialist mode and was effectively a reflection of the colonially organised educational system.

My secondary school was the Presentation Boys College in St George's in Grenada where I was taught by some Irish Presentation Brothers from Cork, in Ireland, very zealous people they were too. Some of them were good teachers, some of them were appalling teachers.And what became very clear to me was that they had a perspective of the island and the social classification which they sought to reflect in the school itself. In other words, those people who came from middle class families, and amongst them were quite a lot of people whom we called 'red-skinned', high yellow, had a profile and a status within the school which was denied to those of us who were black and poor. And one found that reflected in all the school organisation. So I had to think about that a lot as I saw all kinds of injustices happening within the schooling system itself at the hands of those people. But they were also very colonialist. I won't do it now, you'll be pleased to hear, but on any social evening I could regale you with endless madrigals, ditties, folksongs, rude songs from Southern Ireland. I know them all, I know the words of them all even now. We sang them and sang them and sang them. We had concerts for the whole island, demonstrating how we, nice little Grenadian boys, could sing these wonderful Irish songs. And there was an overlay within all of that of a sort of white superiority, which many of the students in the college, sad to say, sought to emulate.

And I well recall one day I went to school when I had just started down there and my mother, as parents would, made sure I was properly decked out and bought me this pair of shoes. Now, we wore shoes only on Sundays. When the priest didn't come to our village we had to walk to a church which was about three miles away. So you tie the laces of the shoes, hang them on your shoulder, walk to church, and as you got to the gate of the church, put your shoes on, wear them in church, come out of church, hang them on your shoulder, and walk back home. So that was my relationship with shoes. It was no close and intimate relationship if you understand my meaning. Come the age of 12 I was supposed to wear these damn things all day long – new, tight, uncomfortable, hot. And I'm walking down the street, in some agony, I have to tell you, and these young women rich – middle class going to the St Joseph's Convent down the hill, in cars at the age of 15 and 16 – saw me and they burst into one helluva laughter. They said something about 'country bookie bumpkin come to town.' And I was bullied with that, day after day, evening after evening. I avoided them. I did all kinds of things and it taught me something else too about class and about economy and about poverty and about human dignity and the rest of it.

One more anecdote and I'll move on to another phase. In the town lived some boys who went to my college. One of them was called Reginald Solomon. I got to know the Solomon family very well. He was a lovely young man. He, myself, the present Prime Minister of Grenada, Keith Mitchell, we all started in my class on the same day and went through school together. My parents got me to take my lunch at Solomon's parents' home. Easter came and he thought it would be a good thing to come and see what country life was about. I asked my mother and she said, yes, sure he could come. He duly came and it was the mango season and he just went wild, picking every mango, eating every fruit that was in sight. Now we boys in the village knew about that and its consequences. He wasn't too familiar with those consequences and the time came, of course, when he began to have the runs. Now the government in its lack of wisdom had decided to put just directly opposite our house a public lavatory. Let me not grace it with that wonderful name. It was a covered pit latrine and was always wet, slimy and decidedly hazardous. I have to tell you I had had the experience, like so many other boys, so many other people in that village, of having some close shaves with that thing. This included having the misfortune of the new belt that your mother had just bought you, after much protestation and stuff, fall into the pit and having to go behind the latrine and lift up the heavy cover and use a bamboo to retrieve your belt and then go to the river and spend some time with some Jeyes fluid trying to bring it back to a socially acceptable condition. I did not quite fancy the prospect of young Reginald ending up where the belt ended up, so I decided to take a chamber pot and give the fellow the stuff to do his business in the house. My mother comes into the house and asks, hot sun blazing outside, 'Who is using the chamber pot inside the house?' I told her and I told her my reasons for not wanting this town boy to go into the public lavatory, and she proceeded to give me the beating of my life. Her logic was that we, as black people, spend enough time, as she put it, cleaning up white people's shit, and so, for as long as she lived, she didn't want to see me carrying the shit of any healthy strong black person.

We had to have a lot of debates in time to come, my mother and I, about that, because there was a whole sub-text to it which was disturbing to me. And part of that was that she, in order to earn money, did something that I understood. In addition to minding her cows and planting her dasheens and yams and stuff; she had to be washing for some of the white people – civil service administrators and so on – and it demonstrated to me how much that woman actually resented what she needed to do in life in order to earn and give us clothes and give us food and so on and so forth. As far as I was concerned, I said to her, 'By doing what I did, to prevent this young man falling into a pit latrine, I didn't feel it was reflecting negatively or detracting from me, or my personality or my character in any way. It was basically an expression of my love for him and his safety. I didn't want either you or me to have to account to his parents how he came to have an accident in the public lavatory.' She wasn't convinced with those arguments and in the end, much later, we talked about it at some length.

So coming out of that background, I went into the Presentation College, did my school certificate examination and then went to Trinidad. My parents protested. They wanted me to become a doctor because I was extremely good at chemistry. My father, although totally, functionally illiterate, was the bush doctor, the herbal medicine man in the village and he particularly wanted his son to be a doctor. I chose to be a priest, much to their complete annoyance. And that took me to the St John Vianney Seminary in Trinidad, next to Mount St Benedict, where there were some Benedictine fathers.

Now the critical thing about that experience in my view was this – that the church in very many respects collaborated with the social divisions and the class divisions in the society. In Grenada, because I was with the Roman Catholic priests I learned a lot about what the ex-patriate priests, Anglican and Roman Catholics, thought of the ordinary people in the village. I went to cocktail parties with the priests. I heard their conversations, and generally they were very, very pejorative. So take the notion, for example, of petty larceny, poor people stealing in order to go and feed their children – the landowners would be invited to supper or cocktails with the Anglican priest. The Roman Catholic priest would go and he would take me with him and they all talked as if I was not in the room, as if they were not talking about people like my mother, or my uncle, or my bigger brother or my father. It gave me an understanding of colonialism and of the church's collusion with injustice, which was to explain many things much later on when I came and joined the

Gus John

Dominican Order here at Blackfriars in Oxford. But that Trinidad experience was interesting for a number of other reasons, because of the role of the Roman Catholic church in social and political life in Trinidad and particularly through the education system, which I won't go into in any great detail at this point.

What I want to say, though, is this. That early experience was formative in a number of respects. For one thing, my father returned from Aruba and immediately got involved in a general strike in Grenada in 1951. Eric Gairy, who became the prime minister of Grenada, a notorious prime minister, for very many years had been a labour organiser in the oil fields in Aruba. My father and a number of other people had worked with him and assisted him in organising the union for their benefit in Aruba and he came back to Grenada and led a general strike. And I have vivid memories of cane fields burning, of the homes of plantation owners burning, and of all sorts of people coming to and fro for clandestine meetings with my father when I was something like six years old.

Another experience which was very formative was when, having saved up a lot of money, my mother went to town and came back one day with a Phillips radio. For the first time there was going to be a radio in the house and we could have communication with the outside world, so I became an avid listener to the BBC World Service. My mother didn't speak a lot about politics in the home but for some reason she was very interested in what was going on in Africa. And I well remember her having discussions about southern Africa, particularly, and about what was happening in the Congo. So we talked a lot about Tshombe, about Kasavubu, and when Patrice Lumumba was murdered it was as if a member of the family had been killed. It had a profound influence on my family in particular and on those people within the village who took a keen interest in what was happening abroad.

Having built our house, my father bought some lands, cultivated those lands and, in 1955, four years after he returned to Grenada, there was a devastating hurricane – Hurricane Janet – which demolished everything. And in less than two years after that he dug up and came out to Britain. 18 months after he arrived here there was in Notting Hill the murder of Kelso Cochrane and I well remember when that news came over the BBC World Service lots of people gathered on our verandah. My mother used some flex, some electric flex, brought the radio out onto the veranda and all kinds of people came listening to the news bulletins to hear how this Barbadian worker had lost his life at the hands of racists in Notting Hill. Kelso Cochrane. And everybody who had a relative in London was worried as to whether their relative was safe.

We had a view of London, which was like a matchbox I have to tell you, because the minute something happened in London you assumed it was near where your relatives lived. If somebody said they were coming over to England, it was automatic they would run into your relative. We had no sense of size or space or the expansiveness of England. So you hear that your relative is in Sheffield, 'When you go give him this letter from me, please.' The fact that you might be in Chiswick till you die didn't matter to anybody. You were going to England, they were in England. So we were very concerned about the effect of that murder on our loved ones, and it was only after people wrote to say that they were all right and these were the circumstances of Kelso Cochrane's death that we got to know what was actually happening. And that taught me too a great deal about what was to come in terms of my relationship with this country.

Having spent two plus years as a seminarian training to be a priest to return to Grenada from Trinidad, I was persuaded by the Dominican fathers in Grenada, who belonged to the English Dominican province, to follow what they considered to be my natural course and come and join the Dominican Order here in England, which I did. I landed here on 20th August 1964, a Saturday, and was quite mesmerised by the sheer physical state of London. I thought it was the most grotesque place on earth and I was just dying to get back on the plane to get back to the beauty of Trinidad and Grenada and so on. That feeling was not to last very long because within a couple of weeks of landing here I was carted off to the Cotswolds, to Stroud in Gloucestershire where the Dominican Order had a novitiate in the village of Woodchester, between Stroud and Nailsworth on the Bath Road. There I spent one year and got involved in some heavy discussions. It was the time when Harold Wilson was doing his nonsense with Ian Smith in Rhodesia, and there was the Unilateral Declaration of Independence. We formed a debating group and got very much involved in activities around that.

But then that experience of being in the church and in the novitiate in Gloucestershire brought me face to face with one brand of English racism. Most people in that area, particularly in that little village of Woodchester, had never seen a black person before so there was a certain exotica about my walking around the streets in these white friar's robes and the rest of it. And then one particular day, this family who used to come and sit in the church – they had bought or rented a pew in the front so they would come, mother, father and children and sit in the front there and I was one of the cantors, one of the novices, chosen to lead the singing. So I was there singing the Latin mass. They would come to Matins and Compline and Vespers and so on, and this lady asked me one day, or asked the Prior whether I could come to her home for lunch. And I was persuaded to go. I thought I would meet her family there – they were about my age, a couple of them a bit younger – I was only 20, 19½. I got there and, to my utter amazement, saw this lady in a dressing-gown. And I thought to myself – there was this elaborate meal she had finished preparing – 'What on earth are you doing in your dressing gown if you invite someone to lunch?' I thought, 'Maybe that's particularly English. I mean the English are a peculiarly eccentric bunch and so I shouldn't think too much about this.' We ate and then she kept on trying to ply me with drink. I was not a stranger to drink because one of the things we did as friars was to brew every week a phenomenal quantity of very strong beer. So although we were very devout and the rest of it we were also solid drinkers of strong ale. So I could hold my drink and stuff and I was basically very keen to know what she was up to. It was soon revealed.

This lady announced to me that she had a sister living in Boston who tells her, every time she writes, that until the first time that you've 'done it' with a black man you can't consider that you know what sex is all about. And as far as she was concerned, the point of having me down there was not to have me to lunch and show me the delights of Stroud and Gloucestershire, but to explore whether this theory of her sister's was correct. I have to tell you that led to a certain amount of unpleasantness and eventually I left that place feeling extremely bruised, confused and all sorts of strange emotions. Here I am, a very holy [audience laughter] – I kid you not, I kid you not – a very holy novice taking the business deadly seriously, believing that these people who came to church were like myself. And then this woman, a lot older than I am, with children, one my age, two younger, actually trying to get me to commit adultery, to satisfy her racist views about blacks and their sexual prowess and the rest of it. And she is being singularly unconcerned about the fact that she was messing up my head and my spirituality, especially when she said to me, 'Now you came here, you met us going to this church, we've been parishioners there for years, one thing you are not to do is to go back and tell anybody about this.' I said I would have to tell my spiritual confessor. She said, 'Blow your spiritual confessor.' [audience laughter]

So I had to deal with all of that. And gradually I began to get a sense of what was going down on the whole issue of race and sex and so on. And I had to be very careful because there is a certain fascination that people, men and women, have with people who wear gowns and cassocks, especially if it is white ['that is true' – from the audience – audience laughter]. Now there speaks a priest, that's Brother Hewie, and he's a Methodist priest so he knows about these things. That was a very salutary experience because, having been armed with that under my belt, it kept me out of harm's way many times subsequently.

The Roman Catholic church did a number of things. The Dominican Order is, in my book, one of the most erudite, intellectually rigorous religious orders. They are called the Order of Preachers. The only thing they didn't particularly deal with was the whole question of sexuality. We did everything from Plato to Thucydides, from Heidegger and Sartre and what have you,

Thomas Aquinas, Augustine, Kierkegaard, all of that stuff. The one thing that they did not do was to deal with the whole question of sexuality and there were lots of very confused and messed-up people around the place, who were trying to deal with their sexuality, as men and women, who had taken vows of chastity. And I used to be very interested in some interactions between certain of our kind, when we went to visit a particular congregation of nuns every so often for the day – most intriguing – but that's for another time.

We went from Gloucestershire to Oxford with a short break in a place called Rugeley in Staffordshire, and it is really in Oxford that the intersection of my theological work and my political work began. I soon came to know, because they introduced themselves to me, Ann Dummett, who was then the secretary of the Oxford Council for Racial Integration as it was called, and her husband Michael, Professor of Logic at All Souls, Oxford. I spent many hours in the home of Michael and Ann Dummett and I became the chair of the education sub-committee of the Oxford Council for Racial Integration, which was later to become the Oxford Community Relations Council. We became very aware at that time of two things: one, of the kind of experiences black children were having in schools – black children whose parents worked principally in two industries – the Austin Morris car factory at the top of the hill there, in Cowley, in South Oxford, and at the Radcliffe and Churchill hospitals. So they the women were principally health workers, the men were factory workers. Their children, some of whom had just come from the Caribbean to join them, were having all kinds of conflicts getting used to parents, whom they had not known, and siblings, whom they had not known and many of whom took a very strange attitude towards them and the way they spoke and their customs and so on. But it was very very clear that the education system in Oxford had little room for those people. It did not respect them, did not respect their backgrounds, didn't believe that they had any aspirations which could be considered real. And in the main the children had to put up with what they found. That led to all kinds of problems, and there were some very bewildered parents. So we worked with those parents. I remember I spent many hours in the homes of parents bringing them together in little groups. In one sense I suppose it was a precursor of what I was to join in London some years later, the Black Parents' Movement. In particular streets groups of black parents would come together. They would talk about their experiences. They would talk about the traumas they were having forming relationships with these children, who had come to join them, after they had been left for years with aunts or uncles or grandmothers or whatever it was. And particularly, they would talk about the fact that they really did not understand why the teachers and head teachers felt that the children were stupid, couldn't learn, or the fact that they spoke Jamaican English meant that they were irredeemable.

So we went in the schools together. We organised meetings, large meetings. Certain members of that community were already members of the West Indian Standing Conference. We had public meetings in Cowley, where representatives of the West Indian Standing Conference came to speak, and so forth. At that time too there were a growing group of South Asian families in a place called Jericho, just within the city centre, and there in addition to all the things that were present as far as the black children, the Caribbean children, were concerned, was the question of language and how were these Oxford schools going to deal with bilingualism. And with that too we spent an enormous amount of time trying to get the educators to have some understanding of the fact that, although those children and their parents were not speaking English, it did not mean they were stupid. They needed to find some way of assessing their abilities in their mother tongue and particularly some way of teaching them, which would take account a) of their linguistic needs and b) their linguistic strengths.

We worked on all of these issues and on employment issues but the one thing, that stands out in my mind more than anything else, is the work that we had to do in relation to immigration matters. Now I'm talking about 1965/1966. We had to form a rota of people who would leave Oxford and drive to Leamington Spa, to Bradford, to Blackburn, to Southall and find relatives of individuals, who were being detained at the Harmondsworth Detention Centre in Heathrow and were likely to be put on a plane the following day, if some relative couldn't go there and say, 'Yes, this person is coming to me. Yes, I have sponsored this person to come here, or whatever.'

There was a viciousness about that regime – both in terms of how people were kept in the Detention Centre and how those of us who were seeking to assist them were treated by the immigration officers, which I never thought I would see in this country. It was a fundamental abuse of people's human rights but at the time, particularly within the Labour Party, no one was prepared to confront the issue. You couldn't be seen to have a liberal approach to immigration issues or indeed to immigrants who were having those sorts of injustices done to them by the port authorities.

And that led to a close working relationship with the Indian Workers' Association, with the Pakistani Workers' Association, the Indian Workers' Association in Birmingham, the Pakistani Workers' Association in Leeds and Bradford and we extended the tentacles and made sure there were advocates in each area who could, like ourselves, act on behalf of those communities. There were other issues to do with the nurses at the Radcliffe and the Churchill, which I suppose you will be familiar with. I won't go into them just now.

So what happened? Why did I end up in London, with Roxy – well, not Roxy at that stage – but with John La Rose, and Jocelyn Barrow and Hewie Andrew, and Winston Best and others, rather than continuing to preach about Thomas Aquinas and Augustine? Interesting question. For me the crunch really came – well, there were a whole number of things. Firstly, we began supporting actively the work of the Student Non-Violent Coordinating Committee in the United States. There were some colleagues from Oxford who were in communication with Martin Luther King. We were heavily into the politics of the middle 1960s, and also communicating with people – James Cone and others – on the whole issue of liberation theology. There were some folk at the monastery, at the priory, who were in touch with Helder Camara and Archbishop Romero and were actively supporting those courageous people, really against Rome, because of the kind of onslaught they were facing from cardinals and others, who felt that they were not fighting for social justice but effectively supporting communism. I mean, it was as crude as that.

But then there was Southern Africa. In Rhodesia, Smith had declared UDI, Wilson had capitulated in Britain here. David Pitt and others in Campaign Against Racial Discrimination (CARD) were campaigning in relation to the 1965 Race Relations Act and trying to get evidence for the government about discrimination for the passing of the 1968 Race Relations Act. And we, despite the fact that we were closeted within this priory place, were in the thick of all of that.

We organised a group called the Christian Marxist Dialogue Group. It included people from the university and further afield. The editor of the journal of that organization, the journal was called *Slant*, its editor was Terry Eagleton, who went on to write about ideology and power and those sorts of things. And there were some radical priests – Herbert McCabe, Fergus Kerr, Cornelius Ernst and others – who spent a lot of time dealing with the dialectics of race and economy and some of us commented on British social policy and so on.

Came one particular day, we were visited by the Dean of Studies of the South African Province of the Dominican Order. The Dominicans had a mission, as they called it, in Grenada and Barbados, but also in Johannesburg and Witwatersrand in South Africa. This Dean came and, after dinner, when a lot of that strong ale flowed, we sat in the Senior Common Room and were talking about South Africa. He talked about wanting to recruit from amongst our group, i.e. people who were just preparing for ordination, to come to South Africa to work as lecturers, chaplains or parish priests or what have you. And again, it was to become a familiar occurrence, I am sitting there, the only black person in the place, and they were talking, he particularly, talking as if I were not in the room. They talked about the students in South Africa, black students being educated separately, even those training to be priests, the lay brothers eating separately, living separately and so on and so forth and I remember challenging him about the theology of all that business. What would Jesus Christ do if he were in that situation? Would he do the same thing as yourselves and so on. And the answers were not particularly convincing, certainly not to me. I was not the best theologian in the world but a very awkward one and I found that very distressing and, given everything that was going on in the world, the United States, South Africa and Namibia, Mozambique and Angola and so on, I could not take it all in.

A decision was made that I was going off the rails, in other words, 'losing my vocation' to use the formal parlance. The Prior of the place was an aristocrat, educated at Ampleforth, and his brother owned a farm in Burnham-on-Crouch in Essex and I was duly dispatched to this farm, in a manner of speaking, for '40 days in the desert to go and find your soul.' I went, had a glorious time, drove the tractor, messed about on a motor bike in the farmyard, fell in love with the farmer's daughter, and did all kinds of things that a young sensible man would do, especially when you had been closeted in that place for God knows how long. And at the end of the day, went back, full of beans but very much convinced that I didn't want to be part of that business any more.

They then thought, 'Well let's try something else.' So they sent me to a Jungian psychoanalyst, a delightful soul called Doris Layard. I was a devotee of Jung. I had read everything he had written and talked a lot about his book *Memories, Dreams and Reflections* and his attitude towards Africa. I had issues in relation to do with his whole business with communism and so on and so forth. To cut a long story short, we spent more time drinking claret and other good wines than talking about the state of my soul. She thought I was a very normal person. We talked about my dreams, home and this and that and, at the end of the day, she told those people that I was very, very normal. And she agreed with me that my soul would be in a state of distress if I tried to confine it to that place so I should be given wings and be free to go.

In due course there was the appeal to Rome so I could get my dispensation from vows and this and that and the next thing. Then

I left Oxford, came to London to join my parents at their home in Acton, and decided that I had been studying since I was four and I wanted to do a real job. So I asked my father for some money. I went and bought a huge old Hercules bicycle, and decided that that would be my means of transport round London. I rode everywhere looking for building sites. I got into this building site one day and I went to the first couple of people I met and I said, 'How do you get a job in here?' One looked at the other, both white, and they pointed me to some foreman. I went and he asked me what I'd been doing and I had to convince him that what I did before England was more relevant than what I was doing most recently, and he said to me, 'OK, come in and start on Monday.' Then he said, 'Let me take you to show you the people you'll be working with,' and he took me to the same two people I had met at the gate. Those two burly fellows waited till the foreman was out of earshot and then said to me, 'Listen nigger, we don't deal with your sort here, If you come back we would drop a bucket of concrete on your fucking head.' They then looked me in the face and grinned.

I was genuinely scared. I rode out of the place and I thought, 'No, not for me.' So I lazed around for a couple of days and then went riding again and I passed a cemetery, Chiswick Cemetery near Mortlake, rode in there and asked these two people, 'How do you get a job in here?' It was my favourite line. They sent me to the cemetery keeper at the gate who asked me a series of questions and I convinced him that I could dig trenches and he said, 'Come next week.' So I went there and was trained in the industrial trade of becoming a gravedigger, which I then proceeded to do for a year. And in the evening I worked at the most wonderful youth club in the world – the Cryptic One youth club, in the crypt of a church in Paddington, run by two of the craziest people I have ever come across – Elizabeth Duff, the wife of the vicar, and her husband Michael, who was a much more laid-back sort of individual and not given to the flights of fancy that dear Elizabeth was. I worked there with a number of people, an excellent youth worker called Vernon Tudor and others and a particularly creative group of young people. They were doing things like sound systems and the rest of it, but also they were into football, they were into drama and a range of other things. In fact, it was that group that organised a meeting later on at the Metro Youth Club at which C.L.R. James came and gave a rousing address one evening, to about 300 young people.

There began my interest in youth work and I became one of the main youth leaders in that place by night and continued my grave-digging by day. And from that, I determined that I would go and train to be a youth worker, which I did. The government had established something called the National Association for the Training of Youth Leaders in Leicester, following the Second World War. They wanted to deal with mods and rockers and the wayward youths of that period. Quite a lot of the people I was training with, unlike me who had come from some very cloistered surroundings, were ex-army people. This training brought me to work with the black community in Highfields in Leicester to a very large extent. I also worked at a youth club in a very poor working class area in Peterborough, white working class, and also in Ely in Cambridgeshire. And that gave me a completely different perspective too on what was actually happening within the cities and so on and so forth.

I finished at Leicester with a Diploma in Youth and Community Work. I went back to the cemetery, but didn't last very long. On one fateful day, it was summer, not many people were dying, the place was full of grass, and they gave me this clapped-out lawnmower to go and cut between the tombstones. To cut a long story short – I won't go into the lattice-work layout of cemeteries, you know that very well – moving backwards and forwards down some aisles, I stumbled on an upturned urn in the high grass. Although I fell backwards, the machine kept coming and mangled up my left foot, ridding me of these three toes here and making a mess of the thing, which was a bit traumatic. But what was funny about it – I held onto my foot and hopped across from one end of the cemetery to the other, where this other fellow was working and, as I approached him and he looked down and saw this blood and half my foot hanging all over the place, he fainted, knocking his head on a tombstone.

The ambulance arrived and there I am worrying that I may be bleeding to death and they say to me, 'He's got a head injury we've got to see to him first.' So they put me to sit down, took him off in that first ambulance while I waited for another ambulance to come. In typical fashion the wife of the keeper of this cemetery went and brought me a huge mug of sweet tea. It might have been good for shock but it's no good if you're going to have your foot amputated or sewn up in the next few minutes. So the ambulance duly came and it rocked and lurched all the way from Chiswick to Isleworth General Hospital and they put me on a stretcher – one of those things that they keep you waiting on now for 24 hours a day in a reception area – and about six different nurses came and asked me what my name was. Now I have the misfortune of having 'John' as my surname. The whole world believes it should be my first name so when the sixth person came to ask me, 'Is your name John Augustine, or Augustine John?' my patience and my devoutness evaporated and I put down some cussing which I have never done before – because I looked down and all the sheets were covered in red and the pain was excruciating – and all these incompetent people were fussing about what my name was – whether it was this or that or the next thing – that's the last thing I remember because I must have passed out or something and I ended up on a bed recovering from an operation where they had amputated bits and sewn up bits and so on and so forth.

Then my mother came to visit me and was absolutely convinced that my accident was as a result of disobedience. She had difficulty in explaining it to all of those good people in the village in Grenada, the whole island, because they had been told by the Dominicans that I was being groomed to be the first indigenous bishop of Grenada. After I had finished at Blackfriars, the idea was that I would go to the Papal College in Rome for two years and then be consecrated a bishop and shipped back to Grenada to do my stuff. And being fiercely independent of mind from day one I decided I wanted nothing of the sort so I did my own thing. My mother could not get over the fact that, having got used to the notion I was not going to be a doctor and set her mind on her son being a bishop, I had ended up digging graves.

Now in our culture, a gravedigger is not somebody with any status. You call a fellow, you give him a bottle of rum, you might throw in three tins of sardines and some crackers, he goes and digs a grave. You might also give him a few dollars, but he would not insist upon it. So the idea that, after all those years of studying and all sorts of stuff her son, in the middle of London, ends up being a gravedigger, nearly killed my mother. She couldn't take it, and for years, she was writing back to the island, 'Oh yes, he's doing very well. He'll be ordained next year. He'll be ordained next month.' And then, I happened to pick up a letter that somebody had written her one day in which they were receiving this news and were very glad to hear – they kept on calling me Gregory, although I had assumed the name of Augustine when I joined the Dominicans – very glad to hear about Gregory. So I said, 'Listen, you've got to end this charade, you know, I mean, I'm grown now. I'm not going to be a priest any more. I will pray with you daily so that you can get it into your consciousness and have the will to forgive me for dashing your hopes, but I don't know what's going to happen after grave-digging but that is what I want to do.' So I bought myself an old wagon and loads of tools. People were dying all over the place like flies, I can't tell you why – maybe there was smog or something. And I was making good money, when I worked in my own cemetery and there was an overload elsewhere. I got into my van and they rang up and I went and I dug two graves, nicely paid and stuff, and then I went to the youth club and I did my thing in the evening. And I was quite happy to go on like that for the rest of my life, except that this accident intervened. And that was another thing that got me to understand something about racism and so on and so forth.

Throughout all that period – all that business of class, and people decrying you because of your poverty and the rest of it – I had not lost my confidence. As a matter of fact I stuck two fingers up at all of the middle class people in Grenada. I felt I didn't want to be part of them, and if my purpose in life was going to be about anything it was going to be about some way of making that whole business egalitarian, and not have people feeling that because they were born with some money, or they have a certain surname or whatever, they have a right to harass others and treat them as inferior beings.

But the one thing that really lost me my confidence was when, as my mother put it, 'You came to England whole, and you decide to go and leave half your foot in the cemetery.' I was given crutches and I used the crutches for a while. I then decided I'm not going to deal with that, 'It's going to make me a cripple.' I discarded them and learned to walk all over again except that I tried doing too much too soon. So one particular day I left Acton and got off at King's Cross for some reason and then decided for the first time to try going up one of these escalators. Now, most sensible people in my condition would keep themselves quiet on the right-hand side, hold onto the railing, hoping that it would transport you to the top without incident. I felt, I'm dealing with the business so I'm walking up the stairs until I got – and I was carrying a bag, I was going to Leeds or somewhere, I had bags – until I got to the top, where it gets a bit wobbly. I lost my balance as I did regularly because when you lose half your foot you have to learn to balance yourself again and I fell backwards. Now to fall backwards on an escalator in the London Underground at 4.00 pm or 5.00 pm is not funny. So there was a domino effect. People started tumbling down all the way down to the bottom of the escalator. Pandemonium. And the abuse was phenomenal, 'Fucking, drunk black bastard.' They were all convinced that I was drunk because nobody in their right mind would just fall like that. I hurt my foot. The wounds had healed, the stitches had been removed, but it was excruciating. I was very, very miserable. Not so much because of the physical pain but because those things that were said to me cut deep into my system. And I decided after that, that until such time that I had completely regained my balance, I would never use the London Underground.

But that soon came to an end because I had to come up to Finsbury Park to see John La Rose, which I did regularly. I met John at 2 Albert Road, spoke with him, spoke with Sarah. I still have these little pictures of Michael and Keith with their big Afros, lovely young boys, being there with us and reading stuff. John gave them books. They were reading. I was seeing all kinds of things and from that time on, in 1969, in fact even earlier, before I left the Dominicans, John La Rose has been a spiritual mentor, animateur, not just of me, incidentally, but of our movement, and I owe him personally a great debt. We have become very close friends he and I and Sarah – a friendship that is over 30 years old – and their home has been my London home even when I went to Manchester in 1971. And between then and now it is my London base. That too is particularly important in terms of what I later did in education. People underestimate how important it is, especially if you are a reasonably intelligent person, to have some of your own experiences and the view you have on life either contested or confirmed by people, who bring a particular art to what they do, by people who make sense through social analysis, political commentary or whatever else, of the historicity of the human condition. So you could relate what was happening to people on the axis of class, to what is happening to people because of race and ethnicity or because of gender or whatever else it may be.

And New Beacon Books really changed my life. I would go away from 2 Albert Road with armfuls of books. I read them avidly. I related them to what was happening around the place. I got to know what was happening around the place through them. I learned about other islands and their cultures through them, from the works of C.L.R. James in Trinidad to the work of Edgar Mittelholzer on the Guyanese axis, to George Lamming in Barbados, Walcott in St Lucia, Naipaul, and you know the rest of it. But similarly I learned to understand our condition as a people in this society, with the past experience of Britain we had in the Caribbean context and the specificities of the black situation and the black struggle in the United States. I formed a very early impression of John – because I had worked and been around all kinds of people – the humility and generosity of the man, the stature of the man was inspiring but, above all, the qualities that I came to love and acknowledge and be grateful for more than anything else was John's capacity as a teacher. He teaches. If universities around the land had characters in them with a minuscule percentage of the qualities which John has as a teacher, the nation would be considerably more rounded in terms of its education outcomes and products.

But that was not just at the cerebral level as I'm sure you will realise. When I worked in Handsworth, Birmingham – having finished at Leicester doing this diploma I was approached by the Runnymede Trust to go to work in Birmingham. Why the Runnymede Trust? Nicholas Scott, who was a cabinet minister in the last government, was then married to Elizabeth Scott. Elizabeth was a trustee of the Runnymede Trust but she was also the chair of the Cryptic One Youth Club management committee in Paddington. We talked a lot. I visited them at their home a lot. She regaled people with all kinds of things about me and the leadership qualities I showed in the youth club. It was she who recommended me to the Runnymede trustees, including people like Geoffrey Bindman, Anthony Lester, Anthony Rampton and Eric Lubbock. Dipak Nandy was the chief executive so he was a worker. The trustees invited me to go and see some of them and they asked whether I would go to Handsworth, Birmingham, to do some work. There was a fellow called Brian Priestley, a reporter on the *Birmingham Evening News*, and he had written a series called 'The Angry Suburbs' talking about black youths in Handsworth. It was a demonic, moral panic type thing about black youths. That was just after the Select Committee on Race Relations and Immigration had published their report in 1969 on *The Problems of Coloured School Leavers*. The issue in Birmingham, Handsworth, was about black youths involved in crime, black youths out of school, black youths being excluded, black youths rebellious and protesting and so on. So I took this brief and went up there doing some, well, I called it action research within Handsworth which involved a lot of participant observation in shebeens. I think I learned how not to sleep when I worked in Birmingham. I would be in these shebeens until about 3.00 am or 4.00 am, go home and cook some stuff, eat, sleep for a couple of hours and be out again at 7.00 am or 8.00 am, sometimes earlier. Because one of the other things I was studying was what was happening to black kids – where parents left them, how they were being minded when people went to work. So it was really burning the candle – the shebeens, the youth activity in shebeens, the police activity in shebeens night and then seeing how black workers organised themselves and their domestic situations in the morning.

That took me into some heavy run-ins with the Thornhill Road police station. I went in there regularly and challenged them. They didn't like that. My car was stopped every two minutes. In fact the *Sunday Times* has this particular picture which I didn't know anyone was taking. I had a little Ford Anglia Super which I had souped up. It was souped up principally for the purpose of playing cops and robbers with the Handsworth police really, because they were doing some dangerous things. They were convinced that I was part of that whole drugs sub-culture in the place and I was very concerned that they were seeking to plant certain things on me. You will remember there were some Hosein brothers who were charged for murdering a woman called Mrs Muriel McKay. The day the *Sunday Times* reported that particular murder they also carried a report, I think they called it 'Must Harlem come to Birmingham?' or some such title. It was a one or two page thing about what I was doing there with these people and the police business and they had a silhouetted picture of me in some corner observing what the police were actually doing. How they were stopping not just young people, but adult workers and so on, on the street. I remember that particularly well. It led to a number of things.

We started the first supplementary school at Westminster Road primary school in Handsworth. There was a group that came about at that time called the Afro-Caribbean Self Help Organisation with Bini Brown and Maurice Andrews who is now a lawyer in Birmingham and so on. They also started a hostel for homeless young people in Forty Hall Road in Handsworth with a lot of support from the Barrow and Geraldine Cadbury Trust and from Birmingham Social Services. That whole movement – the supplementary school work in Birmingham as well as the work that was being done with those young people – has continued virtually to this day.

Come the end of December 1970 I submitted the report to the Runnymede Trust. It was published as a small book called *Race in the Inner City* which, as I understand it, was the first really rigorous analysis of the whole notion of the inner city and the issues around race. I worked very closely with a colleague at the University of Birmingham called John Lambert, who was researching a book called *Crime, Police and Race Relations* which Oxford University Press and the Institute of Race Relations published, a very important book. And when I moved to Manchester in 1971, I researched a book with Derek Humphry, who was a staff reporter on the *Sunday Times,* called *Because They're Black* which Penguin published. It won the Martin Luther King Memorial Prize. And then there was a particularly important book called *Police Power and Black People.* In addition to doing the research for that book and writing bits of it, I wrote a commentary at the end of it all. Now if you were to revisit that book you would be not so surprised to find that all the issues that have been raised in the media recently around the Stephen Lawrence Inquiry and Mr Paul Condon and the rest of it, had been discussed, analysed, prophesied about in that book in some detail as early as 1971 and 1972.

In Manchester I worked with an organisation called the Youth Development Trust. In that capacity, I was seconded to Area Four in the Social Services Department in Moss Side to work with a case load of about 26 West Indian families. What was common to them was that they all had young people who had come to join them from the Caribbean and who were getting into a hell of a lot of problems.

Another issue was the fact that the local authority had pulled down the houses in Moss Side to which many of these people had come from the Caribbean and were building these 1960s sprawling deck-access housing estates. They relocated many of these families to green field sites, as they called them, in Cheshire. One of them was in Partington, very near a Shell oil refinery, one of the most cursed places on earth. And of course, those young people, the children of those families, refused to go with them onto those estates. The estates were planned, there was no social life, many of them didn't have a youth club, they were basically deadly dormitories and the young people continued to make their culture and their lives within Moss Side. That led to a certain amount of homelessness. It made them more visible to the police and the Social Services Department was having to pick up the pieces.

I suppose they saw me as the expert, assisting in sorting these things out. So I was working within the families, doing what I called 'family reconstruction' really. But I was also doing a lot of consultancy work, sensitising these white social workers and their bosses to issues around Caribbean families, the Caribbean community and how it operates and so on. That led to a whole number of issues – policy reviews, some confrontations with the Probation Service and the Magistrates Courts.This was because of the line from police, stopping people on the streets, taking them in front of magistrates, plea bargaining between duty solicitors, the prosecution and so on. It was very predictable, that whole sequence of developments.

I suppose it is that work and the particular approach I brought to it that made me very visible, not just in Manchester but around the country. I was asked to take part in a whole series of media things. There was a programme which Joan Bakewell used to compère called *Twenty Four Hours* on BBC. There was another one called *Late Night Line-Up*. Granada Television did all kinds of things up in the North West. I found myself constantly being asked to come in as a commentator, or as an expert, doing this, that or the next thing. I tried to make sense of some of that by registering with the Sociology Department at the University of Manchester and gaining access to the literature that was around, which would help me to develop what I called some tools for analysis. So that, in addition to the activism within communities, I could actually be writing certain things and giving perspectives that people could make sense of in terms of social analysis and sociological commentary.

That led the National Association of Youth Clubs to ask me to work on a project – they called it the MultiRacial Youth Project. The National Association of Youth Clubs was a national body. The government had a particular concern at the time that youth clubs were becoming segregated. Young black people were not 'integrating', as they put it, with young whites. Young black people were bringing their music into the youth clubs and the young whites, let me be precise, the young white males, were leaving in droves, or having conflict with the young black men, because too many of the young white women found the young black men attractive and pleasing. And that became a big social agenda. So the National Association of Youth Clubs was given this huge amount of money from the voluntary unit at the Home Office or DES or whatever to do some work on that matter.

They contacted me in Manchester and asked if I would apply for this job, which I did. I went for an interview and was given the job and the very first thing I did was to rewrite the brief, basically telling them that they were asking the wrong questions and that we needed to look at institutional practices and policies and not at what different colours, shades of eyes black kids have, or why do they gyrate when they dance, or all sorts of other meaningless things. The National Association of Youth Clubs accepted my recasting of this thing. It led me to be working in 16 different cities, up and down the country, investigating the youth policy that local government was operating in relation to youth clubs generally, and black youths in particular, in cities from Bristol, to Leeds, to Liverpool and so on. That went on for a number of years. To cut a long story short, it was all written up in a quite important report which I titled *In the Service of Black Youth: a study of the political culture of youth and community work with black people in English cities*. And it will not surprise you to hear that I had an argument with the National Association of Youth Clubs, which ran for about three months, about the use of the term 'political culture'.

Generally speaking, people did not like what was in the report. They thought it would make them fall foul, not just of the Department of Education, or whatever it was called then, but of the funders. So they mimeographed X number of copies of it and as fast as it went around the place, it sold out. They mimeographed some more, would not give me permission to publish it myself and so I suppose it could still be found in libraries and in the book lists of some youth training institutions.

The important thing about it is that it gave a very rigorous analysis of a number of things. There was the whole self-help project – the whole business of what I called 'projects versus politics' – the Community Relations Commission funding organisations left, right and centre to do all kinds of strange things, deflecting people from that sharp, cutting-edge political work that they were actually doing, having them fighting about little hand-outs of money and so on, circumscribing them in terms of what they could do because they are receiving the grants and did not want the grants to be withdrawn. Critically important, it talked about the impact of urban aid after Harold Wilson introduced that in 1968 and a range of other things besides. It also looked at why it is and what were the consequences of young Asian people being constructed in a particular manner socially and sociologically – i.e. as people with a culture, people with a long history and tradition of culture and religion etc – while young black people were being constructed as these rebellious children of a very wayward and inchoate, disorganised body of peasants, who happened to come together in England for the first time from these islands scattered around the Caribbean basin. OK, that's a bit of a caricature but, crude though it is, that was the text. So that work looked at all of these issues in some detail. It is my intention to find a copy of it, dust if off, write another introduction and publish it because I believe it will put paid to quite a lot of the nonsense we're reading and hearing now in the wake of that Macpherson Report.

So I've come to the period now where this work has been done, I am lecturing at the University of Bradford, and I want to end basically by saying a couple of things about that and linking it to the work that we were doing within our movement. You won't hear me saying anything at all about the People's Republic of Hackney, that's for another time. I won't say anything about *Romeo and Juliet*, that's for another time. Nor will I say anything about what was hailed by a certain chief executive as 'transforming Hackney', the most radical social agenda since *Das Kapital* which has chronically panned out to be wrecking Hackney, that's for another time.

Bradford. I was appointed a lecturer in Social Policy and Applied Social Studies at the University of Bradford in early 1977. I negotiated with the National Association of Youth Clubs that the work I was directing would continue with the field officers but I would both oversee that and work in that capacity at Bradford University. It was a radical department. The head of it was Professor Hilary Rose, social scientist in her own right, writing on all sorts of issues of social policy, social work, women's issues, wife of Steven Rose the scientist. There I did quite a lot of work on issues of immigration policy, housing policy, education particularly. I joined Bradford Black which was an organisation run on the same basis as the Race Today Collective and, in fact, Bradford Black came to work in alliance with the Race Today Collective, the Black Parents' Movement here in London, the Black Youth Movement and New Beacon Books.

The most significant development – I won't talk about the issues around social work and black families and how social workers were trained and all of those kinds of bewildering issues. I'll just leave them alone for a moment. The most critical thing that happened at that time in Bradford was the fact that George Lindo, who was a Jamaican worker in his 30s, was arrested and charged and later imprisoned for five years in Armley Jail for holding up a betting shop at knifepoint. Bradford Black and the organisations here in London, the BPM etc, organised the 'Free George Lindo' campaign. We worked in Bradford and nationwide to demonstrate that he had been framed by the police and that he needed to be out of jail. My role in that, apart from being a full-time member of Bradford Black and writing for the magazine *Race Today* down here, became quite difficult. One of the many things that I had done up to that point was a very close study of Jamaican English as a separate language. There was the wonderful book, *A Dictionary of Jamaican English*, which became my bible really. It was a matter of saying to these teachers all round the place that they should stop harassing black kids and putting them down with the notion that what they were speaking was broken English and that they should leave all of that aside and begin to understand and learn so-called standard English. Fortunately for us, people like Linton Kwesi Johnson emerged, giving legitimacy to that language in its own right, as indeed Louise Bennett and others had done in Jamaica itself. Young people could identify with the language in its written form being used creatively through poetry and plays and so on and so forth.

The relevance of that to George Lindo is that he had been convicted on the strength of a so-called confession he had made to the police and part of our strategy in the campaign was to demonstrate that that confession was never given. So I discussed the matter with the campaign and that particular Saturday took George with his wife and two other people from the campaign up to the university to my office and there we did three things. With the aid of a tape-recorder I got him to read. He read a long text of something. We had a long conversation – a conversation lasting about half an hour or 45 minutes. And I also got him to write because I wanted to see how his language was constructed through these three mediums – reading, in general relaxed conversation and as he wrote. I went home that weekend and did a thorough analysis, content analysis, of all of that and presented the results to the barrister, in order to demonstrate that what the police were claiming – it was an insulting document frankly – the transcript of what they said was his confession, could not be and that became the deciding issue in his appeal. The confession was shown to be a complete fabrication, produced by people who were simply being inventive with the language.

What I suspect happened is this. The Home Office had issued a pocket guide to police officers to assist them in understanding Jamaicans. It was a very amusing phrase book which would have been of dubious value to police officers in the course of interacting with Jamaicans on the street. You know yourself, if you get an irate Caribbean man or woman, let alone a Jamaican, giving full vent to the language, no phrase book could help you translate. The police who framed Geoge Lindo clearly used some such aid in the calmness of the police station and produced their version of what a Jamaican like George Lindo might have said.

Interestingly, however, the university – well not the university but my bosses at the university – took a rather dim view of all this. The comment was made to me that I was not a sociolinguist and I should not therefore be posing as an expert witness at the trial doing all this elaborate analysis of the man's language etc. What did I know about it?

I soon laid that to rest and, although I had organised with my colleagues to cover my lectures so that I could physically be at the court, I went back to the university to find a long memorandum from this radical professor of mine, the punch line of which was, 'I really think you have to decide whether you are going to be an academic or a political activist.' So here I was, with whatever profile I had. I wasn't born in Bradford for God's sake, I had a life and a political profile before I went to that university which informed what I did with those students. I was demonstrating praxis, the meaningfulness and relevance of being in academia in the context of this Jamaican worker, who had five years of his life taken away from him wrongfully by the British state. And all this professor could tell me was, 'Make a decision – are you going to be an academic or a political activist?' And when I tell you that one of the activities that was considered purposeful and meaningful and relevant for those who made that choice to be academics, was to meet at the home of this professor and sit in sumptuous armchairs, drink vintage wines, eat fine cheeses and talk about Marx and Althusser and Poulantzas and postmodernists and all those erudite things, you'll begin to see the irony of it all. That was the activity they were quite happy for me to be part of. No problem with that. But to be engaging at that level of taking on the Bradford, West Yorkshire police, and so on and so forth, was considered to be not a particularly sensible thing for this particular lecturer to be doing.

Needless to say it wasn't very long before I parted company with the university and went back to Manchester where I had continued to live. I became chair of the Black Parents' Movement there and spent a year establishing the Education for Liberation Book Service, taking books all around the North West to colleges, universities, schools – teaching lecturers and teachers how to use that material and, particularly, making it accessible to black communities by having book stalls in the large shopping precinct in Moss Side every Saturday and by having sessions in my own home and in other young people's homes in the evenings.

I want to stop there. The only other thing I want to say is this. As far as I am concerned there will never be, for me at any rate, a dichotomy between whatever academic work I do and the political activism that I engage in.Those of you who knew me in Hackney will understand that I did not make a distinction between being a Local Government Chief Officer and all the things I had done before I got to that point. And I will have you know that I would never have survived seven and a half years in that completely crazy place but for the fact that it is with all of that and against that background that I went there, with a purpose and a clarity and a vision for education for black and working class white people, which I do not believe you will find amongst most of the Chief Education Officers who run local education authorities in this country at this time.

I've gone on for very long. I told our Chair it was going to be very difficult to condense all of this. I thank you for your attendance and for your patience.

Professor Gus John has been involved in education, schooling and youth work in Britain's inner cities since the 1960s. Born in 1945 in Grenada, he came to Britain in 1964 to become a Dominican Friar studying theology at Blackfriars Oxford.

He became chair of the Education Sub-Committee of the Oxford Council for Racial Integration, then run by Senior Community Relations Officer, Ann Dummett. He worked on education issues with black car workers at the Austin/Morris car plant in Cowley, and their families in the Cowley and Blackbird Leys districts and with Punjabi families in the Jericho district of Oxford.

In 1967 Gus John broke with the Roman Catholic Church, left the Dominican Order and moved to London, where his parents were living. He worked as a gravedigger by day and a youth worker by night and weekends. He later did some journalism appearing regularly on such programmes as *Late Night Line Up*, *World in Action* and *Granada Reports* and contributing as a freelancer to the *Sunday Times* between 1971 and 1973. He wrote the influential little book, *Race In The Inner City,* which was later followed by two

Gus John

publications co-authored with Derek Humphry of the *Sunday Times – Because They're Black*, which won the Martin Luther King Prize in 1971, and *Police Power and Black People*.

During this period Professor Gus John trained as a Youth and Community Worker in Leicester. In 1971 he moved to Manchester to live and work and remained based in that city for the next 16 years. His social work research led to the establishment of the Moss Side based Family Advice Centre. He was a founder member of the George Jackson House, a shelter for homeless black youngsters He also worked in Manchester LEA as an Area Coordinator of Community Education, a Vice-Principal of Community Education in South and North Manchester, an Inspector of Continuing Education and trouble-shooting manager of the special Access Unit at the North Hulme Centre. For a short period in the 1970s he worked as a Lecturer in Social Policy and Applied Social Studies at the University of Bradford.

In 1987 Gus John left Manchester to become Assistant Education Officer and Head of Community Education in the Inner London Education Authority where, with a budget of £80m, he had responsibility for Adult and Continuing Education, Theatre in Education, the Youth Service, Community Schools, the Play Centre Service and the Education Liaison Service. In 1989, when ILEA was abolished, he was appointed Director of Education in Hackney, the first black Director of Education in the UK. When the two departments were amalgamated he became Hackney's first Director of Education and Leisure Services. Since leaving Hackney in 1996 Professor Gus John has returned to Manchester and is working as an education consultant in Britain and Europe and is a Visiting Professor of Education at the University of Strathclyde in Glasgow. He was awarded a Doctor of Education degree by De Montfort University in Leicester in 1996 for his 'profound contribution to the formal and informal education of black people in Britain'.

Throughout his life in Britain Gus John has been active in fighting for racial equality and social justice both here and in the Caribbean. While in Oxford he joined the Campaign Against Racial Discrimination (CARD) and helped test employers and property owners for discriminatory practices. In the early 1970s he was a member of Grenada Cause for Concern, which campaigned against Eric Gairy and his murderous 'Mongoose Gang', and of the Caribbean Education and Community Workers Association (CECWA), which worked on schooling, education and youth matters. When lecturing in Bradford he was a member of the Bradford Black Collective, working in an Alliance with the Race Today Collective, the Black Parents Movement and Black Youth Movement and played a key role in the 1978 campaign to free George Lindo. He contributed regularly to *Race Today* and *Bradford Black* magazines.

From 1978 until he left for London, Gus John was coordinator of the Black Parents Movement in Manchester, leading a number of anti-deportation campaigns and empowering black parents to struggle in schools for their children's education and entitlement. He founded Education for Liberation

Gus John

bookservice and helped to organise the International Book Fair of Radical Black and Third World Books, both in Manchester and London.

Professor Gus John was a member of the panel of inquiry, set up by Manchester City Council and chaired by Ian Macdonald QC, into the racist murder of 13-year-old Ahmed Ullah at Burnage High School in 1986, and he co-authored the full Burnage Report *Murder In The Playground*, published in 1989. He was international secretary of European Action for Racial Equality and Social Justice for three years and chair of the Talawa Theatre company for four years. He is a founding trustee and the treasurer of the George Padmore Institute.

As an ordained minister Professor Gus John works with churches in London, Manchester and Trinidad. He is a member of the board of the Ecumenical Racial Justice fund. He is also currently a member of the Home Secretary's Race Relations Advisory Forum and of the Joseph Rowntree Foundation's Young People and Families Committee. He is a Founder-Director of the Abiadama Centre for Lifelong Learning in Port of Spain, Trinidad.

Right Reverend Doctor Wilfred Wood
chaired by John La Rose (19.04.1999)

John La Rose: The Right Reverend Doctor Wilfred Wood is the fourth in this series of the 'Life Experience With Britain' talks and we welcome him and you here this evening. Please give him a hand.

I have known Wilfred for many years and he knows, and I have said so publicly, the profound admiration I have for him and what he has been able to do and achieve over all the years, 30 years or more, that we have been labouring in this vineyard, in this country. He has a piece which I thought was very perceptive and which he wrote as his contribution to *Foundations of a Movement* published on the tenth anniversary of the International Book Fair of Radical Black and Third World Books. He refers in that to the talks that took place at the West Indian Student Centre of the West Indian Standing Conference and what went on there.

But later there was a much closer bond, which we established from that period, which came through the Supplementary School Movement, through the interaction between the Shepherd's Bush Welfare Association and their school, and the George Padmore school here in North London. Working with Wilfred in that period was absolutely important because he stood out for his commitment, his courage and what he did and what we did. I have a strong memory of an occasion when the members of the North London West Indian Association, many of whom were London Underground workers, workers on the buses and workers on the trains, were demanding something which obviously they didn't have – the right to promotion. The union was not doing it for them. So a lot of us in the Association carried out a programme of informing the public as well as organising ourselves to help them achieve that objective. Well they have now achieved that objective, but I will never forget the day when we picketed outside London Transport headquarters in Marylebone. It was Wilfred, myself, Jeff Crawford and the two Anns, Ann Bartholomew and Ann what?

Wilfred Wood

Wilfred Wood

Wilfred Wood: Evans.

John La Rose: Ann Evans. The two Anns, white Anns, and they joined us outside London Transport on behalf of those black workers who were just afraid to take the risk of putting their faces to their protest outside London Transport. Wilfred and the others that I've just mentioned were there that day for them and they have won, but there are so many other things that Wilfred has done in this society. I profoundly admire the way he has worked. He marched on the New Cross Massacre campaign. I remember him saying when he was asked by another canon – were you a canon in those days?

Wilfred Wood: Yes.

John La Rose: He was asked by another canon whether he would be marching on the 2nd March 1981, the Black Peoples' Day of Action and he said, 'Of course.' That's Wilfred Wood. Thank you.

Wilfred Wood: Thank you very much indeed. Thank you John, for your kind introduction. After that flattery I can hardly wait to hear what I am going to say. Now Mr Chairman, Ladies and Gentlemen, I am highly appreciative of the honour accorded me by the invitation to give this talk and this is no mere pleasantry on my part, because I know that the discriminating perceptiveness of John La Rose and Sarah White has not diminished one jot over their long years of active, steadfast commitment to social justice and universal human rights. So to be asked by them and their colleagues in the George Padmore Institute to share my thoughts in a forum of this kind is no mean accolade. I thank them and apologise in advance if my contribution falls short of expectations. I also take this opportunity to salute them for their contribution to a better world for all us, a contribution which will be valued long after we have all passed on. Mr Chairman, I have been asked in this talk to cover a) my origins in Barbados, b) my social experience as a progressive in British society and c) my experience in the Church of England, on being exalted to becoming its first black bishop. It is perhaps a more self-centred assignment than would be my preference, but I will do my best.

In 1951, parliamentary elections to the 24-seat House of Assembly in Barbados with its 12 double-member constituencies, were held on adult suffrage basis, that is everyone aged 21 and over being able to vote, for the first time. My father, Wilfred Coward, a small businessman managing his own Boston Bus Company and sitting as a vestryman, which was equivalent of a borough councillor, in St Joseph, was persuaded to stand as a candidate for the Planters and Merchants Party – then known as the Electors' Association – against the two sitting members from the Barbados Labour Party, Mr Grantly Adams, who was in fact the leader of the party, and Mr Lloyd Smith, a local shopkeeper. I was only a 15 year-old schoolboy at Combermere School at the time but I became very interested and each night I was out at the various public meetings. One night after my father had made his speech and left the lorry platform to mingle with the crowd, I persuaded the chairman to let me say a few words. It went down so well that I became a regular speaker, usually just before my father came on. To be honest, ours was not a popular cause – my father was soundly defeated – but I can still recall that at the final meeting there was an enormous crowd, mostly hostile, when I went to the microphone. The growling crowd stilled when I announced, 'Let me compare for you, my father and Mr Grantley Adams.' I went on, 'For east is east and west is west, and ne'er the twain shall meet; 'til earth and sky stand presently at God's good judgement sat but there is neither east nor west, border nor breed nor birth, when two strong men stand face to face, though they came from the ends of the earth.' At the words, 'when two strong men' there was such a deafening roar that I had to pause and repeat it because I would have been lynched if I had have said anything against Adams. I can tell you that.

As I said, we were soundly beaten. Adams and Smith were returned, the Labour Party formed the government with a sound majority, the cobbled-together Electors' Association fell apart, later re-emerging as the Progressive Conservatives. I remember some chap seeing a man walk up and down Broad Street and he said, 'Well he must be a Progressive Conservative. He doesn't know if he's walking forwards or backwards.' Having become seriously interested in politics though, my father joined the Labour Party and at subsequent elections we both spoke in support of various Labour candidates. Ten years after those momentous 1951 elections, my father was elected to sit alongside Mr Smith. Mr Adams had gone off to become the first and only Prime Minister of the ill-fated West Indies Federation. There is an amusing footnote to all this. In 1966 here in London, one of Mr Smith's six daughters – Ina – and I were married. So our five children have the unique distinction of being the only people to have had two grandfathers representing the same constituency at the same time.

You will understand that, having caught the eye of Sir Grantly Adams, I was set fair for a political career, and indeed I had decided that I would be a journalist and politician. Meanwhile, like many other people I was regular in church on Sundays, I read the Bible and said my prayers just like most people. While I was growing up, the local parish priest, the Reverend J. T. Adams-Cooper was a Glaswegian Scot, and as far as I know only one woman in the entire parish – the verger – understood anything he said! He retired and was succeeded by a young priest from St Vincent who took an interest in the young people and drew me more into the life of the church. So I found myself helping with the Sunday School, running the Church Lads' Brigade, being drill instructor to the Church Girls' Brigade and the darling of the elderly matrons to whom I sometimes gave a lift to and from church.

Woody Allen, the film maker and comedian, has said, 'If you really want to make God laugh, try planning your own life.' Well, I came to realise, with complete conviction, that God was calling me to be a priest. Since I definitely did not want to be a priest – the life did not appeal to me – and since I already knew what I wanted to do with my life, I convinced myself that I could not rise to the high standards which God would rightly expect of a priest and it was better to be a good layman than a bad priest, so I redoubled all my church work and I shared my thoughts with no one. Then, on 7 July

1957, the Bishop, whose name was Gay Lisle Griffith Mandeville so he rejoiced in the title Gay Barbados, came for confirmation to our church of St Anne, and in the course of his remarks about God's call and our response, quoting an older priest he said, 'If God calls on you to jump through a brick wall, it is your duty to jump. It is God's business to see you through.' After that I had to have the matter resolved. So I was then seen by the bishop, archdeacon, dean, the principal of Codrington College and the headmaster of Harrison College, often, frankly, in a rather questioning and rebellious frame of mind, but the result was that I embarked on a five-year training for the priesthood at Codrington College.

Now we do not have time for a proper description of my time at Codrington College. But I can say that I fell in love with the person of Jesus Christ and knew then that my overriding purpose in life, so far as was humanly possible, was to be faithful to what I came to know of Him. There was no need to grasp at anything – riches, success, acclaim, not even the priesthood itself. Whatever brick walls there were, provided He said jump, I knew what was expected of me. Now I am no Billy Graham, and even if I were, this is not a revivalist meeting, but it still remains true that, in spite of the many charlatans who see Christianity as a safe and easy way to make a quick buck, or of wielding power over gullible and vulnerable people, the call to love as Jesus loves, embracing as it does a recognition of yourself as someone of infinite worth, and yet no more so and no less so than other people for whom Christ was prepared to give His life, that is the true liberation.

I was still a student at Codrington College along with others from Anguilla, St Kitts, Nevis, Saba, how many of you know there's a West Indian island called Saba? Antigua, St Vincent, Grenada, Trinidad, Guyana, Tobago, Bermuda, the Bahamas, the UK and Barbados when the West Indies Federation broke up. I remember it well because, contrary to the rules of the College, we used to assemble in the darkness during the night to listen to test match cricket from Australia, and on the first occasion when the West Indies won, a Trinidadian – who incidentally is now a vicar in Wembley – mounted a small West Indian flag on a broomstick and we marched around in a circle singing, 'West Indian boys are marching.' I then sat down and wrote a National Anthem for the West Indies and some years later it was sent back to me with a sad little note saying, that with the break up of the Federation, there was now no requirement for an anthem.

Because I was paying my own fees at Codrington College, or to be more accurate, my father was paying them, I was not under obligation to any dioceses, and in 1959 came the news of the disturbances in Notting Hill and the death of Kelso Cochrane, murdered by teddy boys. Now, one feature of the ministry of Jesus that appealed strongly to me was that, although he spoke straight from the shoulder, as it were, to rich and poor alike, His message was that they belonged together. I was brought up in Barbados with a very idealised image of Britain – not unlike John Major's old ladies cycling to Holy Communion, village green cricket with polite applause and murmurs of 'Good shot, old boy', a bastion of fair play and British pride, where 'of all the world's great heroes there's none that can compare, with a tow-row-row-row-row row of the British grenadier'. Indeed I was interested to read in the *Guardian* six days ago, an interview with Trevor Hicks who lost two daughters in the Hillsborough Football Stadium disaster ten years ago. He said and I quote, 'Where I came from, it was hard work and play it straight and you'll get on eventually. Britain was the fairest country in the world; there was room for everyone to have their say and what you read in the papers was dead right.' That was also the view that, I, living in Barbados, had of Britain. Hicks went on to say, 'What a load of bollocks!'

So, when we heard that the cause of the trouble was the failure of West Indians now living in Britain to respect the rights of English people to sleep at night when the West Indians preferred to have noisy parties, and their refusal to queue for buses and so on, I felt ashamed that our people who had gone to England were letting the side down. So I volunteered to go to England after ordination for a period of four years to show the West Indians a better way, before returning to Barbados. I saw this as something of a sacrifice because, although the Government (by now E.W. Barrow's

Democratic Labour Party) had intimated that the church would be disestablished, the clergy in Barbados still enjoyed all the privileges of service in a church in which government paid for everything – from clergy stipends to communion wafers – and there were still such things as long-leave passages every four years. So the Mirfield Fathers – that's the Community of Resurrection, who staffed Codrington College at the time – gave me their blessing and made arrangements for me to serve my title with one of their former students, Roderick Gibbs, who was then a Vicar of St Stephen's, Shepherd's Bush. So on 19th July 1962 I embarked on the *Golfito*, arrived at Avonmouth on 6th August and Paddington Station on 7th August.

Some of you will remember, even more clearly than I do, the London of those days. Many features which are commonplace today – underpasses and elevated motorways, central heating, modern office blocks, grime-free houses and so on had not yet arrived. Living conditions for most black people – mainly West Indians and Africans with some Asians – meant one room which had to be bedroom, living room, dressing room everything for both parents and children, sharing a cooker on the dark landing with a number of other families similarly ill-housed. Often the heating was provided by a paraffin heater which meant that one's clothes smelt always of paraffin. My first experience of an English winter was that of 1962 with the last great London smog, when for a whole week you could not see for more than a yard or two around you. I used to go visiting with another curate who was a bit of a wag and he would say, 'Look, can you keep smiling so I can see where you are.'

The English people with whom I had to do were magnificent, and they could not have been kinder. I lived with the vicar, his wife Joan and three little daughters, Monica, Paula and Lucy, in the rambling Victorian vicarage, very much as one of the family. I know this sounds like a cliché, but you really must trust my honesty when I tell you that this was really so and that I will never be able to repay them. There were other members of the church also, most solid working class people. There was, for example, the factory manager Bert James, with his motorcycle and sidecar. With me on

136

the pillion and, believe it or not, his wife and three small children in the sidecar. We would travel to places like Windsor Great Park, Frensham Ponds, Guildford Cathedral, Coventry, Stratford-upon-Avon and so on. Then there was the elderly, retired spinster, Mabel Voller, who had been in domestic service all her life and who took me under her wing. When I married she took my wife also, and when the children came along, one, two, three, four, she took them as well. She was a wonderful person, fiercely loyal to royalty and the Conservative Party. 'Go home Dick Feather!' she would hiss at the trade union leader, Vic Feather, whenever he appeared on television. She would compare white babies unfavourably with our own and then say with a wry smile, 'Makes me feel like a traitor to me own kind.' Even before I arrived, black people had been made to feel welcome in that particular church. I'll tell you a story about Mabel Voller. One day I was in a bookshop, church bookshop in Oxford Street and saw a book *Little Black Sambo* and I got so embarrassed and asked, 'Are you still selling these books?' I bought it to take home and to write to protest about it. I took it home and put it down and one day came back to find Mabel reading it to our little daughter who was enjoying it enormously!

But for most black people church-going was a luxury. Shift work and having to share essential domestic facilities with so many others meant that they were not really in control of their lives. In addition many of those arriving in the 1950s or earlier had had very bad experiences of rejection when they turned up at church, only to find people draw away from them as though they were contagious. So they had resorted to reading their bibles at home, eventually joining others to pray together. Many black churches began in this way. I became increasingly dissatisfied with a ministry to people's spiritual needs which seemed to ignore their obvious physical needs, and I raised this with the vicar. He sympathised with my anxieties but thought that I should first have a proper grounding in the bread-and-butter aspects of parish ministry, supporting people in funerals, weddings, baptisms and illness, before tackling social and political action. The bishop agreed with him so I continued my ministry, still intending to return to the Caribbean at the end of my four years.

It was not easy to buckle down to this discipline. Harold Macmillan's Conservative government was on its last legs, and eventually an election was called in 1964 and Labour under Harold Wilson won a tiny, single-figure majority. But it was a turning-point election. One of the Labour Party's most senior and respected figures who was destined to be the Foreign Secretary, Patrick Gordon-Walker, was ousted from the safe Labour seat of Smethwick by an otherwise unknown teacher named Peter Griffiths, whose campaign featured such slogans as, 'If you want a Nigger for a neighbour, vote Labour'. The Labour government took fright. Too many of their politicians had waited long for their turn in government and were not prepared to miss out over this issue. There was no difference between them, Left or Right, you have only to hear tapes or read transcripts of their answers on phone-ins to spot their unease. Since everyone knew that with such a slender majority a second election was likely, there developed an auction between the two major parties, each striving to show that they would be as tough on 'immigration', which was really a code word for the presence of black people, as the other.

It so happened that the defeated Conservative candidate in my constituency of North Hammersmith was a man called Tom Stacey, who was a journalist and wrote for the *Sunday Times*. He wrote a piece entitled, 'The Ghettoes of England'. I still have it, and in it, by the clever use of words, he purported to show that the prejudices against black people actually had a factual basis. For example, he wrote that he could always tell an immigrant street such as Coningham Road, which happened to be in my parish. He said that the houses would be dilapidated, the front area would be strewn with debris, the windows would be broken and so on. What he did not say was that Coningham Road, with Stowe Road and Cathnor Road on either side, were all of a piece, but that Coningham Road was the only one with black people. He also said that knocking on the doors throughout the day, he found more black men disproportionately home on the dole than white. I knew that often I paid baptism visits and had to speak to the wife while the husband was a bundle under the blankets because he was working nights, and so on and so on. I wrote to the *Sunday Times* complaining and trying to correct the misleading statements. They preferred to publish two short letters, one agreeing with Stacey and the other disagreeing. But I noted that the one in agreement they had chosen was from Barons Court not far away, while the one disagreeing was from someone living in Malta. Quite fair, you see!

Labour did win the second election with a proper working majority and I wrote to and got an appointment with Maurice Foley, the Minister in the Home Office responsible for immigration and race relations. His view was that no special action was needed, because, as people saw how good black people were at their jobs, they would be educated into tolerance. So a black doctor had only to be a good doctor, a black priest a good priest and so on. I was not convinced. The only entry in the telephone directory with race relations in the title was the Institute of Race Relations at 36 Jermyn Street near Piccadilly. So I went to see its director, Philip Mason. Alas, he explained, it was not that kind of project. This was an academic institute concerned with research and study rather than action. What I had in mind at this time was the establishment of a kind of Toynbee Hall in Shepherd's Bush. There was on the Uxbridge Road going towards Acton an army building which had been empty and unused for years, which I thought would be ideal. Youngsters who had no space at home to do homework properly could come there for that as well as recreation and vocational activities. It contained living quarters so university students could come to help the youngsters in the neighbourhood. I wrote to various politicians who had liberal reputations but none could help. One answered asking how did I know this was what black people wanted. This was Jo Grimond who was a great liberal. I did manage to see an official in the Ministry of Defence. He explained that there were plans to rebuild the Duke of York's headquarters in Chelsea and this building may be needed during that time. Years later the headquarters were indeed rebuilt but the Shepherd's Bush building was never used and remained unoccupied.

When in 1964 the Wilson government tried to appease the racists by imposing an arbitrary limit on the number of immigrants per year to be allowed in to take up jobs, and claimed to be doing it in the best interest of race relations, it also set up the National Committee for Commonwealth Immigrants (NCCI), to create a network of local Community Relations Councils. These councils could only be set up with the support of the local authority, who had to provide half of the officer's £1500-a-year salary if the local Community Relations Council was to be recognised by the NCCI. For the most part those borough councils which did respond ensured that the price of their co-operation was control by them. Nonetheless this was the only thing on offer, so I became chairman of the Hammersmith Council for Community Relations. Kensington and Chelsea Borough Council refused to have such a council, so a few of us set up a voluntary group and appointed James Cummings as its first full-time officer. These councils were not an overnight success. Local authority support was grudging. The lone officer, usually called the liaison officer, was often inadequately supported and spent most of his time explaining to needy immigrants why he could not meet their expectations. However, we limped on.

Meanwhile in the wider world the race issue was unfolding. The apartheid regime in South Africa was becoming even more brutal, having jailed Nelson Mandela and his colleagues. Rhodesia was moving in the same direction. Black Power was emerging in the USA and the Kenyan government had put its Asian residents on notice to choose between British citizenship and Kenyan citizenship. White racists abroad and in Britain were receiving influential support and the Wilson government was running with the hares and hunting with the hounds. Multi-ethnic groups campaigning for a genuine multi-ethnic society and strong legislation against racist practices and discrimination were definitely not the flavour of the month.

For some of us matters came to a head when the Asians were expelled from Kenya and the government rushed through overnight legislation to deprive them of British citizenship and the right to enter Britain. By remarkable coincidence at the very same time the Russian troops were massing to break up the movement in

Czechoslovakia and the British Consul there was open around the clock to process as many Czechs who wanted to escape and come to Britain as possible, the British Consul in Nairobi was open for one hour only for passports for those few who could get passports in that hour, while the legislation was going through to deprive them of the right to come here. That was all in the same 24 hours.

Anyway, this exposed the NCCI to be the government's fig leaf that it was, since it had not been consulted and its advice ignored. I contacted two chairmen of neighbouring Community Relations Councils who, like me, happened to be black, and we called a Sunday afternoon meeting in our church hall in Shepherd's Bush of as many councils as we could contact. The idea was for these councils to stay together but independent of the government-control led and discredited NCCI, and so form the nucleus of a civil rights movement. The NCCI got hold of the plan and called a meeting two days before, paying the train fares and hotel accommodation of representatives to attend the meeting, which was a major consideration for those coming from the North and Midlands and we didn't have money to do the same. They solicited their support and sent them back home disinclined to have anything to do with our insurrection.

However, that did not deter us and later, when the government was debating the replacing of the NCCI by a Community Relations Commission, which was eventually headed by Frank Cousins, we submitted what came to be known as 'The Wood Proposals', in which we called for a Committee for Racial Equality. In those days the idea of equality was un-thought of. You couldn't mention it in decent company. You could have integration, yes, or harmony or community relations, but the idea of equality, that wasn't on at all. Anyway we called for a Committee for Racial Equality with membership at least in part directly elected from immigrant organisations and, what is more located, not in the Home Office with its concerns for immigration, prisons and police, public disorder and so on, but in either the Department of Local Government or the Department of Education and Science. Needless to say the Home Secretary, James Callaghan, and his minister,

David Ennals, ignored these proposals. Powellism was now flexing its muscles and appeasement was the order of the day.

On the church front there were a number of individual christians who stood by their fellow black christians. But, in spite of tireless work from people like Reverend John Downing, Reverend Lewis Donnelly, Reverend Alex Kirby, Reverend David Haslam, Canon John Collins, Bishop Trevor Huddleston, Douglas Tilby, a Quaker, and Michael and Ann Dummett, the Church as a whole had no appetite for public opposition to the government and the rising tide of racism. Certainly I can remember church meetings at which people took exception to my call to condemn Powell and some even walked out. It became clear to me that, although there was a place for friendship meetings and tea parties for black and white people to learn more about one another, effective pushing for justice and equality would have to come from us, the black people, ourselves.

So I made a point of attending the monthly meeting at the West Indian Students Centre in Earls Court of the West Indian Standing Conference. The chairman at the time was Neville Maxwell, and its secretary Jeff Crawford. Neville Maxwell was a law lecturer with an extremely fine brain, he was a former Barbados scholar, a man of vision with that rare gift, the common touch. He was a true leader who made allowances for the limitations of those he was trying to lead, and it is not necessarily disparaging to say that those limitations were severe. I remember John here had a regular spot where he gave an erudite round-up of political activity in the Caribbean, but truth to tell the meetings were usually a talk-shop of empty rhetoric where nothing happened and nothing was expected to happen. I remember one person, who shall be nameless, seriously proposing a resolution calling on the Soviet Union to come to the aid of black people in Britain. When I proposed that individual membership should be drastically reduced in order to encourage people to build up affiliated organisations and work through them, and that the monthly meeting should be hosted by member organisations in turn, with the members of that organisation having the right to form a 'public gallery', it was turned down.

That is not to say that West Indian Standing Conference achieved nothing. Joe Hunte's little pamphlet, 'Nigger-hunting in London', drew public attention to police harassment and mistreatment of black people and the campaign to force London Transport to appoint black bus inspectors was successful. Jeff Crawford was an effective secretary and credit for much of what was achieved must go to him. I must say I was very disappointed that in all the great hoo haa about the *Windrush*, the programmes on television and so on, very little mention, in fact no mention was made of Jeff Crawford, and he played a crucial part in those days. I still have a 1968 *Guardian* photograph of him and me picketing London Transport's offices with placards demanding an end to their discrimination. I also remember, because it's written deep in my mind, on that day when we were going to picket those offices at St James, in fact I had been ill in bed with a heavy cold. It was in March, I think, and the weather was quite bad and I got out of bed and was muffled up with lots of scarves and coats and so on. Standing up there with this placard and all the time feeling extremely angry that if I were to get my death of cold, what would I have died for, to have a man made, of all things, a bus inspector?

But self-help had to be bottom-up rather than top-down. So in 1967, after a series of meetings in our home, 12 of us from Barbados, Grenada, Jamaica and Guyana founded the Shepherd's Bush Social and Welfare Association and set about building up a membership. The Reverend John Asbridge, who had succeeded Roderick Gibbs as vicar of St Stephen with St Thomas, was sympathetic and helpful and supported us in obtaining St Thomas Hall, Thornfield Road, for our activities. We were able to get a supplementary school going, and employed one of our own members, Clinton Sealy, to run the school as well as to accompany parents when they had occasion to visit schools in connection with their children's education and welfare. We went on to found the Shepherd's Bush Credit Union and, despite the hostility of one resident in particular who took us to court, claiming a noise nuisance, the Association is still going and there is a full-time day nursery on the premises.

The Reverend John Asbridge persuaded me to join the local

Rotary Club and together we challenged them, as persons whose businesses flourished in Shepherd's Bush because of the presence of black people, to show practical concern for their customers. So began the Shepherd's Bush Housing Association with a committee made up of the vicar, church wardens and me, and a number of people we had recruited, with my wife doing the secretarial work on the church's typewriter and Gestetner copier, all unpaid of course, supported by the local Rotary Club. I remember helping to lay the lino – no carpet in those days – when we secured our first house and moved in a Jamaican family as our first tenants. Since then the Association has gone on to own just under 3,000 properties and to house thousands of families. I was much moved when a few years ago they asked me to return to Shepherd's Bush to open Wilfred Wood Court. In self-help housing I joined Pansy Jeffreys and others to found the Berbice Co-operative Housing Association, and Lee Samuel and others to found Carib Housing Association, which has so far provided four sheltered housing schemes for elderly Caribbean people, where every resident has a fully self-contained flat with bedroom, sitting-room, kitchen, toilet and bath and so on and yet has access to communal facilities whenever they wish to use them. One of them is here in North London and is called Clive Lloyd House.

It was around this time that the bishop decided that the experience I had acquired would be more beneficial to the Church in this country than in the Caribbean and created a post for me equivalent to that of a vicar. I became bishop's officer in Race Relations which gave me the freedom to concentrate on those issues which I thought were important for the Church's contribution to a genuine multi-ethnic, multi-cultural society in this country. The rough deal which black people were receiving at the hands of the police and the courts was presented sharply to me in two incidents at that time.

One Sunday afternoon a Grenadian member of our congregation came to ask me to come with him to get his uncle out of Shepherd's Bush police station. His uncle's story was that the night before in a crowded pub he was trying to get the bartender to change a ten pound note for him. A man who was nearer the bar passed the money to the barman, but instead of passing the change back to the West Indian, put it in his pocket and started to make his way out. The West Indian grabbed him and asked for the police to be called. The police arrived and promptly arrested the West Indian, took him off to the station and charged him with being drunk and disorderly. After retrieving him from the cells that Sunday afternoon I phoned a solicitor who was unable to appear in court next day, but advised him to ask for an adjournment of two weeks and to apply for legal aid after pleading not guilty. As Monday, the next day, was my day off, I was able to accompany him to the West London Magistrates Court. I don't know if you've ever been in a Magistrates Court on a Monday morning but there is a kind of conveyor belt of persons pleading guilty to being drunk and disorderly. A chap comes up, 'John Jones you are charged with being drunk and disorderly. Do you plead guilty or not guilty?' 'Guilty Sir.' 'Ten pounds.' This goes on all the time. Then in comes my man. 'You're charged with being drunk and disorderly. Do you plead guilty or not guilty?' He said, 'Not guilty.' The magistrate (almost annoyed) 'Not guilty?' The clerk says, 'He's asked for legal aid.' 'Legal aid for an offence where the fine is only about ten pounds? No, no. not granted.' 'He's asked for an adjournment of two weeks.' 'Why do you want an adjournment of two weeks?' 'My solicitor ...'. 'You've got a solicitor?' 'Yes, Sir.' 'What's his name?' My man says the name. 'Yes he is a solicitor. Alright, one week. If he were interested he would be here. One week.' I was sitting watching and as it turned out in the end he was acquitted on a technicality, because it was clear that he had been arrested in the pub whereas the charge had been drunk and disorderly in the street.

Soon after that I was called by another West Indian parishioner to Hammersmith police station on a Friday evening to retrieve a young man who had been at my home only the previous Sunday. This was a guy that I knew quite well because I had baptised his baby not very long before and he had had to go home to Grenada because his mother had died. While he was there the priest who was taking the funeral had asked him to remember him to me when he came back. He was writing a thank you letter to the priest and realised that he hadn't done that and left off writing the letter and came around just to do that. So that was a Sunday. On the Friday evening his cousin came to ask if I would get him out of the police cells and I was surprised because he was not that type of person. This is what had happened. He was a motor mechanic and he owned a Morris Minor and he had seen outside a house in Ravensbourne Road a similar car which had been involved in an accident and was obviously a write-off. So he'd made enquiries and discovered it was owned by the people outside whose house it was standing, and arranged to buy the engine from them. This evening after work he had gone to them, told them he was going to work on the car and started work on the car. He was hammering the grille away when he felt someone grab him by the collar, jerk him upright and this young man saying, 'You black bastards can't keep your hands off other people's property. I am arresting you for stealing parts from this car.' So the chap who had done this was about his size and the West Indian chap started to really lay into him. Then a uniformed policeman saw this and came running and said, 'You can't treat a police officer like that!' He explained to this policeman in uniform what had happened and he said, 'Well, we'll see if he's telling the truth.' Took him, rang the door bell and the woman said, 'What are you doing to this young man? I gave him permission to take the engine.' 'Oh,' said the first policeman, 'In that case I charge you with using an offensive weapon,' which was the hammer that he had been using to hammer the grille with.

So once more I contacted the solicitor. At the trial the police offered no evidence and the case was dismissed. The magistrate was quite annoyed actually. I was highly indignant at what the young man and his family had been made to go through and the expense, and I wanted to sue the police for damages. But the solicitor explained that once we started bringing actions against the police, acquittals would be that much harder to obtain so it was better to let the matter drop.

So I was glad, realising all this, to accept an invitation to address four meetings of police personnel, around 200 at a time, on their

Wilfred Wood

dealings with the immigrant community. The hostile reaction which greeted the five mild suggestions with which I concluded my talk is instructive. I still have, I meant to bring it actually, a tape of that talk. I gave it on four occasions. For example, the five suggestions I made. I suggested there should be black policemen and the answer was, 'Why should we lower our standards?' I suggested that as professionals they should make it their business to know something of the culture and background of the people they were policing and they said, 'We are not social workers.' I suggested that they should first warn the immigrant when he is seen to be breaking the law as he might not know he is breaking the law and they said, 'We are here to enforce the law.' I suggested to them that the men and women who are on the beat now should be relaying their experiences to their superior officers, in order to educate those for whom immigrants were not a feature of the population when they were on the beat and they said, 'That's not our business.' I suggested that it was misplaced loyalty to support colleagues who mistreat black people. It was very interesting those talks.

I remember they would get quite steamed up actually, the police, about this and I remember one policeman saying, because we had questions and answers afterwards, 'I think the trouble is that you black people don't have a sense of humour.' So I said to him, 'How many black friends do you have whose houses you go to?' He said, 'None.' 'Black people coming to your house?' 'No, no, no.' I said, ' Now you just heard me speak for about 40 minutes. Would you say I haven't got a sense of humour?' He said, 'Yeah, but you're different.' Another time a policeman said, he was absolutely livid with anger, he said, 'You tell me, why is it that when you arrest a black man and take him to court, he always pleads not guilty?' I said, 'It may be because he isn't guilty.' I mean, even the other policemen found that funny. They laughed.

I was also glad to work with the late Brother Herman Edwards in his efforts to help young people who had fallen foul of the police and as a result had become alienated from parents who, with attitudes brought from the Caribbean, assumed that the youngsters must have done something to bring it upon themselves. So we founded Harambee and Herman now lives on in the lives of the many young people he rescued from a life of crime and helped to make good.

All this showed me how crucial to a future harmonious multi-ethnic society would be the proper functioning of the police and the justice system, so I was pleased to be appointed a Justice of the Peace. I have no doubt at all that my presence on the Magistrate's Bench made a difference in a number of individual cases and to the enlightenment of fellow magistrates in matters relating to black people. Incidentally, it's the only occasion I've been called, 'Your Majesty' and that was, we had this case which came up, a West Indian, a Jamaican chap had an old car and he had bought another car. The first car he had was no good, he'd bought another one and he had transferred the disc from the old car to the new one which isn't legal really, shouldn't do it and a policewoman who had gone down the street looking at the various discs had decided to charge him. He saw her and explained to her what he'd done but she was determined to do him and he was charged. He came to court and explained that he'd been living in this country almost 30 years, he had never been in trouble with the police and he had no intention of cheating and so on. It seemed obvious to me that what he was really concerned about was the loss of his good name, that he'd got himself in trouble and so on. So when we retired I explained all this to the other magistrate and we decided that he would be given an absolute discharge. Because the offence was actually committed he couldn't deny it. He had actually done that but this was a device where, as it were, no guilt is attached, you see, to be given an absolute discharge. So when we came out I explained this to him that there would be no stain on his character, he would not have to pay anything, there'd be no offence registered or anything. He was so delighted he backed out of the court, bowing and saying, 'Thank you, Your Majesty, thank you, Your Majesty, thank you, Your Majesty.'

This in turn led to my appointment to the Royal Commission on Criminal Procedure, which was set up in 1978 in the wake of the Confait case by the Callaghan government, and which reported three years later to the Thatcher government. The Commission recommended the setting up of the Crown Prosecution Service to replace the system where police were both investigators and prosecutors, and also recommended certain criteria that had to be met if an arrest was to be made. Now my membership of that Commission provided me with a number of interesting experiences. For example, I remember a Ditchley Park Conference in 1978 attended by more than 30 police chief constables and some American law enforcement officers including a deputy director of the FBI. This was in 1978 and the theme of the conference was 'Policing in the 1990s'. The FBI's representative confessed that in the USA they had learned their lessons too late so far as the inner cities were concerned. What people in the inner city wanted were reliable and trustworthy police who could be counted on to do their job professionally. To do them credit, the majority of chief constables favoured this approach, so they paid little attention to the lone voice who argued that it was the Northern Ireland experience that had provided the pattern for future policing in Britain's inner cities. However, with the change of government came the time for a successor to Sir David McNee, Metropolitan Police Commissioner and it was this man, Sir Kenneth Newman, who was appointed. The rest is history.

By and large the baleful influence of Enoch Powell made sure that the highest aspiration of officialdom was racial quiet rather than racial justice and, needless to say, it was the victims who paid the price for this quiet. The race relations debate was really between two groups of people, the Powellites and the liberals, with no real attention paid to the wishes or opinions of the black community. It did not help that self-appointed, so-called Black Power activists went around disrupting meetings of any black groups of whom they disapproved. One legacy of such madness is a generation of black people who have fallen victims to the individualistic self-interest quest for personal fame, wealth and power characteristic of the Thatcher era. In spite of this, I do not believe that all is lost.

Now let me share with you two personal incidents that have been quite influential on my own thinking. Some of you may remember the 1963 all-conquering West Indies cricket team which toured England led by Frank Worrell. It was a team that would have beaten any other team in the world. It had the two fastest bowlers of the time, Wes Hall and Charlie Griffiths; the best off-spinner of the time, Lance Gibbs; the most brilliant batsman, Rohan Kanhai; and above all, a unique, one-off cricketer who could bowl both fast-medium and swing and left-arm spin at test-match level and who held the record for the world's highest individual test score, Garfield Sobers. That team would have beaten anybody. I happened to be visiting our scouts in camp at a time when this team had beaten England yet again, and was engaging in banter about this with the scout master when I heard one of the scouts, who I knew to be keen and knowledgeable about cricket, turn aside and mutter, 'England beaten by a bunch of niggers!' Now if you come from Barbados you know that cricket is a religion. So it registered with me then that for some people it does not matter how much of a genius a black person may be, no matter how many inventions, doctorates, Nobel prizes, heroic feats and so on may be attributed to him, for such people he is first and foremost a nigger. Now, such people may never be in a majority but however much we regret that they do exist, they do, and it is really silly and even dangerous to pretend that they do not.

The second incident occurred in 1967 after I had made a broadcast on the BBC. Some weeks later there was a knock on our door in Bloemfontein Avenue, Shepherd's Bush and I found a young man and a very old man, both black, standing there. The old man was completely blind but he had heard me on the radio and made his way all the way from Cardiff to my home. He had been a follower of Marcus Garvey in his youth and he held me in a tight and emotional embrace. 'There used to be thousands of black people in this country,' he said in a voice trembling with emotion, 'Where are they now? Don't let it happen again. Don't let it happen again.' It is my view that ethnic identification in this country will follow the pattern which can be recognised in the United States of America. First there are the genuine immigrants, people who arrive in the country with their own cultural values and practices.

Children born to them in the new country are apt to want more than anything else to be just like their peers, that is, to be normal. They tend to be half-ashamed of their parents' way of speaking, and sometimes dressing or dietary preferences. It seems backward to them. They rarely invite their friends to their homes, much preferring to visit them in theirs. However, it is the second and subsequent generations who are keenly interested in their grandparents and are most proud of their roots and the other identity they have in addition to that which comes with their place of birth. It is said that many almost fanatic 'Irish-Americans' have never set foot in Ireland nor are likely to.

So it seems to me important that black and 'double-ethnic' children – incidentally, that's the term that I'm trying to get into common use. Double-ethnic is much better than half-caste or mixed-race. You see, double-ethnic is positive. It means that you have two of what most people only have one of, you see and, what is more, you are equally proud of both. So do please use that term, double-ethnic.

Member of the audience: I have three.

Wilfred Wood: Or four or five. As I said it seems to me important that black and double-ethnic children of the future must have available to them documentary and other evidence, to show that their grandparents were not all passive receivers of scraps thrown to us, but were proud and resilient people, who, in the face of great difficulties and adversity, made possible the space in which they are now able to spread their wings. For example, whatever good may result from the Stephen Lawrence murder inquiry and whatever credit must go to the Home Secretary, Jack Straw, and Sir William MacPherson for recognising institutional racism, there have been other pointless racist murders of young black men in this country. The decisive factor in this case is the refusal of two immigrant parents, Doreen and Neville Lawrence, to accept the powerlessness which an indifferent society has decreed for them. This nation owes them a great debt.

Wilfred Wood

And now you'll be pleased to hear, I'm on to the third bit. Now to my experience in the Church of England on being exalted to becoming its 'first black bishop'. This is the title given to me, by the way, I didn't choose it. You have been so indulgent an audience that it seems almost criminal to make this demand upon you, so I will be brief in this third section of my assignment. When on the 8th March 1985 I opened a letter from the Bishop of Southwark, Ronnie Bowlby, to read his invitation to become Bishop of Croydon, I handed the letter to my wife and said, 'Well, if this is the latest brick wall, here goes.' You see, ever since I had been Archdeacon of Southwark in 1982 there had been speculation that I would go on to be a bishop, since I was 46 years old then. But it was assumed that this would be somewhere with a substantial black population, and this was hardly true of Croydon. So this was a surprise for everyone, including myself.

Another reason for surprise was that I could hardly be described as a 'safe pair of hands' or an 'establishment man'. Indeed, a parishioner of mine in Catford, where I was vicar, was once attending a conference and mentioned me as the vicar of her parish. 'Wilfred Wood,' said this priest to her, 'I have heard that name. Isn't he someone with a bee in his bonnet about black people?' My parishioner replied, 'You may well have done so because there aren't that many black vicars around.' 'What?' exclaimed the priest, 'You mean he is actually black?' Another friend of mine, when he heard this story, shook his head in mock solemnity and said, 'The lengths some people will go to!' I had taken over the chairmanship of the Institute of Race Relations when its academics, politicians, bankers and industrialists had been ousted from its council and replaced with black people and activists. I had loudly and publicly opposed various racist policies and legislation, gone on various demonstrations against Ian Smith's UDI in Rhodesia and British action in Anguilla, for example, walked from New Cross to Hyde Park in the Black People's Day of Action following the New Cross fire and so on. Above all I had chaired the World Council of Churches' Programme to Combat Racism when we made grants to the liberation movements in Azania, that is South Africa, and

Zimbabwe, Rhodesia as it was, to support their humanitarian work even though they were engaged in liberation wars, and when the Church of England did not lack supporters of white rule in South Africa and Rhodesia in its Assembly, that is General Synod and elsewhere. So I was hardly ideal material really for a token appointment.

But it was not a token appointment. Ronnie Bowlby is a christian firmly committed to equality and justice and made a point of informing me that he had made a list of the qualities sought in the new Bishop by those he had consulted. He could honestly say, having observed me at work as Archdeacon of Southwark, that I met them better than anyone else he knew. It was important that I should know this for myself, he said, whatever else may be read into the appointment. It made me recall being told by a parishioner that there had been some agitation at the time that it was announced that I was to be the new vicar of St Laurence, Catford. She had said to the agitators, 'Look, we've got everything we asked for. We just forgot to say that he shouldn't be black!'

You may remember my saying that my first winter in this country was the 1962 winter, which was extremely cold with the last great London smog. I enjoyed it, simply because having come expecting to be cold and miserable, it didn't much matter how cold and miserable. Well, it is in the same way that one approaches appointments of this kind. In the same way it must be recognised that there are certain inescapable conditions peculiar to all black people in leadership roles in British institutions today. I'll repeat that. There are certain conditions which are peculiar to all black people who are higher, who are at the top of leading British institutions today.

It is rather like being an undersized boy in a school playground. A physically well-built boy may be the greatest coward on earth but is never challenged to a fight, whereas every playground bully fancies his chances against a small kid. A black person in leadership has to prove himself against every sniper who thinks he can do the job better. So when you think, and I hope you do, think about offering a prayer for people like Herman Ouseley and Bill

Morris, because there are certain conditions attached to that which are peculiar. You get to recognise these tiresome situations when the guy is really saying, 'Why should you be promoted when I haven't been?' or 'Why should you, a foreigner, be issuing instructions to me in my own country?' You have to resist the temptation to get your retaliation in first!

Secondly, such black persons are subject to accusations of bias in favour of black people. The result is that if they are insecure in themselves they can bend over backwards too far to avoid appearing partial to black people or even too much at ease in predominantly black situations. Personally, I lost those inhibitions many years ago when I first arrived in this country. Being anxious to be integrated, I went with the other clergy to Tom, the local barber. He had never cut a black person's hair before and hadn't a clue. He was apologetic but I insisted, although frankly the results of his efforts on my head were murderous to behold. It made me feel noble that I was suffering for a good cause. But every time I came through the door I could see his face fall. As a professional he knew he was not doing a good job, and so eventually, more out of compassion for him than anything else, I stopped going. Sometime later I discovered a black barber shop. The West Indian barber who was there was a guy who enjoyed hairdressing and had undertaken an expensive hairdresser's course – white people's hair of course. But after graduation he could not get a job in any white salon so he had to fall back on a black barber's. So here we were, two black people thrown together when both of us would have preferred an integrated setting.

From then on I have not worried about appearances, only to make sure that my actions would have been the same had the person been white. That is why the only priest to take me to an industrial tribunal accusing me of racial discrimination is black. Quite true. He was also the only black priest in my area at the time.

Next there are the relationships with the black community itself. Public office means public accountability and the higher the office, the greater the accountability. It is galling for black people to see white officials play loose and fast with public funds to the benefit of their friends, but find that similarly placed black officials are not prepared to do the same to help them when their own needs are both real and great. But, however sympathetic the black official may be, however trying of his patience it may be to explain over and over again why he cannot follow the practices of his white counterparts, he must hold the line and not cut corners if he is to champion the cause of justice and black people without having constantly to be looking over his shoulder.

All this applies to me as a black bishop in the Church of England as it does to any black person in a high profile public post. But understandably such an appointment when, as was the case with me, it is the first of its kind, receives more than the usual amount of publicity and makes it difficult for one to take it in one's stride. So I was most grateful to the wise old priest, now dead, who was my spiritual adviser at the time. He urged me to see it as just an enlarged arena for the same service to the same God, who had been preparing me all the time for it. He had pointed out to me that few other bishops at the time of their appointment had had my experience of international politics such as chairing the World Council of Churches' Programme to Combat Racism. So much so that I had had discussions with both Joshua Nkomo and Robert Mugabe when they came to London for the pre-independence talks. Few had sat on a Royal Commission, few had established their credentials before appointment as campaigners for racial justice as I had, few had been so well-known from radio and television appearances. He himself had long been praying that I should be made a bishop and I was not to think that I was any less qualified than anyone else.

I think that I can say that in the almost 14 years that I have been a bishop, I have not consciously shirked when it fell to me to say what I believed to be true even though it was not popular, such as deploring the status accorded to Enoch Powell by having his body in Westminster Abbey overnight, or the recent bombing of Iraq. I would like to think that in my endeavour to care for God's people, encouraging them by word and example, and together with them witnessing to God's love of all humankind, I have succeeded and failed in measure common to all bishops. I would like to think that I have kept reminding myself and reminding others that we cannot worship Jesus in church services and efficient organisations if we are also starving, jailing, raping and murdering Him in the persons of powerless human beings of any description. I know that I am not without friends and supporters, and I do not doubt that there are detractors. There is a long way yet to go and a great deal still to be done but I hope with God's help, not to drop the baton before I have reached the change-over point.

Ladies and gentlemen, friends, I don't know what you were expecting but that is what you got and I thank you very much for your patient hearing.

John La Rose: Bishop Wood has said he will take a few questions, so are there any questions?

Member of the audience: I would like to ask Bishop Wood if he would be kind enough to give us a panoramic view of black people in the church, both as lay people, priests, assistants to bishops.

John La Rose: The question is from Professor James Millett who is with Oberlin College in Ohio and is here with some students doing a special course.

Wilfred Wood: Yes, you heard me describe how, for the most part, when West Indians came here they were not made welcome in the churches. As you know, we in the West Indies know far more about Britain and British people than they know about us and they have the notion that black people are all different and exotic and, therefore, they assume that black people who went to church were all Pentacostals as distinct from really belonging to the mainstream churches. When West Indians therefore turned up expecting to take their place as they would at home in churches with liturgies, with which they are thoroughly familiar, and found instead that they were treated as aliens, many of them retreated to non-churchgoing. Now, I've always said that if you have an area where there are a lot of black people and yet the church remains stubbornly white, then it's the fault of the clergymen, because most black people know that they're dealing with white racism Monday to Saturday so they are not all that surprised, frankly, when they find it among the lay people in church, who are the lay people they meet at work and on the streets and so on. They can tolerate that in the sense that they will go to church, worship God and go home again without having much to do with anybody in the church. But if the clergyman is racist or if he is weak on racism then they will withdraw altogether and I think this is what has happened in many cases.

The mainline churches have lost a whole generation of church-going people because even those convinced Christians had withdrawn from the church and could not take their children to church. Hence the children grew up in bible groups and in the independent churches, and I have to say that it really thrills me, frankly, when I go to independent churches, which I do quite a bit, the New Testament Church of God and others and I have to say, too, that many of those churches almost see me as their bishop really as well. It's lovely to see all these young black people, confident and secure and expressing themselves in worship in church without any worry, frankly, about race or being alien or strangers in the church.

So I think that those who remain Christian and for whom religion remains important, will find their feet. They will always be a minority in the mainline churches, but I think it's the black churches that will hold the key. It may well be also that, if black people in this country have to organise for our own well-being and so on in the future, it will be the black churches who will lead in that connection. I would certainly like to think that that is the case because otherwise the leadership will have to come from those who have been, say, in prison. On Easter day, every Easter and Christmas, we bishops in our diocese go to the prisons. So this Easter day I was at Wandsworth Prison and in the chapel, only 100 people are allowed in at any one time. So there were 98 who came to the service and I have to say at least 75 of those were black and I said to them, 'You know, I should be encouraging you, but sitting here and seeing all of you in this place I am feeling rather depressed and I would rather be with you somewhere else frankly than here,' and actually they quite brightened up. When I came to speak to them I said, 'Now tell me, Paul says that there are three things that will last forever: faith and love are two. Can you name the other one?' And one chap says, 'Yeah, Wandsworth Prison!' The answer is of course 'hope'. I think that we still have hope, even in that situation there is still hope. So, I still have a hope that religion will play an important part and that young black people will regroup around it, but it will be in the black churches rather than aiming to be bishops and deans and so on in the established churches. Sorry to be so long, but that's my view.

Member of the audience: I wondered – when the decision was made for you to remain here because your experience was thought to be more useful here than back in the Caribbean, whether you thought that was the right decision?

Wilfred Wood: Thank you very much. I don't have any regrets, no. As I said, I have tended not to think in terms of, 'Now, what's the best deal for me?' What seemed to be right, what God was calling, I followed that. No, there has been a lot to do. My one regret is that I haven't been able to do as much as I would like to do really. It would be for others to judge whether in the end I've made any contribution. My wife knows what I want written on my tombstone when I die. We had a very caustic Latin master at Combermere and once he wrote on a chap's essay, 'You tried anyway!' So I hope that when I die, they'll write, 'He tried anyway.'

John La Rose: Yes, Hewie. (Hewlett Andrew).

Hewlett Andrew: Thank you very much. I want to use the word, foreman, in the colonial sense of the word. I have no doubt that you have been a foreman in terms of the church and society. You know, as most of us know, how effective that work has been. I also know that many people today say – I was glad to hear what you have just said about the black churches – but I hear people again and again say, 'Yes, the black churches are very good at entertaining. They are very good at entertaining but in the true sense of the word they are not liberating black people.' Now I know that liberation or the greater part of it must come from the black clergy or the black pastors of those independent black churches. Have you got some comments to make on that?

Wilfred Wood: Yes I agree with that. It is important though that the membership hold the leadership to account, and I'm glad that a lot of the young black members of the black churches are quite articulate and well-educated now and not prepared just to accept what the old pastor says. I mean, there is a sense in which he has to give an account. You see, as you probably remember, the strength of the black church, particularly in America, was that in those areas where virtually the whole community depended for its living on, say, one enterprise, like a mill or factory or even a plantation which employed everybody, the workers were not in a strong position to make demands because they had no unions and depended on the employer for their living. About the only person in the town really whose wages were not paid by that factory or that plantation and so on would be the local preacher, the local black preacher, because his wages were paid really by his congregation. The result was that he became almost the spokesperson, the trade union man really, because when his members said, 'You must go and speak to the boss about this injustice or that injustice,' he had to because if he didn't and they didn't give their contributions, he wouldn't eat, you see. So you've got a tradition then of the pastor being, as it were, the political leader as well. Now, I think that that will, to some extent, happen here as well. I think the older generation of pastors, the old fatherly type who expect complete obedience, I think that will pass. Their place will be taken by young pastors who have grown up here and who will recognise that they have a political as well as a pastoral and spiritual role. That I think is how it will develop and how I hope it will develop.

John La Rose: Any other questions? I'm very pleased that we were able to have Bishop Right Reverend Doctor Wilfred Wood, to give him his full title, here with us this evening. As you will see from his short biography, he is also a doctor of theology. What has been important for us at the George Padmore Institute here this evening is the unique part he has played in British society. I know it and there are quite a number of people here in this room with us who also know it. And for that reason it is important, and it has been for the other contributions that we have had in this series and the first series, that people of this unique type should be able to speak about their personal experience out of which they have become what they have become and, also, in my view, an important element is that in spite of difficulty they can triumph over adversity. All these experiences we have heard are examples of the triumph over adversity and difficulty, of unique kinds of commitment and of great achievement, and change as a result. I particularly want to thank Wilfred for all he has done, all I know he will continue to do over the wide range of activity which you have heard only partly here this evening but, nevertheless, which we recognise and for which we thank him, for all he has done and for the kind of contribution that is going to come in the future. So Wilfred, thank you very much, thanks for all the analysis that you've given us, thanks for all the information and thank you for coming.

The **Rt. Revd Dr Wilfred Wood** has been the Bishop of Croydon in the diocese of Southwark since 1985. His tireless participation in social and community projects as well as his role as a leading churchman have made him one of the most well-known ecclesiastical figures in and from Britain's black community.

Bishop Wilfred Wood was born in Barbados in June 1936, the son of Wilfred Coward and Elsie Elmira Wood. He was educated at Combermere School and then Codrington College. In 1966 he married Ina Smith, the daughter of the late Barbadian MP Lloyd Smith CBE (MP from 1946-71). They have three sons and two daughters.

The Rt. Revd. Wilfred Wood has had a long and varied career of service in the church in many areas of London since his ordination as Deacon in St Michael's Cathedral, Barbados on 21 December 1961. He was then ordained as a Priest in St Paul's Cathedral, London, exactly one year later. From 1962-66 he was Curate of St Stephen with St Thomas in Shepherd's Bush, London, and Honorary Curate of the same church between 1966 and 1974.

Wilfred Wood

During this period the Rt. Revd. Wilfred Wood was also the Bishop of London's Officer in Race Relations. He took this work further as the Chairman of the Institute of Race Relations between 1971-74. He became Vicar of St Laurence, Catford in London, in 1974, a position he held until 1982. From 1977 to 1985 he was Honorary Canon of Southwark Cathedral. During these years Revd. Wood was also Rural Dean of East Lewisham. Between 1982-85 he was the Archdeacon and Borough Dean of Southwark.

In 1985 Bishop Wood was consecrated as Suffragan Bishop of Croydon in St Paul's Cathedral, and then in 1991 he became Area Bishop of Croydon. Part of his extensive duties in this role include being responsible for 102 parishes in the boroughs of Croydon, Bromley, Sutton and Banstead/Reigate, as well as in the districts of Tandridge and the Mole Valley.

Outside his everyday ecclesiastical duties, the Rt. Revd. Wilfred Wood has found time to be involved in a wide range of social and community work. He was a Justice of the Peace for Inner London for 14 years from 1971. He has been a member of the Royal Commission on Criminal Procedure (1978-81). From 1975 to 1980 he was a member of the World Council of Churches' Programme to Combat Racism, taking on the extra responsibility of being Moderator between 1977 and 1980. He was a member of the Archbishop of Canterbury's Commission on Urban Priority Areas in 1983-85.

Taking some time from this busy schedule, Bishop Wood gained his Doctor of Divinity (Hon.) from the General Theological Seminary in 1986. Thereafter, he became a member of the Board of Housing Corporation until 1995. He is currently a Non-Executive Director of the Mayday University Hospital Healthcare NHS Trust.

Bishop Wilfred Wood is well-known for the time and dedication he has devoted to the black community. He is a founder member of a number of black self-help organisations including the Shepherds Bush Social and Welfare Association; the Shepherds Bush Credit Union; the Islington Harambee; the Berbice Housing Association Co-op; the Carib Housing Association and the Martin Luther King Memorial Trust amongst others. He had a pivotal role in the New Cross Massacre Action Committee in the early 1980s.

For some 30 years Wilfred Wood has also found the time and space to write. *Vicious Circle*, published with John Downing, came out in 1968. *Keep the Faith, Baby* was published in 1994. He has contributed pieces to *The Committed Church*, *Black Britain*, *White Media* and a variety of other publications.

The Rt. Revd Wilfred Wood does find the time to relax, despite his huge commitments to the church and the community. In what spare time he has he enjoys following most sports, particularly cricket. He also admits to being an ardent supporter of Queen's Park Rangers football club.

Aggrey Burke

Aggrey Burke
Introduced by John La Rose (17.05.1999)

Aggrey Burke: The images that I have of life in Britain come from the village. We started off in a little village on the edge of St Ann where Garvey was born. I have very few memories of that period, except that my godmother lived nearby and, though she now has a stroke, she still ranges as one of the three or four people of greatest importance to me. There were these proud, middle class, black people in the villages in Jamaica and only recently I have come to have some understanding about how I might have been part of this business, that is the Jamaican and Caribbean and African experience.

It happened like this. My mother had been telling us for many years – there are six of us – that she had been brought up in Alston. She told us and she told us and she told us. And we did nothing about it. So the last time I was home – not the last time, the time before – I said, 'Tell us a little more about this place, Alston.' She said, 'I've told you the story so many times before, you must be bored with it.' I said, 'Yes, we're bored with it but tell us again.'

And she said about how her grandmother had brought her up for about five years and they had the family land. Her grandmother and grandfather had moved there very soon after slavery. I said, 'Well, I don't understand that.' She said, 'Well, it goes something like this. My great-grandfather must have had good times on an estate and was given this whole village or bought it, whichever the truth is, and the family moved there and owned everything there.' So I said, 'You know something, tomorrow morning I'm going to drive there.' So I went down there and met the one remaining cousin who was rather old and decrepit but he gave me a little more history of that early life in the very desolate grim hillsides of Jamaica.

It's quite important because nobody in the family wants to stay in that village now. The rock is so hard and the trees seem almost bare that the land, the many hundreds of acres of land, has simply been given away or occupied, possessed by the people there. And my relatives have moved away all over the place. But when we

163

went – I went with my brother to this village – one had a sense of this dignity and lifestyle that must have been so prominent in that period of Jamaican life, early in the century. But one saw alongside that dignity a certain poverty as well. The people could hardly eke out anything from the land. There was nothing to sell. The yams looked bad to me, the banana trees looked bad to me. So I wondered about the life I had in the early period of my days.

We moved from St Ann to Clarendon very early on in my history and the culture change, only now I understand, was massive. Clarendon is hot and the dignity that made Garvey and other great Jamaicans from St Ann was very different in Clarendon. We had lots of estates in Clarendon. St Ann didn't have estates like that and St Ann has Ocho Rios. The nearest thing we have to that in Clarendon is a place called Milk River and you go there and soak your body. But we were up in the hills – a place called Goshen – and we had mainly orange and pineapple. We ran a farm, my mother did it.

And so the second bit of my life, my godmother had been important, my mother very important because she had to look after us whilst my father worked for the government. Life in that village called Goshen was very odd for me. We were the main employer of the village. We had the property, not a sugar property, you know, a property. You had to break stones all day, cut wood all day, the cows sometimes looked so maaga but we used to get up in the morning and milk them nonetheless. Cows are wonderful things, even when they are like that you can milk them. And the village was somewhere where we employed some of the people.

So when I went to school, in my early days, the people I went to school with didn't know what to call me, the boys and girls, because their parents called me 'Mr Aggrey' and they didn't know what to call me. So I had a very strange existence with them. But I was very much aware from then of how I had clothes and I had shoes and we had running water. And if there was a killing which we had to do regularly – a cow killing was the one I liked the most, but goat killing was good too. If you have a goat feed in Jamaica is a big thing you know. In fact we learned as little boys to run the goat, not that we were doing it to be employed, as the people in the village were, we were doing it to be with the people we employed. We would go with them and see what they did.

But my father felt that this business of being at the local school wasn't the right thing, so he sent us across the island to a place called Jericho in Hanover. And we had again another totally different experience because at Jericho you could look down and see the sugar estate. You were very much aware that in Jericho you had a sense of being totally dominated by that estate. You really were in another world, totally dominated by the sugar plantation economy of the Caribbean. We lived with the teacher who was my father's friend. We were amused by the teacher, because sometimes he would lose his glasses and everybody would be looking for his glasses and then we would look at this man's face and they were on his face. One day he lost his hat and we had everybody looking for his hat and it was on his head. But teacher Mac was a wonderful man and he gave such good education in Hanover.

And at night we would listen to people chanting from across the hills – it is in a mountain range – and we would know that this meant there was someone dead and people were on a nine night or 40th night. Whatever. We were hearing that all the time. Subsequently I got to know that Hanover is the heartland of obeah. Quite important because of the superstitious aspects of life which seemed to be most preserved in those areas where the sugar estate dominated to such an extent that the people had to resort to their own thing. And I became part of that thing.

The differences of these three areas were really quite stark and the religion in these three areas was again very different. Jericho, for example, was a Presbyterian place, the Scots – in Mocho, and Goshen, where we were before, it was a Church of England place and on Sundays my father had to go and preach if the bishop or parson wasn't there. St Ann's people had their own churches, much more so than Clarendon or Hanover people. You had a sense that Jamaica had every bit of every thing.

When I was about eight or nine, I passed some of the government exams and my father decided you can't get enough education down there, you'll have to go to Kingston. So the family moved to Kingston and I went to some local schools again.

Now Jamaica was a harsh reality for me and for many people. Moving between these different areas was fun. But you were very much aware of the differences which existed between you and them. You were always very much aware that you weren't part of the total thing. We were living at the teacher's home. Your family was the main one running the 'business'. My mother, not my father, ran the business of living.

Anyway, we got to Kingston and I went to the local school in Rollington Town and came face to face with the Jamaican, how can I describe it, the real ting, what people regard as the Jamaican, the Kingston boys. I couldn't fight then. I still can't fight. They loved me and I loved them but their style of operation was really very different. I tended to argue my way out of one or two spots. And in fact I was a favorite at school from many points of view because the school needed its own dignity and its achievers. I stayed there only a short time, probably a year and a half. We were very close to the head teacher and his family. They were my father's friends. I then went across Kingston to another school, All Saints, where there was great achievement from the point of view of the Jamaican school movement. And I was very much part of that and was very happy to be part of that – debates and this and that. I was still quite young and then, lo and behold, I got the first Garvey Scholarship, for going to the secondary school. Well, this was a bonus for the family because I feel that probably they would have made some way to pay for me but this way I got not only my fees paid, my boarding paid, but I got a book grant, which I'll come back to in a moment. And I arrived at J.C. – Jamaica College – in 1955.

The period was a period of great growth in Jamaica. My father had been very close to Norman Manley and that was in many ways a plus and a minus for us. During the period of hurricanes back in Goshen, for example, if you had to give out rice our family gave out the rice. You could tief some of the rice too, you know, because you have all the rice. My father was amazingly religious and didn't go in for any thieving. And we had to somehow look after the people and there was a whole sense of being part of a looking-after population and my father's work was community development. Manley had set up this Jamaica Welfare and it was really mainly around my father – to try and build people in the village areas, and to give people a sense of hope. Our history had been so short and the few black people who had the possibility of making sense of the society were part of that movement. Linton will know because he went to school with my grandmother, Mammy Watts, in Chapelton, where my father was from. And Mammy Watts had a little school and so you had people who were before those who seemed to be achieving. The population I came from didn't come straight off, out of the oven, at one time. There were two or three generations of achievement or freedom, whichever comes first.

Well, J.C. was tough. I arrived at this place thinking, 'I'm a Jamaican and the very best.' And when I got there not only did I speak a different language but when the boys wanted me to sing a song – and I remind you that Paul Robeson, he did not influence me in those days, but Paul Robeson faced with the same thing – of wanting to sing negro spirituals – was being urged by people to sing opera. He said, 'No, I'm a black man. I want to address this issue first.' Well, when they wanted you to do an initiation song in J.C., I was foolish and decided to sing a Jamaican folk song. Most of the boys had never heard such a thing before. They had been to schools where they sang the same sort of thing you learn round here, in Britain, you know, and they spoke a language identical to what you hear round here. So you had this layering in Jamaica – oh, the other thing was they looked lighter in skin colour than me – so you had this new movement of education in Jamaica which brought in black people and it's really no more than 45 years that the Jamaican education movement has been going strong and it's slightly after my time.

Well, they beat me and they fought me and I fought them back – now, I could really take up what I had learned from some of these boys at school. It's at J.C. that I decide I going to show them one or two things because these boys believed they owned Jamaica completely. They had no sense of village life, no sense of the traditions of the society, and yet they were in charge. I found that daunting. I found it very difficult. I pondered on that issue so much. Fanon talks about them, the petty bourgeoisie, he talks about their racism very openly. He says that this is a very difficult group. Well, I was there with them. I loved them, they loved me – eventually. I am reminded of Joe. Joe was a Lebanese from one of the village structures – small town, his father ran a shop. I still had some country clothes, and Joe would lend me his suit and his this and his that. He would say, 'I have to bring you up to a level you know.' I would say, 'Boy, I have to bring you up to another level as well.' And so this exchange was going on. It was a wonderful thing.

But J.C. was difficult as well because what it really led me to believe was that there were really great problems in bringing together groups of people, who had come out of the business at different rates and at different times. I had gone there with a capitalist group and I was very much aware of the capitalism at school. Eventually I had a major conflict with – I think he was the bursar. I was reminded of him the other day by a friend who was here, a J.C. friend, and he said, 'Remember you used to ask about the book money?' I said, 'Yes, I remember.' And the book money was this. The bursar and the headmaster would use the book money only to buy books from here, Britain. And I was saying to them, 'Look, don't bother buying any of the Keats and all them things for us. I am used to some proper Caribbean literature. We have plenty of it at home. If you don't want to buy books come and borrow some of those at my home.' So they said, 'But those are not books, those are not written by the proper people.' I said, 'Don't bother with that, you come and see the thing.' But the second thing was that they used the money for their own good and that bothered me. So I got together all the scholarship boys and I said, 'Look, brothers, we have to plan this thing properly. 20 per cent of the book money must go on proper books this year. And it must increase gradually.' And indeed this is what happened.

Well, my life and schooling was interrupted once again when the Notting Hill riots took place here in Britain. Norman Manley came to Britain to try and patch up things, and you know, we were in this business all along, of trying to represent the interests of our people. And here it was, we were being attacked in Notting Hill, in Nottingham, all over Britain, and we didn't know what to do. Manley, as it turned out at the time, was very concerned about how he would move forward. So he suggested that my father should come here. So we all had to come.

Well, this England here was another kettle of fish. It was a very, very, very curious area at that particular point in time. Village structures were not here then. Hornsey, Nottingham, Willesden were the three that I remember most during our early period. We got here in 1959 and we spent our whole lives trying to make sense of this betterment of the relationship between a mainly Jamaican group of West Indians living here, black people living here, speaking mainly patois, and the middle class and the student group around Hans Crescent. We were having some good parties for that group too. Good parties. Every so often people remind us. But our people could not be expected to negotiate a position in this period – we were trapped, we were very much trapped during that period of time. And my father and others were striving, seeking to make sense of it.

Of all the things that have influenced my being, I think it is that threat of death and death itself that comes from race, racism, that has affected me most. One remembers so well the experiences – I went to school for two years here. The past head boy had left me to run the Christian Union. In those days I was into this business of God, you know. We had a very active religious knowledge group, sort of contemporary religion and we were talking about everything under the sun. And I was in charge of that. I was a deputy head boy and all of that for a short time. Running the cricket team, I may say I was a good athlete at running and all that. But I was very much aware of how much it was like an island as though – Ngugi talks about it in 'Being Detained' – I had that sense, you know – it was an amazing experience. And one day I went to this past head boy's home to see him and his mother called the police because somehow she thought ... and I had a funny tie, and blazer and all that, you know. And only the boys who were the leaders in the school had this special badge you know, so everybody could see it. And you said to yourself, 'Well, what is it all about?'

And that's the experience I have had, the main experience I have had, of being like – in these modern days of course one has a sense of O.J. Simpson. I haven't done anything as bad as O.J. Simpson, or as good. Because O.J., you know, is the Othello, the real Othello, in every sense the Othello. The hero who marries into the white community and so bridges that important gap because to join up, you know, it's the same thing we're dealing with now. Eddie Brathwaite talks about it – creolisation. The conflict of creolisation during slavery. And that conflict of creolisation we have again here now. In modern day Britain we have it very, very powerfully. But I was aware that even from those early days at school that O.J.ism was something which was very powerful. You had a challenge to join up but there was the very real sense that, when it came to the crunch, like a river that knows that certain fish do not belong, we'd throw them onto the banks. That's the sense one had. And yet there was ... like Claude McKay talks of this desolation and yet he found the possibility of great creativity in Britain and indeed, in Europe.

Well, when we were growing up we had to choose what we wanted to do and I wanted to be a doctor. And so it was, as though God would bring it down on you to be a doctor and that was it. So I went to Birmingham and we were so few in number – the black students – mainly African, a few of us Caribbean. The ones from the Caribbean, like Gordon [Rohlehr] with whom I lived, were going home without a doubt and formed themselves, with myself, into I think we called it the West Indian Student Group or something like that. But anyway, the headquarters was in our house, my house, with Gordon – Gordon joined me and we rented over a shop. And the boys – there was one girl – she had a real problem because all of us wanted to go out with her. She married one eventually and I don't think it went too well.

But we had this sense of being trapped, you know, and yet because of my own experience of having been to school for two years I was also in the other group. So I became the head of athletics and became in a way an ambassador for Birmingham

University because we travelled a great deal on the continent. So I was in these two groups. One group of which Gordon was really the president. In some ways he was the president but he couldn't speak the Jamaican, you know. I was the Jamaican in down town Birmingham where we played dominoes and I was good at the dominoes and the Eastern Caribbean guys, they weren't too good at the dominoes. And you know the rice and peas, you have to enjoy the rice and peas. And ackee and saltfish. And sometimes they'd give you things which the Eastern Caribbean guys didn't really know, 'The students must enjoy the food properly man. Have seconds on us.' And we had this tremendous relationship with the people in the town because we knew, better than anyone else, that if we didn't have that relationship, we would lose. So we had dances with them. Gordon had a steel band. I think he went half-deaf you know. And we had a folk group which I was very actively part of and we had this ceremonial, regular Saturday evening party. That was a multi-cultural affair, much more than any other. So we had this sense of an eliteness, an 'elitedom' almost, needing to make sense with the people from our population. And that was the theme running through my whole experience.

It is during that period that we started to get our heads around some of the things described by negritude and in the literature and the theatre that were about. One started to look at how the theatre itself was a reflection of the political structure of society. And that, depending on where you are in the theatre, on stage or in the audience, you can have a position of being part of the ruling class or not. And it is for that reason that we felt that the Caribbean Artists Movement, the whole 'book movement', the musical movement and the theatre itself are crucial to a progression within society. All of the artistic fields seem crucial.

It is there that I had this great urge to have an understanding of happiness and what is it about. Having been Church of England, I went to one or two other churches down there in Birmingham and had to run out of them as quickly as I went in. They were grim places. The Church of England was a grim reality. The people with the black churches – and Wilfred Wood talked about it a bit last time, a month ago – were developing a way of looking forward. The institutions we had were of home, that was number one, home, back home, going home. Language was an institution for us during that period. We didn't have the shebeen but we set up these dances which were sophisticated shebeens of a kind. And then we had the church. That was an important institution during that period and continued to be. Cricket was an institution. I remember so well when Frank Worrell came to Birmingham.

And then we had this business of being attacked. It became an institution in our community. Racial attack. We were under seige as a people. During that period, Powellism and other things came on stream. There were many places I've been to in Birmingham where I couldn't go in because of being black. And certainly if you were with a white student you couldn't go. There were many times. But during this seeking, this search for a meaning of what is happiness, one was very very struck, and I think, in some ways, put off, by the ideals of a world which would have been more easily defined had one remained in the Caribbean, of the kind that one grew up in in that period. Was this happiness, simply, you know the kind of thing you have now, having things and enjoying them? Or was it seeking glory, and if you are seeking glory – Ball talks about it – glory in what setting? I've had this tremendous difficulty myself. If I have to speak to an audience, if I have to write. To whom? Where? When? Why? What is it all about? Or is it something to do with some virtue in one's life? Some average position? We were struggling with these issues in Birmingham, and indeed, most of the lads, most of one's colleagues went back home. Eventually I shared the view that the most legitimate way forward was to go home. And yet, one remembers so much, what Birmingham gave. It was the threat that this group of our people living here and ourselves, would merge or would be destroyed.

We're a small people and one was very much aware of that reality. We are small and one is struggling all the time with the history, the history that we have, the tremendous problems of death and destruction that slavery brought and the atrocities, the cruelties of slavery. We were always struggling with these issues. We were always struggling with how do we come to be a people, when there have been these tremendous hurdles to clear and all we seek is a sense of ourselves as people, and protecting the institutions that we have. So we were clear during those Birmingham days that the institutions were important. What became true was that for people from the countries of the Caribbean and Africa, the movements we had there in Birmingham and here in London were precious. I had this curious life of being named after Booker T. Washington and Aggrey of Africa. My father was meddling with these things of names during that period. By then quite a few people were doing likewise in Jamaica. And I had this sense that we had to find a way to maintain the traditions of the African people in the Caribbean.

Returning home to Jamaica was a curious business. Everybody seemed to have a little radio at their head. Ska or rock steady was the way. Nobody seemed to be working. Everybody seemed to be moving in a very wonderfully attractive manner and I went to do 'house' jobs as a young doctor. The society was in a state of turmoil. It was all over the place. Guns were now widely available. The drug trade was in motion. And my first recollection going back was meeting the same boys, probably not the ones I was at school with, from the area where I went to school Kingston. None of these boys had work. They had either been at the front line of destruction by the police because they had been hired to be involved in political whatever, and at the end of the political whatever, then things had to be cleaned up a bit. Or they were living orderly lives. But there was no order.

It is of interest to me that some years later I worked there when I came back from Trinidad. This school I went to was near to Bellevue. What we found in places like Bellevue was that you had some very great Jamaicans, like Don Drummond, who had been there, and there was Audvil King who wrote a very, very scholarly piece, and so one had a sense that the people who were involved in struggle are likely to be caught up with the struggle of the mind as well. This is the point. At that stage I hadn't decided to be in psychiatry, in fact I was far more attracted to these obeah men than psychiatry. But it seemed to me that there was no way that we could bring resolution to the people's ills without a political structure and indeed, within a short period of going home, Walter Rodney was excluded from the society and those of us remaining there came together. Some of us were lukewarm and some of us were hot. I would put myself in the lukewarm group, in terms of trying to find a way. I was too busy to be hot and I don't know if I am capable of being hot in that political structure.

Abeng was formed. There were some wonderful people, some of them very solid in their ideology. They thought that the ones of us who were lukewarm weren't solid too, but I think we were. But there was rivalry of that kind. And there was also within that movement the rivalry of those who went to prep schools and those who went to ordinary schools. The prep school boys could not make sense of the society, no way.

Well, Walter was excluded and that was a grim reality for us. It was worse than anything you can imagine. We had colleagues like C.Y. Thomas and others from Guyana. We were moving around the place. The year after Walter was excluded I went to Trinidad with my girlfriend at the time, now deceased. And within a short period Trinidad went through the same thing. And a lot of intellectuals were locked up in prison. The Caribbean is a strange place. Because I am Jamaican I was there as an ex-patriate so I could move around as a diplomat. It was a joke. John La Rose came down there during that period and we wanted him to stay, because it seemed that there was a possibility that a movement could get somewhere. But it was the intellectuals who prevented the movement going anywhere. But Trinidad was wonderful because half the population is Asian and this was for me quite a wonderful thing. We had Asians living – we call them Indians in Jamaica – next door to us in one or two places.

In Trinidad there was this vitality. It was like a Western country, that was the first thing that struck me. You had the groups. The French Creoles, the Indians, a black élite, this was wonderful to see. And the Indians were also the poorest. And I had this very odd experience of working in my first job in psychiatry which I started in the General Hospital, Port of Spain. All of the psychiatrists there were in private practice nearly all the time. So, poor me, the first trainee down there. I had to learn how to deal with the Indians and our own people one time. And there was a whole mix-up down there you know. Trinidad's a mixed-up place. But there was so much enthusiasm and vitality in Trinidad as well. We were able in six months with Elaine Arnold, a social worker now living here, and with one or two other workers, to re-house many people who were in the mental hospital. The vitality of the people was amazing. And Trinidad had resources which we didn't have in Jamaica. But Trinidad was also not my home. I think it's a place I would live, but it seemed to me after a year that, with the carry-on with Eric Williams and everything, I should go back to Jamaica, which I did.

It was a new phase. Jamaica, Trinidad, Barbados, Guyana were all now in a political phase. Our lives were no longer simply our own. People had to take positions on the political fray. Many of the people I was close to in Jamaica joined up with the Peoples National Party, the PNP, with Michael Manley. And those of us who didn't join up were in a state of either stupidity or something else. And so one can see that if at critical periods in one's life, one is ambivalent to the political process, one will either be excluded, killed or incorporated in the system in a different form. Well, I think from about then, which was about 1970, until now, that political period of flux has bedevilled, I would say, it's bedevilled us and me.

I think essentially to be part of society one has to be clear on the politics. I think so. The experience I have had suggests to me that it runs through everything. It runs through one's work. It runs through one's community. It runs through one's whole way of thinking. You could say that as West Indian people and as African people we had a struggle here. But indeed when it came – I returned here to Britain in 1971 – when New Cross occurred in 1981, it became clear to me that the political struggle was one which had to be waged within a political framework. It seemed to me that here we have had experiences in Britain repeated from the time I came here in 1959. They've been repeated, all along they're repeated. Threat of death and extinction is the main theme leading to political struggles, leading us to have to either join up willingly or unwillingly, or be thrown out. It is as clear as that.

Aggrey Burke

Well, going back to Walter Rodney's exclusion which I want to touch on because, you know, I hadn't been accustomed to being afraid. In fact I had a great deal of self-confidence. I thought I was a mighty man, young man, at the time. But when Walter was thrown out I came to my senses. There's no might against the state. This is the reality of the business. And it seemed to me that what Walter had done was bring into the frame the possibility of liberating our own people. He could communicate with them. I don't know the extent to which Walter did it. But I know the extent to which we all tried to do it. We were very busy. I worked six, seven days a week, and on the little one-time drive I would have out at the weekend we would go and sell papers, meet people and so forth. But I think Walter had a message. Rupert Lewis has just written a book about Walter's sojourn and Walter, even when he met me in Jamaica – there's a little bit in it – he was concerned about the differences between the people that he was part of through his intellectual activity and the people who had nothing. He was very aware of that.

Well, we became very fearful in the Caribbean round about that time. We became fearful of all kinds of things. It reminded one, and we were debating it, about the issues that Fanon had been discussing. It reminded one of the great problems and the great needs to make sense of the relationship that we had with the former slave masters here. It reminded us of how we would become extinct unless a clear position could be determined. I've had a great sense of travel and enjoyment in Britain and I often, when in great periods of frustration, go off on a trip. Sometimes on my own. And in the Caribbean you don't do anything like that on your own, you know. Nobody's that crazy. But here there is space and time to do things like that and certainly when I came back to England, I continued doing that.

I remember once, and I want to mention this, going to a place in Denmark called Langeland, a little island and for two days that I was there, or the day after I got there, there was great jubilation. I couldn't understand this business. And then I came to my senses when I read Barry Higman's account of slavery in the Danish

Caribbean. And I tell you that because it seems to me that there is this very, very vital relationship between the two groups of people. Those who have enslaved us and those who we are. And that somehow it is never understood until people have a chance to understand it.

Well, in 1971 I came back here to Britain. I think I had a British passport but I didn't know what that meant. But I was very promptly told in psychiatry that they would have me, but only if I was a student from the Caribbean. So one had this sense of the most prominent places and wherever one went for a job would have you, if you were going home. I was a bit brash even in them days, and I found this alarming, that I had no freedom. I was now firmly labelled as 'Caribbean only' because I'd been back you see. British medicine is something like that but here I was then, up against it. And one was very amazed, I was quite amazed by what was going on and what goes on in professions.

I want to skip somewhat because I don't want to be here all night – certainly I don't want you to be here all night. But this business of how one experiences life within a profession. Well, I have had difficulties making sense of it. It is making sense of the task ahead. In the Caribbean it was very clear. And even here in London I've been far more directed, firm, confident, clear, when doing things relating to the Caribbean. I think it would be the same if I was doing things related to Africa or India. Here I'm very clear about things that are related to our people, very clear.

I had the experience the other day of going to see a woman who in fact is from India, I think. And there was an interpreter offered to me but I noticed I could talk to the woman better if the interpreter kept her mouth shut. And I noticed that when I'm talking to the woman by telephone the thing gets even clearer. There must be commonalities in how we relate. But when one has to relate within one's profession one has to use their language, their norms, their systems. One has to divest. Become two or three people. Change up. Sometimes lose yourself. Well, I can't claim that I've done that yet. But there is always the challenge and the threat that if you don't do that you will lose. It's implicit. Believe me. It is implicit. And when the system says you behave in a certain way, if you don't do that you will be up against it. So I've had this great difficulty which I will share, which is that I believe that the critical issues that we are about, relate to us.

It was New Cross more so than anything else which was a reminder of the reasons why I came to Britain. It was an alarming experience. I was looking at the detail of New Cross. The 20 families that we followed up for three years. The difficulty we had in reporting it because of course New Cross ended – in one sense it hasn't ended – by this alarming dispute between the parents, which we had to take note of, regard, and not become involved in. We couldn't take sides. We were there only as volunteers. We were there as professionals. Some formed the action group. John was involved in it. But we had a support group and the support group is very, very intensely involved in activity throughout the country. And I followed up one family in Jamaica for five years. And I was struck, looking at the notes of following up that family in Jamaica, of how the whole village, this person told me, cried when the village heard that her son was dead. The whole village. The structures of support that this person went back to, and I met them in Jamaica. Sadness remained with them for a long time. And when she went back she went and planted her yams and bananas and finished building the house. She could take the chance to find solace, to have comfort and to be understood.

Here, New Cross reminded us more so than anything else that if we don't have a system, we will be destroyed. And what is this system that we have? It is going back to the village and trying to support initiatives, trying to work closely with people, trying to make sense of the possibility that we will one day come out of it in one piece. New Cross was hard work. My car had a number of incidents which I never quite understood, but I paid for the bills quite happily or willingly. I was struck by many of those New Cross families, how they were from the villages. They were from different backgrounds. There were mixed race families, black families, migrant families, Indian families, you know, African families. But the sense of shock and of grief was so pervasive, and was so much part of us that both the Action Committees and the Marches and the Inquest and the aftermath of all that, but also the way the families have had to deal with their losses. And we say, was that the last?

But of course we know of Roger Sylvester, seeing Sheila there and Beverley there, recently. But when you read the paper these days, I know three families now who have had sudden losses like this, without reason. And you say to yourself, 'Is that our history?' Well, of course it is. But what supports do we have to make sense of it?

I work in another area which involves death and suffering and which has to do with mothers, who are under pressure, finding it impossible to look after their children without support. I perhaps know better than many that we are up against it. We are highly over-represented among such mothers. Highly over-represented among their children who get into difficulties with the state. Highly over-represented in the prisons, and in the locked wards of mental hospitals. And recently it has come to the fore, but it was known about from the days of the Educationally Sub-Normal (ESN) debate, that exclusions from society and from school are part of the thing we are struggling with.

But when one starts to look at the manifestations of this grim reality – at one level we do have a grim reality, at another level we have an exciting reality – I think one needs to balance the two. I think for many one is blinded by one or the other and survive by so doing. When one looks at one group, say excluded from school, one sees all the other things happening in these families, far more than other families. And when one starts to look at these realities, Caribbean people and African people, in one way or another, are the people most highly represented. If Mr Blair and his officers, being ministers of government, are going to do anything about it, co-opting us on committees won't do it. We have to be given the privilege and right to do a number of things ourselves. I'm very clear on that. I somehow see a process going on, which robs us of the possibility of achieving our worth. And I think that this is affecting certainly a third of our population all the time. And then when one sees the reactions of our people, the kind of things one is seeing is fairly harsh things between members of our own community. You hear this thing – 'black on black'. And I just hope I'm not tiefing anybody when I see them. I just hope I'm doing the right thing or a good thing, as an ideal. Because there is the possibility now that we will exploit each other by virtue of the fact that there are so few of us. And it is in this field that I find it most challenging trying to come back to this sense of the village.

The loyalties we had. We used to sit and sing together. The women would break stone. The men would set coal kilns. And the hurricane, Andrew Salkey talks of the hurricane. I was home for Gilbert. Gilbert was bad, you see. It was a bad one. But these natural disasters that we have may not be as intensive in their effect, in my view, as this ongoing sense of conflict within this society. So what hope is there? And this is where I think the George Padmore Institute and the groupings of people in various settings become crucial. I've spent my life trying to make sense of those things which I picked up in the village, and sometimes I think I've made some sense but sometimes I think I haven't. I think there's time to do a number of other things. We have laid the foundations in a number of areas.

One day, you know, an obeah man came to me and said, 'I not feeling so well.' So now you know I catch my fraid, you know. Obeah man, you know. And he come into your surgery, and you know these obeah men. And he had some bush in his bag as well, you know. And anyway they say he so sick that he must come in. This was in Jamaica. Anyway I talk to him and I find out what his situation was. I said, 'Boy, I fraid you, you know'. And the shame that comes from obeah is amazing. People here now, plenty people say, 'I don't mix up with those things.' But when it comes down to a death, or these things you know, everybody mix up with it. And everybody fraid. I mention that because when I hear the stories from people from, Angola from the Congo, from Dahomey – I meet Africans from everywhere in my work – they have the same systems. And you say a lot of what we have are survivals of the crossing. And it is the wonderful aspect of life, I think, which we have to make sense of. And you know we have had so many crossings. We have crossings from China, India, the Middle East and, of course, Europe and Africa. I mention that because it seems to me that we are still at this point of choosing a direction and the direction that I think we have attempted to make sense of here is a direction which comes out of, I think it's Garvey.

Garvey said, 'Race first.' And you could argue with that. But you could argue with it positively, and say, 'Did he not choose to come to Britain despite it?' He came you know. He came right up the road there, buried him right up the road there. Probably the same cemetery there. And I think it is Garvey. I think the Rastafarians and Bob Marley and Linton Kwesi Johnson have been disciples of a tradition which starts to make sense of the superstitions, the myths and the fairy tales that come out of Africa. I think the struggles that I have been struggling with are struggles related to those things. Certainly it has been a challenge to me. I have been reminded that I had a Garvey scholarship, you see.

The question for me, and I think for all of us, is how can we have a shared consciousness, through the systems that we're dealing with? And I think the shared consciousness of the African and Caribbean people is a very important one to promote. I think one has to pay tribute all the time to the musicians. I was so amazed at the extent to which we depend on our musicians and artists. More so than anyone in this society. They seem to get the message out. Caribbean Artists' Movement was getting the message out through art and through written material, and I think the black churches, as Wilfred Wood says, are getting the message out. But does psychiatry have a message to get out?

I think I'm very struck by the sense of great fellowship and dignity which Roger's funeral was. I was very struck by it. I found it a very sad occasion. Sad because I didn't think it would happen. And it happened in such a grim way. Roger Sylvester was known to me. I met him about ten years before his death. I was very struck that he came from a very wonderful tradition of Eastern Caribbean people from Grenada and they were there at the funeral in such fine form. I saw some of the Jamaican boys from Tottenham moving round and I moved with them, because I say it's a Jamaican offshoot.

So I thought there was this possibility within Britain of maintaining strong elements from particular village or small island structures which we have to preserve in whatever way we can. I think people will do it anyway, because of their sense of place and their sense of tradition and their sense of the foods they eat and the things they know best. But I think that this is a challenge that we now have. The Jamaican differences that I grew up with from village to village were very, very sharp. The differences that exist between the islands are sometimes also quite sharp. But the similarities are so rich and so evident all along. And it is that, more so than anything, that I use within my work. The similarities of experience, the similarities of tradition, the similarities of lifestyle, the similarities of experience here in Britain struggling against a mammoth, struggling against the possibility, the threat of death that one sees all around.

I have a sense that I've said enough, but perhaps there is one that thing I would wish to go back to which has to do with this business of the creolisation of Britain. Are we faced with this possibility that there would be two movements. This is what I struggle with in my work. There would be the movement to protect the cultural entity where we would find commonalities and similarities, but there will also be a tendency to accept that creolisation and being part of a structure is legitimate. And if we have those two tendencies, how do we begin to respect each other if we are not part of one and we're part of the other? You can see that it could be so evident in the theatre, coming back to the theatre. You could say it's a black play but you say that it's a creolised black play. And the other person say, 'Boy, me don't want that, me waan the real t'ing.' You could say you'll have a restaurant and you say, 'Boy, you'd better make it so that people from Italy will want some of it, creolise the thing properly.' Him say, 'No, man, the brothers them want them rice and peas and run down.' You could go on like that and I think that is how the society is indeed taking itself forward at the moment.

So I think there is a sense of, even within psychiatry, having to acknowledge that there are two tendencies in front of us, but alongside those two tendencies, and this is what I find most difficult, is what a patient said to me. She said to me, 'I feel confused. I feel angry. I feel depressed and I feel it's impossible to go on.' And I think there's a sizeable population of our people who feel like that. And so, that's where I come in. I think I have a role with that group. But I think I have a role with the other two as well, you know, and it is balancing which of the three groups I will most be involved in.

I wish, you know, that I could get my little radio from the time I went back home, that was playing ska and rock steady, and just listen out, and continue to listen out, because the themes that were evident then were real themes. And I think we need to continue listening to the themes of the Carnival, to themes of calypso, to the themes of our artists much, much more to get a direction. I'll stop there.

DISCUSSION
John La Rose: There was one person's name you did not get. And I want to give it to you. His name was Aggrey's father, the Reverend Eddie Burke. And I remember a writer who's become quite famous, Erna Brodber, saying to me, 'You know we grew up on Eddie Burke's stories told to us on the radio.' And Aggrey once showed me the book of those stories which explained some of the background that he did not quite explain. The Reverend Eddie Burke who came with Norman Manley to form Jamaica Welfare, the first of the kind in the Caribbean at that stage. And then who at the same time came to London after the riots when the three people who came here in 1958 were Carl La Corbinière, the Minister of Finance at the Federation, Norman Manley and I think there was a third whose name I don't remember, who helped to form the West Indian Standing Conference, which became the leading organisation to deal with problems of West Indians after the Notting Hill riots. And the Reverend Eddie Burke and Aggrey came after that, as he says, in 1959. And that is just a part of the history he did not mention. The philosophical ideas that came out of that experience, both in Jamaica and the Jamaica public school, because

we don't have public schools in the rest of the Caribbean, like you have in Jamaica. J.C. was an English public school in the English sense. K.C., Kingston College was an English public school in the English sense of a public school. So J.C. and K.C. were leading public schools in Jamaica and that Jamican elite which Aggrey entered into at Jamaica College who knew nothing about the folklore, that is because of the Jamaican public school system which existed at the time. What we have are elite secondary schools in the rest of the Caribbean, but they are not public schools. Jamaica had public schools.

Gus John: That obeah business interests me a lot. And what I think is interesting about it is this. We as a people, and that's true of all the islands, not just Jamaica. I grew up – I mean my father was a bush doctor and the shango queen was my godmother and we lived with the Roman Catholic business and that African religion stuff throughout our childhood and adolescent years. What I find interesting is that because of the European religions, Roman Catholicism principally but then the rest as well, we have been encouraged to, if you like put the fear into obeah. And many people even now have some vague notion of where it came from etcetera, what its actual essence is. But the predominant thing is the fear. This is what people could do to you. This is what happened to this person down the road and so on and so forth. But what is not known is the actual origins of the thing and that those origins were and are positive and were part and parcel of the whole cycle of people's lives and our communication with the earth and those forces and so on.

So my question really is this. Insofar as it continues to have a role, sometimes linked to organised religion, as in the Spiritual Baptist faith for the Orisha tradition at home, sometimes because of the survival of traditional medicines, how does one relate to those people who continue to see it as having a function in their lives but, at the same time, because of all the negatives that are associated with it, they don't want to be associated with it either? But for many of them they know that it has a powerful effect within their lives.

Aggrey Burke

And when push come to shove they don't bother with all of this anopathic medicine business they go and see the man [audience laughter]. Including the politicians. I mean a number of politicians in Jamaica and Trinidad who go by night in the wee hours. I meet them all the time in Trinidad. So my question is, how do we begin to legitimise that and assist particularly our children right now in understanding and valuing it so that it's not seen as some kind of devilry and the rest of it, but as being as important to us as all of those other African retentions that they want to celebrate and they consider to be legitimate?

Aggrey Burke: I must declare my hand. I haven't been to an obeah man for any treatment [audience laughter]. I think it's quite important, that, because I have been struck by the history that I gave of being in Jericho and hearing nine nights' singing going on and 40 nights. And when I lived in Trinidad, I had a friend, Compton, and his grandfather I think it was who died and he couldn't come, and he phoned me and he said, 'Boy, you go down there and lend them some money.' I became a grandson, foster, or substitute or something. And all of this grief business, this thing about death, seemed to have a lot of food, a lot of drink, a lot of chanting, a lot of singing, a lot of life. And what struck me about the funerals in New Cross was how much of the process of mourning had gone from most of the families very very rapidly. In fact, I was quite surprised that even my little recollections from the village settings where I grew up – it seemed that people had moved away from them fairly rapidly. And I was surprised.

In my work, I meet quite a number of refugees and from certain parts they bring a child quite often. And then they have a dread about the child flying back to Africa and all kinds of things because they haven't really made a proper parting and now they can't go back. Some very prominent African people are here as refugees and many of them have no real future because they have had no parting, no closing on a grim reality. There is a group of people I have seen who go to obeah men. And what I find with them is that there is a tremendous amount of shame about the fact that they are doing it.

185

Usually, you know, people have affairs, you know, affairs between men and women and that kind of thing. And about things which they can't make sense of, and I think that there is a problem, Gus, which has to do with making sense of things and I want to diverge a little bit on that.

The single woman and her son and how in the mythology of the African past – I don't have any clear idea of the things that were prohibited or allowed – I know a lot of the stuff from Jamaica comes from Ghana but in the Caribbean a lot of people came from the Central African Congo as well. But when you read Greek mythology you see all kinds of things that are happening to people – you know, boy is taken away, kills father and takes mother, you know, the Oedipus thing – and girl does this and there are lots of issues about incest in the mythology and we have real problems – and did have real problems coming to terms with the fact that there's really quite as much abuse in one setting, whether island or continent, as another. Everybody doing it. But I think it is not what one is doing which is critical, it's how one responds to it and responds to the cupboard getting opened.

Then we have so many of our people thinking social workers were good, you know – and go, stupid, stupid, telling them a whole heap of things and of course, once you do that, your systems break down. The Asians have been very much more together in not breaking down systems, the Chinese and the Indians and so on. But the middle classes, you know, they have these big houses but when they lock up you see, nobody goes in there boy, everything is secret. And so I think that this business of over-spilling too easily and actually not understanding one's own reality, going back to the single mother.

I don't have a number against single mothers but I think it's an important issue. The single mother with a son. And one has a sense of so many of the youngsters' sons who get into scrapes with the law have no structures within their own framework. If they had an uncle, or a big dis or a dis or a dat, it wouldn't be too bad. But just the one deggeh-deggeh adult with no sense of – when I go in there, they not taking me on, you know. And I worry about this, because

I worry about the closeness that sometimes develops and how one can offload. Any mother, single, married or whatever sometimes wants the girl or the boy to go up and stay with a grandmother once in a while. Of course we have no structures. And what I think is developing is a situation where we do have an isolated community without networks. I work with this all the time. Sister Monica is working with it all the time. You work with it in schooling, you know you are responsible for that. I think that eventually we start to accept certain things that are not normal, even for us, as normal. And I think that's a danger. So I think two things are necessary. One is to separate abnormality or unusual activity from normal activity, and the other one is what you are asking. And if what you are asking has to be understood properly one has to apply it both to the abnormal and to the normal. Well, the rough and ready, struggling within very poor conditions here in Britain.

I didn't say it but it is my impression that it is the most grim reality in the black diaspora – that we have a large amount of poverty here and poverty in modern-day Britain is a very, very grim business. It's on bad estates with bad education, bad housing, sometimes bad services generally and people having to make the best out of a pretty sloppy existence. Drug use is very high and all kinds of things. I think, for that group, holding onto a belief system is a very difficult task. I think that the mothers in those situations, and fathers, are finding it difficult to even believe in the gods that are round the corner. They really do find it difficult believing in anything. They don't know who to turn to, they're in real problems. And yet they come from families that, surprisingly, have given up on them more often than we realise. And that's a worry that we are caught in that. But then if you move away from that group to the other two groups, the groups that I say are creolised now, trying to make their life within multi-racial Britain if you want to call it that and those who are getting into their frameworks – I think that you're right – that we must try to find ways to address both groups. I think we shouldn't give up on one or other group because I think both pathways are legitimate as I see it. But this is where we then have problems.

The religious elements are struggling and the belief systems of obeah, and the superstitious systems don't fit easily with some of the Pentecostal and Baptists, you know. They don't fit easily. I don't think they do, you may feel they do. They fit easier with the Pope, you know, and the Church of England, they easier with that (laughter), because those guys who come down, let's not call them 'guys' – they are bishops and others. They are saying that you have to follow a certain pathway and that you have to firm up your belief system towards them. Many of them make it into a personalised thing and sometimes I say, 'Well, this thing look good, but it shaky as well.' So I think that we are going through a very great struggle because people are being asked to look at traditional superstitious systems alongside powerful Pentecostal and Baptist systems, they're very powerful. And then we have what we call the 'backsliders' who are saying, perhaps we should give up on the whole thing.

The final thing, Gus, my experience of the extent to which it can work, suggests to me that the obeah men who are here are doing a good job (laughter), it looks so to me. The East End has a few of them. I don't have their names and addresses, but I hear they are doing a good job. And in one other setting I know of a number of people who have had some real crises like their children killing themselves and things like that, they can't get sustenance here and they have gone home in secret missions to see obeah men. I see that quite a bit.

Linton Kwesi Johnson: In the early 1970s did you come across any evidence of the forced deportation of mentally ill immigrants?

Aggrey Burke: Yes, indeed. I went home and I have done some very crazy things, but one of the things that I did – I was very worried that my colleagues were saying that going back to a nice orange grove and cane piece was the solution to mental problems. And I got the Jamaican High Commission to help and I went home and followed up about 70 people. And it was a very, very sad thing that people were being forcibly repatriated because of mental problems or being in prison and, as you know, Linton, we are faced, and I am faced not infrequently with problems of people being here illegally, who have carried out serious crimes and other misdemeanours. And the state in that period of the early 1970s was repatriating quite a lot of our people because of mental problems and in fact, the outburst that we are the maddest people in the world, and we have more schizophrenia than everybody else, didn't happen then because people were being sent back. The outcome of that group who went back because of mental reasons was pretty grim. Many of them lived in the bush. Nobody wanted to touch them because already, when you go home, I don't know if you've been home recently, Linton, they say you're mad, I think they might exclude you (laughter). And so when you have a definite diagnosis of being mad and you go back and they see that you're mad it is bad business. So there were high suicide rates. A lot of people wouldn't live in their villages and they were rejected by the population.

Alex Pascall: You haven't spoken at all about yourself as a pioneering person and obviously the challenges I'm sure you have and continue to meet, because of the visibility of who you are in a very difficult community as we have here in Britain. Everywhere someone has a problem and in particular the black people they would say, 'Have you seen, could you get hold of Dr. Burke?' Tell us a little bit about that, because sometimes nobody would know the pains you may go through and the challenges you meet and how it could be misinterpreted in so many ways. While you are trying to do good and to meet the needs of everyone you may be doing yourself in.

Aggrey Burke: Yes, I go walking you know sometimes and I try to reflect on exactly the question, Alex, that you asked. But we've had a tough period and I'm very much aware, Alex, that when you addressed this gathering you looked at it a bit. We had a period in the early 1980s and the latter 1970s when we believed we were moving forward on many fronts. Ken Livingstone might have been part of that but I think it might have been other factors as well and you remember that Paul Boateng and others were warriors within the Livingstone movement – they are now incorporated in other movements (laughter and applause). I'm not saying that one is better than the other (laughter), you know history moves on, Alex, you know that. I can only tell you that during the New Cross period as we know, Alex, the radio stations, the black radio stations and the black media – it's difficult to give them marching orders in the same way, like the national radio stations or the national newspapers. I mean there is something about disloyalty during periods of a country at war. And the question really is who is employing us and which country are we part of? And so this split loyalty is a major problem.

In my own workplace New Cross created a bridge which really did mean that I could lose everything by going on that bridge. But I was aware of going on the bridge and how fragile that bridge could be and how it could be destroyed. Nowadays you have cruise missiles going for bridges. I think I'm still on the bridge. I don't have a sense that one has another land to land on in that simple way. And I think it's the same for all of us. We are on one bit of land only and that when we go on a bridge joining that bit of land with another group, a group that we define by virtue of its experience of our experience, then we can be gunned down, that is the simple fact. And so, whilst one is on the bridge one can reach out and try to make sense of the realities of the experiences that one would have and that the people are having.

During the last 12 or so years I had to diversify very, very sharply. Perhaps it's a little longer, I considered it carefully. I had other issues to deal with – my relationship with the Caribbean – at about that time I went to India and Pakistan to see what was going on there. I had the possibility and went and that was a very rich experience. The South African struggle was very, very important to me. I worked closely, in my quiet way, I like being quiet, on a number of issues linking the miners' strike, the struggles here in Britain and the South African struggle. They seemed to me to make sense and to fit together.

So you could say I have a political view. And perhaps others believe that I do. I don't know. Some will say I don't or some will say it's weak, some would say it's strong. But during the last 15 years or so I've had to address the point you are asking about, Alex, in a very real sense. And I've been seeing a great number of people and making sense of what I would consider to be my life, in certain situations. For example, going back to the O.J. thing, Alex, and I know you are very close to the thing. Not O.J. But you were O.J. once, weren't you, by being on the radio, you had the possibility of being O.J. But O.J. made the link, you see, by being with a white partner, that was the crucial thing, and by being a famous star and the society of America, and here in Britain too, has had to deal with many people, men who have been through that experience. Now it's women but I don't know the equivalent of O.J. for women. And what I've seen, Alex, is that when a black man is in a certain situation, he is really mocked and the papers and the media and everything goes to town on it and the theatre goes wild.

Certainly one sees a sense of injustice, I guess injustice is the best term, not oppression, I think there is oppression, but I think injustice is what one sees within the criminal justice system much more and within other areas of law a lot. And I think it is this business of the extent to which the state believes that we have joined up or not which is the crucial factor influencing, for example, the way the police deal with us. I have to work, as you know, very closely with the police because psychiatry is part of control. And so I would be the last person to be critical of the police unless the situation seemed such an over-statement of fact if I didn't join up with the people. But certainly one sees the police are responding all the time to society's wish to continue to see us as monsters and as people who can be stereotyped as bad, violent, mad and all the other things that go with it. But why I say O.J., Alex, is that O.J. was also a star, and continues to be a star, stars don't die, you know. And so society continues to see that the best newsreaders should be black. It still does. It still believes that the best – you know, not just Lara, you know, it believes these things. It seems to have us in these two frames.

Aggrey Burke

Roxy Harris: Could you tell something about your campaign about the doctors, would-be doctors who are discriminated against, what happened and how you got involved in it in Britain? You know the young doctors who are black or Asian who are discriminated against trying to get into medical school?

Aggrey Burke: Yes. I got involved, and I hadn't mentioned it, in a number of political initiatives in medicine, both in the Caribbean and here.

The thing in the Caribbean I'll start with first and in Africa too. We believed that a kind of socialism in the Caribbean public sector was important. We believed that. But it now looks as though there is a common acceptance, a wide acceptance that the American way of life is here to stay, certainly in our lifetime. And that struggles of the kind which were attempted during the early periods of independence will be snuffed out if they take root. It looks so. Which then means that we will continue to have large sections of the populations of black peoples, wherever we are, poor. That will be one consequence of accepting the American way of life.

But here in Britain, when I was a student at Birmingham University, my parents had gone to work with the United Nations in Africa and they worked in Ethiopia where I went to see them, and in Zambia and in West Africa. I went down to Ethiopia, but as it turned out Birmingham University had a strong link and I could do an elective period in Ethiopia. Birmingham also had a strong link, and in fact set up a university, in Zimbabwe, Southern Rhodesia but in fact, no black could go there and I had a real crisis in Birmingham University because of that. I mounted a campaign around that, because here you had a crazy situation – I was a student of a university running a college in southern Africa and there was no way blacks could be involved. But in Ethiopia we could, and when I came back I did an elective at a place called Sutton Coldfield with one of the Ethiopia mob, so to speak. And we had these African, mainly Nigerian, registrars, and Asian registrars, trainees. I was a little student. But because I was a prince from the Birmingham set up I was treated as a prince. I could walk on carpets of any kind and do anything, you know. I said, 'No, this can't go on.' I had a difficulty because when the day finished these African guys were cooking up some good food and I found that I was enjoying the food. But I went back to the University after the elective period and said to them, 'This can't go on. You're treating doctors in training as nobodys. They're telling me this. I'm going to represent their interests. It can't go on.' And they branded me as someone political.

Later on, at my own school in St George's Hospital here in London, we discovered that there was a computer set to discriminate against people who had foreign names and women. And it was set in such a way that the admission of those individuals would be reduced. One can understand it to some extent. We're in a male chauvinist society and though the professions are now taking women, women certainly don't become the judges. They still don't and they won't for a while. And the same was happening in medicine to some extent. But it was the threat of Asian takeover and Asians now make up something like 25 per cent of all medical students in Britain. Clearly, you know, not only in general practice but in all areas of medicine, come back in 30 years, it will be a different ball game. Within our group, the African group, there have been real problems and the problems are compounded, not only because of South Africa and Nigeria, but because within Britain there is no common acceptance of the need and right we should have to see people who we feel comfortable with. The argument is extremely complex and recently we had a meeting of the African Caribbean doctors group to say, 'Why black doctors?' And I had the sense that even my colleagues were ambivalent on this issue as to how to mount a campaign to have more black doctors here in Britain. I tend to want to see it in a political way but I don't think I have, or I am likely to have, the support of large sectors of the small group of black doctors here now. I don't think I will.

Nadia Cattouse: What about the children and the influence of the peer group? But that's not the most important thing so I'll set that aside for the moment. But will there ever be steady progress so long as we remain as what we are, a fractured community, I'm talking now nationally across the country? I did not come to feel a Caribbean person until I came to England as a student. None of the islands or other places were independent and so we were altogether Commonwealth to begin with and then Caribbean again. Because we were under the aegis of one body, the British Council, and we shared so much at that time. Now Bishop Wood brought out the expression, 'Double ethnicity.' And I thought it would be much easier because for so many generations we have been British and Caribbean. It would be so simple to just be Caribbean British and that would involve people up and down the country, whether we come from one island nation or another island nation. It has a ring about it. It has a ring of identity, culture, everything about it. And this has struck me from time to time that we are so splintered. We have tight communities here and there but we are splintered as far as the nation is concerned.

Aggrey Burke: Thanks Nadia. I think you know, we shouldn't despair. That's the first thing I'd say. But you see – when we came here, I think Stuart Hall is right – he said it the other day, there was some assimilation thing going on. But it was only the middle classes who wanted that, you know, because of our experiences in work and so forth. I think our people really had strong networks wherever they were. I think they had strong networks. But within one generation, or half a generation, because we have a lot of split off generations. Remember the migration was really 1955 to 1962. And then the children came from 1962 until whatever. So you have a lot of people who were born here in that first period and a lot who came at the same time. And so the ones who came were brought up half and half you see. So we're looking at split off half time generations going on. It seems to me that we shouldn't despair for these reasons, we've had a lot of people who have gone back. We now have a lot of people who are coming in the last 15 years, mainly from Africa and refugees. People have gone to the States and to Canada. If you go to Toronto, you find that most of the Torontonians, or many of them, were here. It was a staging post we used here, like the Irish who used Liverpool. And it seems to me that, though the situation is very very grim here in many ways, there is a group making headway and so we have to see what are the possibilities that that group making headway will continue to grow and will continue to make headway. I think we have to look at that possibility.

Irish female member of the audience: It would be easier for me to bring up white Irish children here if there was that reconciliation, that peace within my soul, but there is not because I am here in Britain and still the North of Ireland is colonised and we're still with mental slavery, we're still sort of entrenched. We haven't loosened the shackles, we haven't broken the shackles, and we need to start loving ourselves which is very important.

Aggrey Burke: I think you're right but the issues as I see it, and this is a basis for a real debate, have to do with the institutions which we have and the likelihood that these can survive or will be demolished. For example, the link you're talking about of Ireland and the Caribbean – but in Ireland and in Britain this river comes down and the Burkes somehow don't seem to hold together if one is black. You see and I think that the Irish have also had to contend with the issue of being in Britain like we have, but it seems to me that we shouldn't despair because there is the real possibility of something coming out of the experience we have had in Britain. I went to Antigonish, Nova Scotia, some years ago when my father was given a degree. And I was surprised that there were so few, there were no black achievers remaining in Antigonish, and I think there's a risk that this could happen here, but the risk will be offset, I feel, in time by virtue of the continued movements of people from the African continent itself and from the Caribbean. We'll be moving up and down. That's my sense of it. I think this question of identity is complex.

Burt Caesar: I just wanted to ask Dr Burke about this notion of the village as a model of a supportive community. In the first instance, even in the West Indies the village is breaking down, in the sense it's getting older in terms of population. It's a shock to me to realise in the West Indies there are old people's homes. And you have these children who live in special homes. Even in the Caribbean the village can't support people. But I agree that its values need to be sustained and transferred to this urban setting. So the question is two-part. How do we set up the possibility, the rivers to use your image, of communication between the village and the urban setting? But also, most important, how do we avoid the kind of claustrophobic conformity that villages are about? A lot of people came to this country in the 1950s, they weren't just economic migrants, a lot of them were escaping claustrophobia and small villages which were oppressive. You know, they thought coming to England would be a kind of existential freedom. How do we sustain the benefits, but also how do we avoid the conservative and repressive elements of village life, living in London?

Aggrey Burke: I think your question brings one back to the attempt at an analysis of the lumpen group, the group struggling on benefits unemployed, many of our people will never be employed, and whether that lumpen group is simply caught in the trap of the state or can start to see its possibilities outside of that, that's the first thing. But this religious group, or the group that have managed by some hook or crook to keep some of the traditions going, are they using village networks? I go to Birmingham, for example, a place called Greatbridge which is near Dudley, and when I go there to see this old lady who is my friend and my friend's mother, sometimes I have to go down to the Pentecostal Church with her. And there's a great sense of fellowship remaining in those small areas like Rugby, you know, still quite a lot. And I have a sense that in certain areas of London it still exists. So I'm just wondering whether this ideal, and I think it is idyllic, of a village is being maintained by having the same kind of basic structures – I think a church might be one part of it, but the difficulty is that these churches don't mix up too much, you know. And so they become church communities rather than village communities. And we don't have much tolerance

– Nadia's point about being splintered. The churches don't have a lot of tolerance for each other here. Whereas in the village I grew up, everybody got a bit of the cow. I can't believe that people didn't come and get a piece of the pig. But then plenty people when I went back who said, 'We're doing pork.' So I wonder whether there is something about 'shared experience' – the hurricane is a very powerful bringing together experience, drought is a very powerful bringing together experience. In the village, a disaster brings us together immediately. If I want to give away £100, something happen in my village, I go back and give it away one time. Because people need the money right there and then you know, a disaster. So, do we have anything that brings us together? And I say I think we do here in Britain, and the difficulty is will the Blair state, Mr Blair and his ministers, allow these networks to develop. I think at the moment they are reluctant.

Dr Aggrey Burke is a leading psychiatrist and a pioneer in his field both in Britain and the Caribbean. He has been particularly involved in the field of transcultural psychiatry and in issues of access to mental health and other services for people from the ethnic minorities.

Aggrey Burke was born in 1943 in Jamaica in a period of profound social change in the Caribbean. His father, the Revd Eddie Burke, worked very closely with Norman Manley and was a leading member of the Jamaica Welfare Association which was involved in the movement for community development, particularly in the rural areas of Jamaica. Aggrey's mother ran the family farm, while he and his brothers and sister went to local government schools where they were exposed to the rural structures and mixed with the villagers though their family position was that of employer.

The family moved to Kingston in the early 1950s and in 1954 Aggrey won the first ever Marcus Garvey Scholarship. This was for the best student in the whole island, and on the strength of that he went to Jamaica College, one of Jamaica's leading private schools.

When the Notting Hill Riots took place in 1958, the Revd Eddie Burke was appointed by the Caribbean High Commissioners to work on improving relations between the black and white communities in the UK. The whole family moved to Britain in 1959 and Aggrey finished his schooling here. He continued to be a successful student and became head of house in his predominantly white school. There was also one Asian student.

In 1962 he went to Birmingham University to study medicine. There he became engulfed in the struggles of the migrant population in Britain and with initiatives to bring together the students of the university and the migrants. He was active in the West Indian Students Club which formed a folk song group and steelband. He was also President of the prestigious Athletics Club, being a very good sprinter By this time Aggrey's parents had gone to work for the United Nations and were based in Ethiopia. Aggrey joined them for three months in 1965 and elected to do three months of his practical medical training there at Addis Ababa General Hospital.

Aggrey Burke qualified as a doctor in 1968 and, deciding that he wanted to practise in either Africa or the Caribbean, returned to Jamaica to work doing general hospital medicine This was the year that Walter Rodney was banned from returning to Jamaica after attending a conference in Canada and Aggrey was active in the political and intellectual ferment that arose from that banning, in particular he became involved with the *Abeng* and *New World* groups.

In 1969 he went to Trinidad and began to study psychiatry which was the area of medicine he had been interested in since being a student. In Trinidad he began his early training in psychotherapy and started to research the kinds of mental illness occurring in Trinidad and in particular studied suicide among people of Indian and African descent. Again this was a period of radical Caribbean politics. The black power uprising of 1970 in Trinidad was the most important event of that period and Aggrey became drawn into the intellectual and political activities which arose at that time. He returned to Jamaica later that year and worked mainly in approved schools introducing psychiatry to sections of society that otherwise would not have had access to it. He also continued his research.

Aggrey Burke returned to Birmingham in 1972 to continue his studies. He qualified in 1973, having become a member of the Royal College of Psychiatrists the previous year, and moved to London in 1976 as a consultant psychiatrist and senior lecturer at St George's Medical School.

On his return to Britain in the 1970s Aggrey became re-exposed to the reality of disadvantage of the black migrant population and, within that context, the difficulties of ethnic minority and black doctors. He carried out research on many related areas including the returning and repatriated migrants, the difficulties of people living here, suicide, facilities available to treat patients from ethnic minority backgrounds and issues of access.

He wrote many important research papers on these issues which were published in the *British Journal of Psychiatry* and other professional journals. His work on the distribution of psychiatric illnesses in Trinidad and Tobago and Jamaica and his comparative work on suicidal behaviours among the African and Indian populations in Trinidad and Tobago represents an important milestone in the development of psychiatry among these populations. Subsequently this work was continued in Birmingham with comparisons of suicidal behaviour among migrant populations and related groups in India and the Caribbean. Since then he has completed the first study on suicide in the Caribbean. A further interest has been the fate of psychiatric patients repatriated to the Caribbean, where it has been believed that this procedure would be beneficial, but his research has shown that a good outcome is unusual for these patients.

Aggrey Burke has been clinically involved in increasing access to services for persons who have suffered trauma or death by virtue of work practice or attack, access for persons involved in the criminal justice system, difficulties of immigration, mules of drugs, mental health review tribunals and a large group of persons at risk of losing their children. He has been an expert witness in a number of important court cases and has also given evidence at several independent inquiries.

He later became involved in the Transcultural Psychiatric Society and in 1979 was elected chair of that group. In 1981 he helped to set up the support group for families who had suffered bereavement and injury through the New Cross fire. This group provided much needed counselling and support and was the first of its kind in the UK. In 1984 he edited the 30th anniversary double issue of the *International Journal of Social Psychiatry* which was dedicated to the theme of 'Racism & Mental Illness'. During the 1980s he worked with various organisations including the Westminster Pastoral Foundation, a professional body of psychotherapists, the British Agency of Adoption and Fostering, the Family Rights Group, the Inter-Country Adoption Agency, MIND, the Church of England Board of Social Responsibility, and psychodrama groups.

At the end of the Greater London Council (GLC) period and with GLC funding he co-founded the Ethnic Study Group. This group was aimed at identifying gaps in services to ethnic minority groups and in improving access for people in these groups. A particular interest of the Group has been to help the education of social workers and other professionals working in mental health and childcare. The group also set up an ethnic switchboard and established a code of practice for interpreters. Aggrey Burke is currently President of the African and Caribbean Medical Society and is particularly concerned in helping black students interested in a career in medicine and in educating the wider population on health care issues.

Aggrey Burke has always been concerned and involved in wider issues apart from health involving the migrant population in Britain. He gave the key address at 'Salkey's Score' the tribute to Andrew Salkey, the Jamaican writer, essayist and broadcaster, held at the Commonwealth Institute in 1992. He gave the seventh Martin Luther King Memorial Lecture in 1994 entitled 'In Search of Freedom'. He has provided practical support to the Talawa Theatre Company and is a trustee of the George Padmore Institute.

Yvonne Brewster

Yvonne Brewster
introduced by Aggrey Burke (17.05.1999)

Yvonne Brewster: I tell you, I was really scared coming here today so what I did was to write my talk down, because I thought my whole life has been a ramble and if I got on to all the tangents we'd be here till midnight. Well I might be, everybody else would be gone. So I've done a few pages which I typed out. So here goes. I will read it because I'm trying to stay focused and I'm trying to do what John asked me to do, which was to deal with the early years, and then use them as a kind of a backdrop for what really happened here. Because the early days is 'Life Experience *With* Britain' not '*In* Britain'.

The title of this series has always had a strange fascination for me. Over the years I've learned to listen well to the subtle nuance in everything which has the John La Rose touch. So not 'Life Experience *In* Britain' but '*With* Britain'. The devil I decided would be in the detail of how one perceived oneself – British, Black British, West Indian, Jamaican. I decided to apply the Norman Tebbit test to my own sensibility. The outcome was still a bit ambivalent as I definitely cheer for the West Indies but I'm happiest when there are at least some Jamaicans on the team.

I have had a varied and multi-faceted life in England but I will try and concentrate on the bits which have to do with theatre direction, as this has been my major interest and where inroads, if any, have been made. This is not to say that I have not really enjoyed the radio, the television, the film, the mental health work, the advocacy and even my feeble but numerous attempts at acting. Alistair, do not laugh. So it's 'Life Experience With Britain' as a black theatre director, calling upon the Jamaican upbringing which formulated and acted as a focus to my time here.

My earliest memory of things British was being made to plant a tree at the end of the war to mark the safe return of my uncle, who had been flying with the Royal Air Force, and we sang 'God Save The King'. There was a fight among the siblings because I got to plant the banana tree, and so we then all had to plant a mango tree, and so it went on.

The real influences in my early life were my four grandparents – all migrants to Jamaica from different cultural backgrounds, but all robustly Jamaican eventually. It might be interesting just to spend a few minutes on them. The first pair, Polish Jew married to Indian. He, the Polish Jew, was the wealthy black sheep of an émigré family to America who had stumbled upon Jamaica in a spell of youthful, I think they call it beach-combing. She was the child of indentured Indian labourers. An unlikely combination, these two. He loved Ella Fitzgerald, Chopin and Dickens. She loved shiny baubles and status, not in that order. My mother was the child of this Jewish Indian combination.

The second pair – African married to Scot. He, the African, was somehow mysteriously connected to a runaway slave in Cuba. It sounded very dramatic – I don't know if it's true – the grandson possibly. What we did know was that he used to make shoes of kid leather for Batista. But more important for his grandchildren was that he made the workings of a merry-go-round with six horses which he carved himself. She was the child of a Scots planter family, Cook Hylton, and Jamaicans will know that's very posh from the west coast of the island and they now claim some relationship to Captain Cook. Though we don't know if that's true either. But we had to live with all these people claiming all these wonderful relationships. That couple had to run away and hide in the cane fields in the face of fierce opposition, barely escaping the dogs and the deliberately set fires in the cane field, which were intended to flush them out – burn him if possible and re-capture her. My father was the child of this African-Scot combination and if you're feeling sorry for me, I accept it.

In both families mystery abounded. No one was allowed to delve too deeply into the detail of their individual lives and histories. What I can say is that Christmas dinners were a veritable international gourmet feast as each culture tried to outdo the other. Curry, haggis, fu fu and herrings – indigestion. For the purpose of this reminiscence I'm going to concentrate on my maternal grandfather's taste in the arts and on my father's social conditioning. These were the most enduring influences on my life and on my life experience in Britain, with Britain. Sorry John.

Old man Sam, that's my mother's Jewish father, was a rich, handsome blonde. He had flair, owned race horses and was loved by a great number of women. He was the sort of man who, when Jamaicans found his Polish name, Lejinski, too foreign to pronounce, had it changed by deed poll to Samuel Abraham Isaac – three forefathers of the Jewish faith, just in case anyone thought he was hiding his Jewishness. His was the lesson that I have learned latterly of cultural specificity. He was a born businessman who cast aside the wig and gown for the undertaker's parlour and the crematorium, when he spotted a gap in the Jamaican market. 'These people will pay to bury their dead in style,' he said. So he bought up some cheap land downtown and set up shop. Sam Isaacs and Sons Undertakers is a pretty well known name in Jamaica. My mother runs it now. He built a fortress type house in the hills above Kingston, which was pretty spectacular. But for him the best thing about it was the cellar-study that he dug out of the rock. Under the house, away from the disapproving glances of his wife, he could read Dickens, recite Shakespeare and listen to Ella Fitzgerald and what I then called, 'No other love have I'.

I was his favourite grandchild and plenty jealousy. Probably it was because I adored his flamboyance and as such was allowed into the underground hideaway. There he told me about *King Lear*, *Macbeth*, *Othello*. He would recite the purple passages with such understanding and the incredible voice control that he had, that I was totally transported. When later in Britain I learned that the norm for Shakespeare was to be spoken with a plummy English accent and that my wonderful grandfather's interpretation would have been considered amusing and ethnic, I determined to prove this wrong and myopic. As far as Ella Fitzgerald was concerned, my grandfather taught me how to listen to the artistry of her scatting. He gave me set passages to learn and then to perform. It was on one such occasion when the door burst open and my irate grandmother took up the record player, threw it across the room with the words, 'A big white man like you teaching Yvonne all that black woman singing. You should know better!' And that was when the rebel was born.

My father, his idea of what was right and proper, his family was more simple. He and two brothers were all scholarship boys with burning ambition and careful habits. No gramophones flying across the room but, rather, quiet storytelling by candlelight. He grew up to love England and everything English. I grew up hearing non-stop praise for the excellent jurisprudence which the British colonial system had left us, the two-house system of government, the tradition of impartiality and fair play, the dress code and so on. He would almost stand to attention when it was time for the world news from the BBC twice a day. He drove Jaguars. He ordered his shoes from Churches. He sent his children to study in England. Where else?

In preparation for this we were sent to St Hilda's Diocesan High School for Girls, Brown's Town, St Ann, situated in the middle of the country set way up high on a hill. The city, you must understand, that is set on a hill cannot be hidden. Us St Hilda's girls were expected to set shining examples to all. The exemplars were the staff, all were female, mostly from Yorkshire, but all reigned over us with a fury and a missionary zeal that can only be imagined. I remember my reaction when I realised that the only West Indian member of the staff, one of the music teachers, was only allowed to sit on the platform with the other teachers if she was hidden by the piano. Our school motto was 'Res Servera Verum Gaudium Est' – 'True Endeavour Has its Just Reward'. This was sung in Latin as a climax to our school hymn on important special occasions. Well, in secret now, I trained the fourth form to sing the line in English to a blue beat rhythm. Thus 'Res Servera Verum Gaudium' (singing) became 'And a hard, hard ting is a true true true true joy'. Now, disaster, expulsion! My father was sent for. My sister asked to be taken away from this school as I was too great an embarassment to bear. She's younger than me. I escaped expulsion, however, as my father thought and told the headmistress that it showed an imaginative twist and it was an exercise which would help me in my Latin viva. In fact, and I couldn't write this down in case John read it, but the thing is that he actually said, 'What did she say?'

And she said, 'I couldn't possibly say.'

'What did she say?'

'Oh, I couldn't possibly say.'

Eventually he got it out of her.

'Well, she translated our school motto into "a hard thing is a true joy".'

And he said, 'And you don't find this to be the case?'

He got in his car and drove down leaving me packed on the quad with my suitcase.

All right, it was late in September 1956, because ladies and gentlemen I am quite ancient, when the SS Queen Mary pulled into Southampton with me on board. I'd been watched over for the entire voyage from New York by a chaperone specially engaged for the purpose. On arrival at Waterloo we were met by my father's Masonic colleague, a large red-faced man. And I'm saying all this because it's a contrast to what happened later. He met us in a Rolls Royce and his name was Benson Greenhall. He lived in Upper Brook Street. He took us to the Cumberland Hotel and then finally me down to Sidcup to Rose Bruford Training College of Speech and Drama. Everything changed. I watched this really comfortable car speed away from the suburbs, you know Sidcup. And there I was at 17 on my own in Sidcup. The first conversation I had with Miss Bruford, who unfortunately is still alive, went something like this, 'So you are the girl from Jamaica? Well, your father is paying for you, isn't he? We will take the money but I must warn you, you will never work. You may go.'

Well now the gramophone flying across the road, the jurisprudence, the sense of fair play, the 'hath not a Jew eyes and doth he not bleed', the blasted heath and all of these things dancing in front of my eyes and demanding of me that I would work. But not only that I would work but that I would be the first in my year to get the coveted Equity card. By the way I was the first full-time female black drama student in England, okay? History does suggest that I did work a little. Indeed I was the first person to get my

Equity card, because I stole out, and that was as the genie of the ring in the pantomime *Aladdin* in Colchester Repertory Theatre. And just for the record I am now patron of Rose Bruford College. Okay, 43 years with Britain, 43 years as a Jamaican in Britain.

But back to college days. There were other challenges which complemented Miss Bruford's kind words. For instance, problems with Africans. Imagine my delight when Janet Bajan from Ghana turned up. Another black woman, and I did not say coloured, to join me in my isolation. I can't tell you. But that delight was very shortlived. She objected to me and told me in no uncertain terms that all West Indians were mongrels and she dealt only with thoroughbreds, and would I please refrain from engaging her in conversation. Then there were the people on the buses or on the trains, who either wouldn't sit beside you or deliberately sat beside you to find out if the colour would rub off. You know that thing? (laughter). Right.

As I approached my final year in college it became clear that there was every likelihood they would fail me. This was because of my attitude, I admit. You know with hindsight it must have been a bit much to put up with, because I was fighting from the word go. How can you learn? For instance, I refused to use received pronunciation. In fact I still do, for my verse speaking. It seemed to me that poetry was a personal thing and to use someone else's accent was to render the exercise a sham. I was good at phonetics and I could do any accent required of me and was quite willing to demonstrate this from Blackpudlian and all down, but not with poetry. They even got the then poet laureate, John Masefield, brought him to talk to me. I think the word was remonstrate, no good! But he had an accent you see. So I said, 'Well that's an accent. I don't understand what you are saying.'

'I don't understand you.'

Anyway, I'm going off. So the writing was on the wall. I was going to fail. So my father now was paying for me, as I mentioned earlier, but expecting a piece of paper. You don't send your girl child all that way and pay Queen Mary prices without a piece of paper at the end, you know, to prove. I knew I could not go back to

Jamaica without this piece of paper. So knowing what was good for me, I enrolled with the Royal Academy of Music and lived a double life. I shunted between Sidcup and Baker Street. I did some wicked stuff with tickets because I didn't have the money. I used to buy a return to the first stop and then hope to God they didn't catch me in between. It's too late now for me to be prosecuted. I was at two colleges at the same time and neither one knew about the other. Anyway, I ended up taking both sets of exams at the same time. But luckily the Royal Academy was announced first and I did quite well actually. I am not really showing off but I got a big red, yes! So they phoned up Rose Bruford and informed Miss Bruford that her student had done very well in the exam.

'Which student?'

'Why Rose don't be so silly, if there is only one black student.'

'What?'

I was called up there.

'I have just had a phone call from the Royal Academy of Music.'

'Yes, Miss Bruford.'

'And what has this got to do with you?'

'Absolutely nothing Miss Bruford.'

'Well, I'm here to tell you that you have got a distinction.'

I said, 'Wheee!'

And immediately I said, 'Well, baby you can fail me.' I went on so bad, 'You can fail me if you like. I don't care. I don't need your little foolish piece of paper when I have a big ting from the Royal Academy of Music.'

Well they didn't fail me. They couldn't because the Royal Academy was slightly better, i.e. got you better pay.

So I went back to Jamaica and I handed the two cerfiticates, as we say in Jamaica, to my father. He was delighted. I don't know where they are now because he framed them so well that they probably became stone.

Now we go back to Jamaica and life back in Jamaica in those times was not simple either. I wanted to act but there was nothing happening. One must remember that there was no professional theatre in Jamaica at this time. The annual pantomime was the only production which paid the actors and most of the other productions were funded and directed by Paul Methuen, an extraordinary man from Scotland, who had adopted Jamaica as his spiritual home. The Jamaica Operatic Society was another expatriate outfit and it mounted Broadway musicals. Fully qualified, I auditioned for *South Pacific*. After a few call backs I was offered understudy chorus. Even bloody Mary was sung by a Canadian. Well, I did not join the understudy bench, but I sulked. And Wesley Powell, a fantastic man, got me out of the sulk. In fact he called me some bad words and implored me to teach drama at Excelsior. Now they had never taught drama at Excelsior before as a bona fide subject and the Ministry of Education would not approve the pay. So Mr Powell, or Wop as he was affectionately known, called me into the office, 'Now, Yvonne to establish drama in the Jamaica schools curriculum I will have to enter into a long battle with the authorities. This means you might not get paid for quite a while. You might never get paid if I lose. Will you stick out the siege with me?'

This appealed to me and battle was engaged. We won and that was the beginning of paying drama teachers in Jamaica. It's really nice to be at the forefront of these things because people don't really know how those things happen. But that's how it was and it was Mr Powell.

I was soon back in England though. The island is very small, you know. And then I came back again and I worked at Kingston College. There were people like Rachel Manley, Trevor Rhone, Marjorie Whylie, sister of Dwight, and we worked at the school. We produced lots of people like Willard White and stuff like that. Then, because there was nothing to do in the afternoons, we formed the Barn Theatre.

John wanted me to spend some time on the Barn because it's not that known and it's quite an interesting little exercise. It's still going strong, you know. It is 34 years old now and it still produces four plays a year. The primary objective of founding this little theatre was to have a fully professional theatre company in Jamaica within 12 years, that is by 1977. Many of the company are trained in the theatre arts, either in Britain or in the USA. On their return home they met with little welcome and some hostility from the existing theatre establishment. At the time there were so few scripts that existed which interpreted the contemporary political and social concerns of Jamaicans. We first produced Strindberg's *Miss Julie* in a double bill with Edward Albee's *Zoo Story*. It was a financial disaster. I think one night there were four people and my mother had bought all four tickets. But we had to go on. So we persuaded Daddy to make his garage at 5 Oxford Road available. We'd been rehearsing there as a performing space and that is what has now become the Barn Theatre. We call it the Barn. It is named after Barracca, Lorca's *Baracca* and also, as a kind of ironic gesture, the practice theatre at Rose Bruford which both Trevor and myself had been in, was called the Barn. So we thought we would call it the Barn.

We put on a few plays from young English cutting-edge authors – Joe Orton, Roger Milner. And then we did workshops in order to make new plays for people who could see themselves on the stage. Up until then there were no plays, because Derek Walcott's plays weren't done in Jamaica, and Stanley French every so often but we had no plays where we could see ourselves. So we were doing the recordings of the workshops on a large reel-to-reel machine. Someone had to write it up and it fell to Trevor Rhone. And that was the beginning of his career as a playwright. And he's probably the best known playwright in Jamaica. I mean people have heard his name, I suppose. His play writing career had begun. Someone had to direct them and, since I was a bit bossy, I got it and so my directing career had begun and so it went on. We worked with people like Janet Bartley, Mervyn Morris, Denis Scott, John Hearne. Oliver Samuels did his first piece of acting at the Barn, I've got to say. We brought directors and designers from all over the world including England, and Sam Walters' Orange Tree is probably the most successful fringe theatre, well it was for many years in this country. He got the idea for this fringe theatre from our theatre in Kingston, Jamaica, and he will admit it.

Now we had a lot of political stuff and this all has some

relevance to what's happened later on here. The political thing of the work in England is something that I've got to get to so I'll use this kind of example. We were putting on stuff at the Barn and trouble brewed when Michael Manley was told that a Barn review was taking pot shots at him. The offending sketch had been written by the late Ken Maxwell. It portrayed a handsome young politician, recently returned from studying at the London School of Economics, promising the workers the world and having expensive lunches with the bosses and the workers ending up with Rediffusion – which is just speakers, light music, muzak in the work place. Well, that's rather tame actually. But Michael Manley did not find it funny, and I was summoned to his residence and told to take it off. There's something running through this, you know, because you see what threats do. He threatened to get an injunction and I heard myself say, just because I don't really care you know, I said, 'Well m'dear if the cap fit wear it.' Lord have mercy! Bad move. Michael Manley leaped across the table, grabbed me by, not quite the throat because he couldn't get at it. But then Beverley Anderson Manley, well she was Anderson at the time, had to appear in the room and stop him and his henchmen. I did not take that review off. It's a stupid piece of undergraduate nonsense and you do not give into threat.

Another threat was Robert Hill who is now a very, very elegant and well-respected professor of something somewhere. I came up to London sometime in the 1960s, I can't remember exactly when. And I met this amazing man called Ed Bullins at the Ambience Lunchtime Theatre in Queensway. And a Trinidadian man, Junior Telfer, was very instrumental in doing that. We started lunchtime theatre too, you know. Do you know that? Anyway, we saw this play, and it was called *Electronic Nigger* and it was a pretty difficult, well, a difficult play to put on. It was wonderful and Ed Bullins was a very important playwright and still is. So I got permission from him, and he said, 'You know, you're so charming I'll give it to you and you can do it, ya, ya ya, ya, and come up to the Lafayette.' I go and take the play and run. So we go back to Jamaica. We put on the *Electronic Nigger* and it was probably the most political piece of work that we were trying to do at that time. Robert Hill saw the title of the play, so he picketed the Barn with banners. He'd not read the play. He did not know about Ed Bullins. So when good sense prevailed he left and went to America.

Well, I came back to England in 1972, and my first experience was sort of digging some people out of a very deep pit. There was this play, which was on at the Institute of Contemporary Arts (ICA), and it was written by Sally Durie, the English wife of a very wealthy Jamaican businessman. It was being directed by Gillian Binns, wife of my one-time Radio Jamaica boss, Graham Binns. The piece was called *Lippo the New Noah* and it had been written as a tribute to Kapo, one of Jamaica's most celebrated intuitive artists and revivalists. The production ran into some trouble. Indeed some culturally specific guidance seemed to be necessary. In other words the cast was on strike. Phone call from Mona Hammond. Could I help? Well I wanted to get into this directing business and so I said, 'Yeah,' and therein lies the rub, ladies and gentlemen: an all-black cast with an all-white executive.

That's what Talawa as a theatre company, from it's formation and up to today, has been trying to work against, this kind of thing. I think the Jamaican background of that kind of 'in your face', it doesn't get you anywhere really. You remain poor but you don't remain bowed and I think that's what the company's done. Talawa was formed, almost by chance, in response to a phone call from Lord Birkett of the Greater London Council (GLC). 'So Yvonne, why haven't you put in an application for funding? I mean the council is being wound down. Isn't there some sort of play you want to do?' Well yes there were. I wanted to see C.L.R. James' *Black Jacobins* on the stage. Why the *Black Jacobins*? I simply wanted to honour C.L.R. James, even though he's a Trinidadian! I wanted to prove that 50 years on from the first production done in this country in 1935, with Paul Robeson at the head of a top cast – Paul Robeson was the only black man in the cast – and I wanted to know that 50 years on we could mount the production with the right people. So I put in an application and I put in for a certain amount of money. The cheque came and it was £80,000. That's like a lot of money, you know. The cheque came written to Yvonne Brewster. Well my husband Starr said, 'Send it back! If this scheme don't work, we (he's a very modern man) are not selling the house. So send it back but form a theatre company and get it redone, reissued in the name of the theatre company.'

I thought, 'Form a theatre company, my God.' I sat up. I phoned up Carmen Munroe. I said, 'Carmen you want to form a theatre company?' 'No!' I phoned up Mona Hammond, 'Mona, you want to form a company?' 'No!' I said, 'Well, you are!' And I phone back Carmen, 'You are! What shall we call it?' I'll never forget that Carmen said, 'Something round.' You know how gorgeous she is and she said, 'Something round,' and put the phone down. Mona said, 'I've no idea and I couldn't care less. But, okay, I'm there, do it if you want.' So I got this dictionary, Cassidy's Jamaican dictionary. I started at the back and the first thing I came to was 'zuzu wapp' and I didn't think that would quite work as a theatre company so I went a little further back and I came to T and I found 'talawa'. So I phone up Carmen, phone up Mona, poor things. I say, 'Listen, talawa?' Carmen say 'What's that?' She's Guyanese you know, naturally. Then Mona say, 'Chilli caboshe talawa, yes man!' So tallawah is spelled T-A-L-L-A-W-A-H but me, thinking I'm an artist, thought that the graphics would look better with talawa. So quickly wrote up this application – Talawa Theatre Company and some fictional company number – and the cheque came out, because remember the GLC was coming to an end, in the name of Talawa Theatre Company for £80,000, and we did the show. We were innocent because what I'd put the application in for was exactly what I spent. That has been why we still exist actually. The problem was that I had forgotten to put in an income. But with C.L.R. James in a 400-seater, three week run at the Riverside Theatre, and a second Haitian revolution taking place on our first night, well we had to do it didn't we. So it was very well attended and we made £30,000. So when we looked at each other, we said, 'What, we spent the money on the production, we didn't think of the income.' So that started the company because we now had £30,000 in the bank. Nobody believes me because they know I'm a business woman. They think I'm a business woman. But we really did not put in an income and that was an oversight because the GLC was ending and here we are.

Now Talawa's been going for 13 years. It's in its 14th year. We started off, we were in, say, like sections. The first section was because I overheard Peter Hall one day when I was acting, doing Tituba (in Arthur Miller's *The Crucible*). Well I did do it for the National Theatre for my sins and it moved into the West End and we were doing the 'get in' (technical theatrical term) at the Comedy Theatre in the West End and I was up in the circle, Tituba doesn't have much to do, when Peter Hall came in at the back of the circle and I heard him talking to some other guy that looked quite like him in silhouette, actually, 'Well of course, quite impossible to cast these black actors in Shakespeare, because simply darling they are just not up to it. They just simply can't do it.' Now that's why I told the story about my grandfather at the beginning, okay. So hear me (makes coughing noise). 'Oh, there you are Yvonne,' and they continued in the same way.

I thought, mmmhhh, right. We're going to do Shakespeare and we're going to do *The Importance of Being Earnest* and we're going to do all those things that they say we can't do and we did that for about four years. We got hell from the critics, especially Jane Edwards at *Time Out*, who really thought, she actually said that we should know our place. But the only thing is that they did quite well with the black people. We found a black audience. And in fact it did very well with the white people too because we weren't trying to prove anything you know. This is not antagonism. This is just give us a break. I remember when we did *The Importance of Being Earnest* and when the chap's only grandson, the chap being Oscar Wilde, the only living relative, he came to the production when it was at the Bloomsbury and he said – we didn't know he had come– he sat there and he said at the end, 'I must meet these people.' So he popped around and he said, 'I'm Merlin Holland (because he had to change his name to Holland), I'm Merlin Holland and I wanted to tell you, I need to talk to these actors,' and I thought, 'Oh my God, here we go, he's going to take the show off or whatever.' And he went back and he's become quite a good friend actually. He wrote in my script, 'This has put back 20 years on my life because this is what he meant. He wanted to take the piss.' What we did was do the words and when it came to 'blue eyes' Gary Macdonald said to me, 'How can you say your eyes are so blue. We're all black people and we don't have no blue eyes. Shall we put in contact lenses?' And I said to him, 'Do you know, I don't know how I could cast you, a man of so little imagination. You will find a way of saying to a woman with black eyes, "Your eyes are so blue".' And I knew, I knew what I wanted but just in case he didn't come up with it. It was like a school you know, how can we get these blue eyes in? Finally, we only had three weeks rehearsal I said, 'Listen to this. (Sings Blues style) Blues! Your eyes are so blue, yes.' So every time we came to the part, the yardies go ooh (sings), you see it's putting a specificity that was not necessarily meant but which was taking your own cultural background and that is what we are about.

We won't go into Talawa's productions because that will take too long, because we've done over 45, but those are examples of the way we approach the classics from a kind of stand-off position of saying, 'No, you don't tell me I can't do that!' Anyway Wole Soyinka did say that Shakespeare's real name was Al Shacklespeare. Now the second thing that we did because they said alright, alright, and a lot of those people like Jeffrey Kissoon, Dona Croll, David Harewood who did Othello at the National, every one of these people, Harewood's first Shakespearean role was with us. Yes and he played Othello at the National. We don't need to do that anymore, unless we really want to. Maybe we will, maybe we won't. But then we have the second role, because where are the classics? There are no black classics. So Derek Walcott came to see *Anthony and Cleopatra*. Derek Walcott is a big supporter. He will fly the Atlantic to see the shows which is more than some of the locals will, and he said at the end, 'That not bad you know, it's really not bad.' He said it in a very poetic way. 'You're opening this new theatre, I think you should do something really difficult.' 'And what is that?' – because there are lots of people I'm in awe of and

I shake – John La Rose is one and Derek Walcott is the other, and I go; 'And what is that, Derek?'

He said, 'Well, you have to do *The Road*.'

'Why *The Road*?'

'Well because it's difficult, I don't understand it and you must do it.'

'Yes Sir!'

So we did *The Road* and in fact many people said that was a bad mistake because it was so esoteric that nobody knew the hell what was going on. But, in a way, it set a sort of thing that we were going to be difficult and it didn't do that bad at the box office anyway, in spite of all these people saying, 'Why are we interested in what the Nigerians eat?' So the riposte was, 'Well cucumber sandwiches are equally uninteresting.' So you just have to be there for it. So we did this whole section. We did Derek Walcott, we did Trevor Rhone, we did lots of American, African-American playwrights for the simple reason that I could find very few West Indian women playwrights. Isn't that a shame. Things are happening now because we've got the lovely, the inestimable Miss Pat Cumper and I want her to keep writing but, apart from Sylvia Wynter-Carew and her lovely *Masquerade*, it was really difficult to find. Cicely Waithe-Smith just can't go down in the 1980s. I couldn't find a way of doing it anyway, and I couldn't find the women, you know, historically had written these plays. Although Sistren did one of its first productions at the Barn. But they were doing their own stuff, you know. So it was really difficult. So we did a lot of male stuff and we did the female from Endesha Ida Mae Holland who you may not know about, but she wrote *From the Mississippi Delta* and is a wonderful woman. Ntozake Shange, who turned my hair grey, but we're still very good friends. Pearl Cleage who is a really lovely woman, *Flying West*. We did a lot of those. That was the middle section.

Now we're into saying, 'Well we don't need to do that unless we really want to.' So our kind of reincarnation now is to approach what is being written by the young, Black British writers and over the years we have run lots of courses. We do a lot of script reading. We're very political. Notice that I'm not talking about art in this,

I'm just talking about the politics, because this is not for the art. We can decide whether we think things are good or not but if the politics aren't right we are really going to get left. So for the young people, we run these things called Zebra Crossing. And why Zebra Crossing? It's because you don't want to say, you know, black beauty because you're excluding too many people. So the Zebra Crossing – the zebra is crossing. It has been really extraordinary because some of the things have been absolute rubbish and some of them have thrown up new talent, this last Zebra Crossing, which was a series of eight new plays written by young black people, directed by young black people, have thrown up three excellent directors we didn't know about before and a couple of playwrights. What more can you want? You go and see the terrible one and you think, 'Well that one didn't work.' But you see we have to have the right to fail.

So in a way that's where we are at the moment and that's why at the moment I'm planning my exit, because at 60 years of age I do not want to be doing young experimental drama. Me like the big tings, right. So I go to the States and I do my big stuff in the States and I come back and I'm behind the scenes trying to get the young Black British people so as to be able to give them the voice, them the time to go forward.

I'm going to finish just on a note here which is, in 1985 there was a review done of the black and Asian theatre companies existing in Britain at the time and this has been quoted many times but perhaps not to this audience. Dr Elizabeth Clark from Barbados did it, and the Black Theatre Forum found the money and there were 35 theatre companies registered, most of whom had some sort of funding. Well ladies and gentlemen at the moment there are four; two Asian and two black. We received the largest amount of funding and it's pathetic! There's a history here. When theatre companies reach a certain age in some disciplines they are told, 'Well have a rest and come back refreshed.' When Temba got to that sort of stage they weren't told to take a rest and come back refreshed, they were told to get the hell out. So 21 years of public subsidy and investment went down the plug and I'm as sick as a parrot because that leaves the other ones that are left isolated. Black Mime, and there's a whole series of theatre companies that when the people who formed the companies get old or tired and it does mean jolly hard work, instead of saying, 'Well why don't you shift and we'll get someone new in,' like they would do at the National, when Richard Eyre decided he wanted to be a knight, he went off didn't he? We got the next one to come in to be a knight in three years' time. It's cool. But with us they cut the company and that has happened. So that is why I have taken the political stance to tell them that I am going and try it. Just try it! Because you've got to be active about this. I do think that for the community, the black community and because half our audience is white, God bless 'em, right. But I would say it is there. You still have two theatre companies that do black work and there's two Asian companies and I would say as a kind of huuugh to sit down, use it or lose it! Thank you.

Aggrey Burke: Well, thanks very much, Yvonne. Use it. Use it yes. In essence Yvonne is saying to us that at 60 she is going to reform or transform her life and I think it poses a challenge, which I would have liked to have heard a little more on as to how you see the next phase. We have a very challenging period ahead. You've told us of just four left – two black, two Asian. I think some of the things you've said represent real threats but opportunities. Both, I feel. And then you've brought us in on the context of the Sam Isaacs, Polish Jewish origin with the road to eating Indian indenture on that side trying to keep things happy, and then your father's side and how these two themes have been so powerful in shaping your vision and your life. It seems to me that insofar as you've started off there, do we now accept that, at this junction in Britain, we go out as a unified possibility or we seek to be part of the four that you mentioned. It is a real issue. Do we keep the four separate with the black, the Scottish, the Polish, Kosovan almost and the Indian or does one bring them together in some sort of rigmarole? I think what you have said is so challenging. Thank you a great deal and I think we should open it up for some discussion because it needs some rapping and some thinking. You might say you have the final word in that you have decided at 60, but I don't know if that is so. So questions, thank you.

Quintin Yearde: My name is Quintin Yearde and I'm somebody I suppose. I'm a Jamaican. You were telling us about some of your experiences when you first came. Is it that those experiences continue as you progress? Have you met people like Miss Rose Bruford 20 years down the line and have these experiences kept happening in different ways perhaps?

Yvonne Brewster: Okay, quick answer. I directed *Raisin in the Sun* in 1984, I think, with Carmen Munroe – we keep it in the family you know – at the Tricycle and it went on a national tour and it was a really very successful national tour. I was asked by Methuen to write the preface for the new publication of *Raisin in the Sun* in 1980 something. Now at the National Theatre of Great Britain they are in the middle of a series of the 100 great plays of the century. Each week they do two, right. They came up to 19 whatever and they wanted to do *Raisin in the Sun*. That was one of three or is it two black plays out of the 100, so I suppose the proportionality ain't that bad. August Wilson being one, James Baldwin being the other. Three Americans. No Africans. No West Indians. Okay, that's fair. Now I'd also directed at the National Theatre a couple of times, you know, been around, you know. Actually the telephone directory does have my name. The man sorting out these platform readings, when it came to *Raisin in the Sun*, 'Now who can do this? Oh who could do this. Oh yes yes, I think we'll ring Nick Kent.' Nick Kent is the gentleman who runs the Tricycle Theatre. So they rang Nick Kent to find out who he thought should be the person they should ask to direct this little stupid platform performance which they used to ask me to do for nutten' when I was working there. Sorry about the dialect. So Nick Kent then said, 'Well I think you should phone Yvonne because she did it here sometime before me and I think she's written the preface and I think she's got quite a few papers written on it.' They phoned me and said, 'Nick Kent thought you might be the person to ask to do this reading.' I did it because, if I didn't do it, then they would say I think I am Kofi Annan and I don't think that. I have no ego. But I do think it's a bit much that they have to ring up Nick Kent to find out his advice as to who to ask with all the galaxy of black directors, and we do have about six or seven people, to ask him who! That is facety. However we did it and luckily it has gone down as one of the really exciting ones, so Lorraine Hansberry power! That's an example to say it wasn't only Miss Bruford saying, 'You'll never work.' That just happened four weeks ago.

Pearl Connor: Can I comment about that? *Raisin in the Sun.* We're now talking about the 1960s, before your time Yvonne, when we put it on. Sidney Poitier was brought from America, we brought him to play the lead. And we put some black actors who were here. That was a long time ago. We had some good people, Johnny Sekka and others for playing it. But because we have no directory or record of what we have done in this country, they have to phone Nick Kent 20 years later to ask him who there is? It is an insult. The whole of the situation here is an insult. Not only are you mad but I'm madder, because I know from way back that we were doing these things. We had competent people doing it. This play is a well-known American, you know, it's an amazing play and we shouldn't have to suffer by that nonsense. So that when you came along, I mean that was really an abuse. I mean you heard about it. That's why John and this place here or any publisher maybe can record the things that have been done. You must put it in print. Because they can't refer to any book. Can they turn back?

Male member of the audience: I am moved to ask your opinion. It's a continuing problem as Pearl and many others know, it's been going on for a long, long time. I'm not in the arts but what I'm talking about is the ability of Black British people to gain jobs here in all plays, but being constrained from time to time from getting a chance to act in plays which are American but over here and constrained, if you like, in taking up positions that black actors in the United States have taken up. So we have a kind of transatlantic problem. Now I don't know what black actors over there are trying to do, but on this side of the water I don't know that there are any major black members of Equity whose voices have been heard recently. If there are voices I haven't read them in the press. The question being politics. Jobs are politics, employment is politics, good plays are politics but jobs and the opportunities to present themselves are extremely important. How can black members of the profession and of the trade union help resolve this culture problem, this problem between black actors on the Atlantic, on the US side and black actors here?

Yvonne Brewster: Well I don't know. You see, I think that we're still young at the game. I work in America quite a lot now because I can be really outrageous in America and they just kind of say, 'Oh okay.' Not here. There's a kind of forced greenhouse, exotic orchid situation and I think that's something to do with it. Because I think that we are at the state now where some black actors, and I'm just talking about people of the African diaspora now, not of the Asian diaspora because I think it's different for them, are between a rock and a hard place.

You can have a company at the National which has quite a few black actors in it. But when you look at it they're all born here, which is great and they are told, and I've spoken to nearly all of them and it is this thing, 'Well, I'm not really a black actor. I'm just an actor who happens to be black.' And that is a political thing that goes on and in a way you've got to see that position. You're talking about money, politics and stuff and often people say, 'No, no don't call me a black actor,' and in a way Carmen says that as well, 'I'm not a black actor. I am an actor and I am black!' She doesn't say, 'I'm an actor who happens to be black.' She says, 'Yeah, I'm an actor and I am black!'

And, please, there is this thing about blind casting. That's what it's called, that you're blind. And that's why I get into trouble because I was told this by a very posh and important person. Yes, artistic director of the National, so I don't suppose you get bigger than that. And it's that blind casting is actually the answer to everything. And my response to that, and it may be very old fashioned because I'm not really that hip hop anymore, is, 'No thank you. I don't wish you to be blind to me. I want you to see me.' So that it's alright, I mean Mona Hammond can play Lady Bracknell, Dona Croll can play Cleopatra, but she looks just like her anyway, you know, and that's okay. But I want you to see what I can bring to the part that is specifically mine. Don't be blind to me. So we're caught in this kind of thing of what you call something, terminology, and you get caught up in terminology and the next thing you get caught up in quotas. When they try to do a four per cent of every theatre company in this land, the Arts Council tried that some time ago, to have four per cent of the people working in the theatre, every theatre should have four per cent.

Well now, a man that used to run Shared Experience, a friend of mine actually. I'm surprised he's still a friend as well so I can call his name, he said to me, 'All this four per cent rubbish.' He said, 'Look I've got to paint my little finger black and that's four percent of me because I'm the only one,' and I nearly killed him. We actually fought physically because he's a friend, you know. I said, 'Don't come with that,' and then I was on the Arts Council at that time. I was an officer. I went round as the officer for Guildford and I was at my first meeting and this was when this four per cent was coming and I said, 'Well, where is the board room?' and they said, 'The board room is there M'am but you really want that entrance,' and I said, 'Oh is that the better entrance?' and she said, 'No that's the canteen,' and I said, 'Well, I would have thought as your new Arts Council officer that you might have offered me a cup of coffee. Where's the board room?'

Okay, because that staff out in Guildford had increased by four per cent in the canteen! So quotas don't always work. Terminology doesn't always work. So what I believe that an actor has to have is a position for himself that he's willing to go down with. A lot of the youngsters come into my office, a lot of them. I mean today like three of these big young stars, because they feel very outside. They come into the office and you say, 'We don't have no coconut water but we have plain water. You want some water?' And they sit there, sometimes you know sit just to be quiet and read the books and look up the archives, because we do have archives, to see the history such as we can get. So that they can go back outside and say, 'Well, I'm just an actor who happens to be black.' It's really difficult. It's very de-racinating, yeah, but it's a matter of working. I think the stalwarts within this society can help those kids because the history isn't long enough. As Pearl [Connor], my mother, says here – she wouldn't want me as a daughter so she's not saying yes [laughter] – she says, we haven't written it down. We haven't written it down so there's no reference point. Whereas our African-American brothers and sisters, they're more into it, but I have to say they've had longer and when we get into our stride they better watch out!

Aggrey Burke: Allister, do you want to come in on that?

Allister Bain: Well it's a very difficult track but we can't stop. I'll give you one example. An English Canadian actress once said England would go down as traditional because they are not changing anything. It might seem like change but it isn't. I will give you one example of what we're talking about. Many years ago a director cast me in *School for Scandal* as Rowley – it had never been done in this country before, right, and of course I was up against the odds. The cast didn't really see how you could have a black man playing the role. But Rowley really could be anyone if you know the play. Rowley could be one of the eastern boys that they brought over or whatever, but he's always played by a white man. And of course I had a lot of pressure. The first time the play was supposed to go on the leading man fell ill. There was a lot of tension. The point I'm trying to make is they say that people, the audience, wouldn't like you playing in that role. What happened, it was in Watford and two elderly English people came backstage and said, 'Could we speak to the gentleman playing Rowley?' They said, 'Thank you, we really enjoyed it.' So that's part of the answer, but how do we solve it because the ones who dictate and the ones who hold the purse won't allow us. It's control. I mean there are various aspects of it and I can't split it up enough to explain how I feel. What Yvonne said about, 'I'm an actor.' But still they're going to cast you black, this is a fact. On this same point about Rose Bruford, there was a seminar some time ago. We all attended and we were broken up into groups and one section of my group asked one of the teachers, 'How do you see this actress,' who was black, 'What prospects are there outside when she leaves drama school?' Just because she was a black actress. I said, 'So you had already put that label on. She's not going to get work apart from only as a black actress. So I said, 'But I thought she was an actress! But if you are preparing her as a black actress, she's black already.' So the problem is very, very difficult. It's very hard to crack but I think we've got to crack it.

Roxy Harris: Can you say something about television and film because some people might be interested to hear about that.

Yvonne Brewster: Oh yes I can very quickly, because I decided at the beginning to deal with theatre, because you know I've had a varied life including television and film. When I was teaching drama in Jamaica with Mr Powell at Excelsior Perry Henzell had this text and Trevor was trying to make it into a script and said, 'Leave the work, man. Cho, teaching is not on.' And we went off and did *The Harder They Come*. I was production manager. I didn't produce a fly before in my life and that was really interesting and I think that's why we need to get back into the work that we do, not to follow the pro formas that other people give us, you know. Because that film *The Harder They Come* is actually, whether we like it or not, probably the single most successful black film ever been made. Because I'm here to tell you that the royalties still keep coming in after all this time – 2nd November 1970 it started and it's 1999 now. Mind you, I don't get the royalties you know, and they might be tuppence, but they do come actually. And there is somewhere in the world at some time in every week that that film is played. We had four different cameramen because we ran out of money, you know. We had a nice pretty little English man first and then the money ran out. Then we went to Chappie St Juste and then the money ran out. And you can see in the film some exposures are really, really, really much too light and some exposures are really, really, really much too dark. But it spoke, because it spoke from a culturally specific position and we knew about Rhygin.

Trevor and I have just decided that we are going to do a thing that we call *Top Ranking* and we're going to do it next year. We don't have any money but we will find it and we're going to go right back to *The Harder They Come* and do *Top Ranking*. *Top Ranking* is *Romeo and Juliet* in Trenchtown. That's what we're going to do. We're going to have war in Trenchtown. But we have to go back and not say what Ridley Scott likes and, you know, whether we're trying to be *Alien*. We should do that.

Now the radio is interesting because I'm going back into radio and I've done quite a bit – I'm doing radio criticism these days. Well you know you have to keep the shekels rolling in somehow, Miss Pearl. Television is very interesting in this country, because that's where we're cracking it actually. If you did but know. I was at a conference over the weekend of women in television and film. They have a black section of that and it was the best attended conference at BAFTA for years. It was just Friday night and Saturday and they wanted to bring out all the women that we would recognise and so some of them like Paulette Randall and all the youngsters phoned up the old folk and Dame Jocelyn, bless her heart, she turn up and that puts a kind of a oomph! Baroness Amos, she turn up and as you go down the line we all turn up. Carmen turn up. Mona turn up. This one turn up and support the thing and it's changed the commissioning editors' point of view and a lot of people got commissioned out of that day. Because they're young, you know, and they're bad. They're braver than we are in theatre. So you know what they did? They did *Birds of a Feather*. They took a scene and then they said, 'Watch dis!' So we had Meera Syal and Dona Croll and some other woman who is in *Goodness Gracious Me* and whose name escapes me, and they re-did a scene from *Birds of a Feather* with a black actress and two Asian actresses, and it was funnier. So they said to the commissioning editors, 'So come on now what are you going to do? We got ten scripts.' And they just give it to him, and he was so confused I think it got commissioned.

But we're a little bit politer in theatre because in theatre we come out of a British tradition, but the problem is we don't. Theatre started in the church and the church never start in England. That's what we need to be brave about but we're no fellow travellers because as the first bullet, gone! Norman Beaton would stand up and then they say, 'Oh, well he don't count because he's a drunkard!' You know. So you destroy the man but he was one of the most brilliant people around. And that is it, in the theatre we tend to eat at each other and divide and rule and follow that rule so well it that will never get anywhere. That's why I want shot of it.

Aggrey Burke: Well I think we've come to the ending of what seems to me to be an opening of something really new. It seems to me that even though Yvonne at 60 ...

Yvonne Brewster: You keep on with this 60 business. You keep on with this 60 business [laughter].

Aggrey Burke: It seems to me that there is a real possibility now that with Pearl, yourself, the kind of work you've done that you've told us about today is inspiring, and we would wish to thank you for that.

Yvonne Brewster is a foremost theatre director, with an international career of over 35 years spanning work in theatre, film, on radio and television. She has been a teacher and lecturer, edited plays and advised arts organisations. The scale of her ground-breaking achievements has been recognised by a string of awards in Britain and the USA.

Yvonne Brewster was born in Kingston, Jamaica and attended St Hilda's Diocesan High School there. She later came to the UK and was educated at Rose Bruford College and the Royal Academy of Music.

As a theatre director, Yvonne Brewster's career began as early as 1962. She has now directed over 100 plays in various parts of the world. Her directing credits include: Lorca's *Blood Wedding* (Royal National Theatre, London, UK); Pinter's *The Lover* (Florence, Italy); *Nanny, Queen of the Maroons* (Apple Corps Theatre, New York, USA); Wilde's *The Importance of Being Earnest* (Newcastle, UK and Cork, Eire); Shakespeare's *King Lear* (England national tour); Derek Walcott's *Tijean and His Brothers* (The Wright Theatre, California, USA); Femi Euba's *The Eve of Gabriel* (Baton Rouge, Louisiana, USA); and Wole Soyinka's *The Road* at the Talawa Theatre's opening event at the Cochrane Theatre in London. Yvonne Brewster has also directed radio plays and documentaries for BBC Radio Four and has most recently directed *Shakespeare Shorts* for BBC Education Television.

In 1965 Yvonne Brewster became one of the founding members of the pioneering Barn Theatre in Kingston, Jamaica. The Barn was set up in an old garage space with the aim of providing Jamaica with a fully professional theatre company. The company found that new scripts which related to contemporary social and political concerns of the island were few and far between. From 1970 Yvonne Brewster, along with Munair Zacca and Trevor Rhone, began to conduct devising workshops to remedy this situation. Trevor Rhone found himself working as a playwright as he wrote up the scenes produced at these workshops, whilst it fell to Yvonne to take on the directing and Zacca the acting. Since then the Barn Theatre has created some of the Caribbean's best loved plays and has been the starting point for many actors who are household names in Jamaica today. The Barn continues to present four plays a year despite its economic strictures and the need for renovations.

From 1976 Yvonne became more involved with the administrative side of drama. Having served her apprenticeship as a production assistant for BBC television, she then took on the role of production manager for the highly acclaimed film *The Harder They Come*, which was directed by Perry Henzell and which won the Editor's Prize at the Cork Film festival. She continued to work as a production manager for various film companies including her work with Knuts Production/Smile Orange Films. She later became administrative director for the Jamaican Government's Festival Commission and then worked as drama officer for the Arts Council of England.

In 1985 Yvonne Brewster co-founded, with Mona Hammond, Carmen Munroe and Inigo Espejel, the Talawa Theatre Company, which has since then moved from the back bedroom of Yvonne's house to become an important and innovative theatre company at the forefront of black European theatre. Talawa has sought to provide middle scale, high quality productions reflecting the significant creative role black theatre plays within the UK. Talawa has continued to use black culture and experience to enrich British theatre. Yvonne has been their Artistic Director since 1985 and has directed many of their productions.

Yvonne Brewster edited *Black Plays, Volumes 1, 2* and *3* whilst maintaining her directing career. She has also been involved in education, teaching at Kingston College High School and Excelsior High School in Jamaica, and at Fulham Grammar School in the UK. She has lectured at Rose Bruford College in London, where she was once a student. In the US Brewster was Artist-in-Residence at the University of California and a Guest Lecturer at Louisiana State University.

Yvonne Brewster

The last 11 years have seen Yvonne Brewster take on a number of advisory responsibilities within the arts. From 1988 to 1994 she sat on the British Council Advisory Panel on Drama and Dance. She was part of the year-long Gulbenkian Enquiry into Theatre Direction in 1989-90. Yvonne Brewster currently does work for the Theatre's Trust (since 1991), the London Arts Board (since 1992) and the Arts Council of England Regional Theatre Initiative (since 1994). On a community level, Yvonne served on the Riverside Mental Health Trust from 1994 to 1999. She is now a non-executive director of the new Brent-Kensington-Chelsea-Westminster NHS Trust.

From the early 1980s when she was first awarded a Director's Bursary by the Arts Council of Great Britain, Yvonne Brewster's potential and talents have been recognised. In 1992 Brewster received a Woman of Achievement Award from the Arts Council of Great Britain and in the same year she became a Fellow of the Royal Society of Arts. This was followed one year later by an OBE in the New Year's Honours List. In 1997 she was awarded a Living Legend Award at the National Black Theatre Festival, USA. Yvonne Brewster has also received the accolade of a BAFTA Award for *Shakespeare Shorts* (BBC Television) and a Royal Television Society Award for *Romeo and Juliet* (BBC). Her entry in the world famous publication *Who's Who* confirms Yvonne Brewster's place in history as one of the most successful black women on the international arts scene this century.

Alexis Rennie

Alexis Rennie
introduced by John La Rose

John La Rose: I want to welcome you all to this last session in this current series of 'Life Experience With Britain'. I also want to thank those of you who are here and, in their absence, all of those who came during the series. This area holds 60 people. It was intended to hold not more than 60 and our average attendance is between 40 and 50. So we have been succeeding with the varied attendances that we've had in producing the kind of results which the George Padmore Institute has sought for the sessions we've had on the 'Life Experience With Britain'. But that is not all, as you will see from each of the talks we gave in the first series and now for each of the talks we did in the second series, seven each. We've published a short biography of each of the persons who have contributed to the sessions – 500 of each of those biographies. So the biographies are intended to go beyond the numbers who can attend our sessions and they have and they continue to do so. But even more than that with the book that we've just published on the first series, *Changing Britannia: Life Experience with Britain* – not in Britain but with Britain – what we've been able to do is to make it reach way beyond the George Padmore Institute's attendances to people all over the continents, which is what our intention is.

For example, I was in Trinidad in the Caribbean in the last four or five weeks and there it was that someone told me they'd seen a reference to *Changing Britannia* in the weekly *Guardian*. The *Guardian* is published every week and circulated internationally. So those who read it will have seen it in the weekly *Guardian*. There are other people in Barbados who have seen it and quite recently other people told me they had seen it from Nigeria. So it means that the talks are important documents and I hope that undergraduates in universities in Britain and in Europe will be able to use this as a text in certain courses in the future. That is our intention, our hope. That is our aim. We hope that sixth form studies will also embrace this documentation which we have been preparing as part of this series of 'Life Experience With Britain' in the George Padmore Institute because that's the way that cultures are reproduced through schooling and education. That's important in a written culture like this is, that not only that orality should be preserved, but also the consequences of the productions from orality are also preserved in books like this, *Changing Britannia*.

So again I welcome you all to this talk this evening by Alexis Rennie, who we also call Gentle. He may tell you why he is called Gentle. In the modern state, in the modern economy, science and technology are dominant with finance. This is what is dominating the modern economies of the world at the moment and with the IMF, the World Bank and G7. But it's important that the new technologies be understood and we've tried our best within the George Padmore Institute to concentrate on an understanding of the modern technologies. It's not surprising that in a short period of only two decades that the computer has dominated. Not only that, but the most important modern company, as mentioned by *Fortune* magazine, is Microsoft and its founder and managing director, Bill Gates, is the dominant person in terms of fortunes in the modern world in terms of business, in only a short period of 20 years, two decades. We have to consider what was accomplished before that, the energy companies, oil companies, took much longer to be dominant in quite that way. So science and technology are really important and key components of what we have to understand and grasp and it's important tonight that we are approaching that phase of our work. There'll be more of this kind in the future, in the kind of varied way we make our presentations. But we are approaching that with a person who comes from that tradition of building. Monuments and buildings are important features of the modern world and of the ancient world. We don't have pyramids without builders and we don't have any of those things without architects and builders and scientists and mathematicians who can make computations. Algorithms, as we know, are part of the quest of the modern computer. So I am very pleased to have with us tonight, in fact a builder, a civil engineer who in the course of his life has dedicated his life to this and we welcome him and we welcome you to hear what he has to say. Thank you very much.

Alexis Rennie: Thank you John for this very kind introduction. I hope you don't mind if I sit. I think it's a warm day and I would much prefer to sit and I hope you don't mind if I take you back, say, three generations.

I want to go back three generations because it's around the time when slavery was abolished by the British in their colonies. Around that time, from 1834 to 1840, there was a gentleman, James Rennie, who was my father's father. He was born in Grenada shortly after slavery was abolished in the British colonies. Academic education may not have been a priority for the descendants of slaves since consolidation and coping with the new way of survival were very important. At that time agriculture in its most organic state – there were no GM foods then – was the industry of the day. The estates were managed by allocating portions of lands to the more capable workers, who cleared this land and cultivated it firstly with short-term crops and then with long-term crops. The workers were allowed to reap the short-term crops for their own use and were paid in this way. When the long-term crops were ready to be harvested, that land was taken back by the owners and the workers were then given another portion of land for clearing and cultivating. This process was repeated and repeated and repeated.

My grandfather worked diligently at this process and, from the earnings of the short crop, bought some of the uncultivated lands at a low cost and developed those for himself. He was thus able to academically educate his children. It was those lands which later became his legacy to them. My father, Linus Daniel Rennie – my mother called him Ray – became a policeman in Trinidad and when his father died he returned to Grenada, claimed his inheritance, bought off those of his brothers and sisters who had travelled abroad and pursued other careers, and so kept most of his father's lands together to start maintaining his own family. My mother, Agatha, and father proceeded to have nine children after their marriage. They had seven boys, two of whom have died, and two girls, one of whom is here with me this evening. Joyce Rennie-Pascall, there she is.

Being the sixth child of the family, I had a lot of high standards to live up to. My elder brothers, Raydon and Neville, had already gone to the best schools on the island and had good results. Neville had also excelled in his sporting activities. Joyce was diversifying, becoming a very good pianist. I was so proud attending some of the concerts in which she was taking part. She also fought many of my battles. I'll give you an insight into one of them. We were at the time attending a primary school in Grenville and I was kind of troublesome. There was a schoolboy who had a slit on his lip and his lip was turned up so we decided to call him 'Skinny Lip'. In those days, when we attended school some of us who did not live far away went home for lunch. One day, returning to school after lunch for the afternoon classes, I met 'Skinny Lip'. I started teasing him and calling him 'Skinny Lip mess in your pants' because 'Skinny Lip' had an unfortunate experience in class, which soiled his pants. 'Gentle, I tell you to stop teasing me!' said 'Skinny Lip' as he became angry. I took no notice of him and continued to tease him. 'Skinny Lip' suddenly bent down and picked up a stone from the side of the road and threw that missile towards me. I tried to avoid it hitting me but the stone struck me on the side of my foot. In those days boys wore short pants, the blood started streaming down my foot so I had to attend to the injury. Joyce was some way behind me but she flew past me and landed on 'Skinny Lip' before he could even think of running away. They fell in a ditch on the side of the road. When 'Skinny Lip' managed to escape from Joyce he ran away and did not come back to school for two weeks, he was so scared. So as you can see my sister fought many of my battles and that's just a mere one of them.

I, like my older brother Neville, attended the Presentation Boys College in St George's for my secondary education. I have actually much fonder memories of the days of my primary education than those in Presentation College. I think mainly because it was obvious, though not an official policy, that the white Grenadian students and those of mulatto origin were treated more compassionately and caringly by the all-white Irish brothers, who were the main teachers and who controlled the college. My education there was also left wanting. I had a thirst for knowledge that was never quenched there. I could not see how the knowledge I was acquiring was going to help me to play a significant part in the development of Grenada. I liked the science subjects – Chemistry taught me how steel was made in a blast furnace; in physics I learnt what size gap must exist between railway lines to avoid them buckling as the temperature changes – but I felt that we were being educated for export. I now know that the University of the West Indies has addressed these issues in formulating their syllabuses, adapting them to meet the needs of the local people. I'm glad that has been addressed because our syllabuses were all to do with the British system. We were never ever going to be having trains there. We were never ever going to be laying railway tracks and we were never ever going to have the raw material to produce steel. So our education was not directed to the development of our own country. I think that was the kind of thirst that I felt was never quenched.

I wanted to become a civil engineer. Part of the syllabus for this course is surveying and mapping. My brother, Neville, had taken up cadastral surveying which he made his career. I sought his help after leaving college and pursued a correspondence course from International Correspondence School (ICS) in London, England, and obtained practical experience by working with Neville. I thoroughly enjoyed that period of my life. I was about 18 years old then. All the girls I knew and grew up with had blossomed into very beautiful young women. I began to take special notice of one of the five young beauties that I can refer to as the girls next door. I was well liked by their father, Mr Pierre. He was a head teacher in an R.C. school in Grenville. Our families were friends and that helped the acceptance of our love and marriage. At this point, let me take this opportunity to introduce to you, my wife, Curl Theresa, one of the girls next door.

In 1955 there was another woman who set my career on its way. She was called Janet, Hurricane Janet. She took Grenada by storm, so to speak. She demolished the St George's pier among other things. The pier had to be replaced by a new construction which is known today as the St George's pier and wharf. For me this was an ideal opportunity to launch my civil engineering career. An English company, Holland, Hannen & Cubitts were the appointed contractors. My passion for civil engineering drove me to seek employment on that project. I was successful, so successful that at the end of the contract which lasted about two years, I received a letter via the administrator of Grenada from H, H & C's overseas director, no less than Brigadier Edney, thanking me for my good work and enclosing an award of £50. This, he said, was meant to be an encouragement for the younger students who showed particular diligence and promise, and at the same time I was invited to work in London with the firm, where I would be able to pursue my course of studies in civil engineering if I so wished.

That was an offer I could not refuse. It was like receiving an Island Scholarship. I say Island Scholarship, because at that time in Grenada, the sixth-form boys and girls from the four main secondary schools offered up a particular subject when taking their Cambridge Higher School Certificate examination, and the most outstanding candidate was awarded the Island Scholarship, just one scholarship for the whole island. It was this scholarship that the late Lord David Pitt won and he chose to go to Scotland to become a doctor of medicine. The offer from Holland, Hannen & Cubitts to come to England and study in my chosen field was an equally valuable one. However, I had one concern when I took up the offer. Would that beautiful girl next door want to stay behind while I checked out the scene in the UK or would she travel with me? I was happy she chose the latter.

We were married the day before we left Grenada, travelled on the ship SS Irpinia and arrived in London at Waterloo Station to be greeted by my sister Joyce and her friend Alex Pascall, whom she later married. Thus started my life experience with Britain. Joyce and Alex informed me that they had secured a flat for us in Islington and the rent was 30 shillings a week. It consisted of a little box room and a cooker on the landing. I can still visualise the look on the face of our first landlady, a Jamaican. It was a look of pity and compassion for these two innocent and naïve newcomers to London.

I reported to work at number one, Queen Anne's Gate, the head office of Holland, Hannen & Cubitts. I was taken to meet Brigadier Edney, the overseas director. He was a fat, chubby, white man sitting on his green leather chair in his plush office with thick green carpet. We chatted about the function of the new pier in Grenada and he then told me that I would be working on the Hyde Park Corner Scheme with Arthur Shallcross, who had been my senior engineer in Grenada. Afterwards, Edney's secretary took me to the office of the civil engineering contract manager. 'You're just the man for the new job at Southbourne!' he greeted me. 'I see you have worked on that sea defence contract in Grenada.' My studies being my main concern and wanting to be not far from Joyce and Alex, our only support in London, I asked, 'Where is Southbourne? Can I do my civil engineering there?' 'You won't be able to start your course until September so you will be alright there.' I then spent the whole of that week in London. I visited the Hyde Park Corner Project to meet with Arthur Shallcross who showed me around the site. On the following Monday I was on the train bound for Southbourne near Bournemouth in Hampshire.

Hotel accommodation was made available for me until I found private accommodation for Curl and myself. Curl was left in London. There was lots of accommodation advertised in Southbourne. The site office arranged for me to view a great many. One after the other doors were closed in my face. 'No longer available.' 'Just taken.' 'Sorry.' And sometimes just the bang of the door when they saw my black skin. My colleagues in the office and even the workmen on site were very supportive and helpful. Eventually, I was accepted in a bedsit in Boscombe and several months later we obtained an attic flat in Southbourne not far from the site.

The contracts manager did not release me from the job at Southbourne in September so that I could attend college in London. I had to remain on the job for its duration early the following year. My work on the contract consisted of making all the necessary calculations for laying out the intricate curved wall and promenade between the beach and the foot of the cliffs. Groynes were constructed to ensure that the beach was not eroded and an access road was constructed from the promenade to the top of the cliff. I was responsible for ordering materials for the construction. My job included checking on the fill materials, concrete control, making sure the right sand was used as there are different sands for different structures in the construction industry. I also provided the levels and alignment for the structure. Spring gave way to summer on the coast. Joyce visited us sometimes and our first son Newton was born in 1961 in Southbourne. The contracts manager then sent me to another sea defence contract at Birchington and when that was completed he sent me to another similar contract at Dymchurch. I thought I was never going to get to London to do my studies.

Early in 1963, I found accommodation in London for Curl and our first son Newton in readiness for commencing my studies in September. It was not until August, when my special surveying skills were needed to lay the base lines for the five bridges that brought the M1 into London (the Mill Hill Bridge, the Salvage Lane Bridge, the Deansbrook Viaduct, the Edgware Road Bridge extension and the Scratchwood Bridge), that the contracts manager summoned me to London by saying, 'I have just the job for you and you will have day release to attend college.'

Before I continue with my experience in London I want to flashback to the Birchington contract. When we were there my elder brother, Harry, came to England and to Birchington. Harry was a motor engineer and informed us that he had driven tractors in Grenada. At the time we had two D8 tractors being delivered to the site to spread the fill behind the sea defence walls and we needed tractor drivers. I spoke to the foreman and secured the job for Harry. The day before Harry started the job, we decided to go down to the site so Harry could familiarise himself with the controls. After Harry got in, I was standing on the beach, Harry got up and he started the tractor. Harry pulled a lever, the tractor shot backwards and took off. I could see Harry, 'Which one to stop it and where are the brakes?' And this is a D8 tractor. Harry somehow got it out of reverse and it shot forward. Harry tried to get it into neutral but it took a right turn towards the beach heading into the sea. I saw the anxiety on my brother's face. Somehow Harry got it to stop on the edge of the water. He then stopped for a moment, scratched his head, he did not even realise that his hat had gone. He then moved one of the controls and I saw the tractor reverse. He stopped it, turned it round, manoeuvred it to where it had been parked before he switched it on. He then switched it off and then said to me, 'Let's go and have a drink.' Anyway he kept the job of driving that tractor until of course the weather became too cold for comfort on the coast and he headed for London.

So, after carrying out the surveying and establishing the base lines of the M1 bridges, I was employed as a senior engineer, supervising and guiding other site engineers who were mostly carrying out their first jobs straight from university. I was also responsible for the planning and programming of the construction of two of the bridges, and liaising with head office as to the extent of the temporary works design and requirements of various trades and plants, and that was for the duration of the contract.

Holland, Hannen & Cubitts went through a significant change then, because of the severe economic conditions. They were the times when – some of you young folk don't remember it but I'm sure John would remember this – when there was a limit of £50 on the money you could take out of the country, when Harold Wilson, the British Prime Minister at the time, introduced severe economic controls. Holland, Hannen & Cubitts made many of the staff redundant, before the redundancy laws were introduced by the government. I'll tell you how that happened. I was in the head office at the time, working in the planning office, servicing the contracts which were mainly coming to an end. There were a few of us in the office, and some of us got a brown envelope on our desk and some of us got a white envelope. I got a white envelope and the white envelope said that I should report to the board room at 5.00 pm. The board room was about as big as this section of this room and when we all got in there, there were bottles of gin and whisky and brandy and a few snacks. The managing director of the company was there – he was a good friend of Lord Cubitts, Harry

Cubitts. He started the meeting by saying, 'Well I just want you all to know that all those in this room are with the company and all those who are not in this room are not with the company.' We were standing around the room, and everybody leaned forward to note who was present or absent. I'll never forget that. That was more or less the case apart from the few foremen and agents who were on site and were needed until the completion of the job. Everybody else, all the people who got brown envelopes, were dismissed. About two months later the introduction of the redundancy laws came into force. That must have saved Cubitts quite a lot of money, because they got rid of an awful lot of employees then.

Now I was among the nucleus of the staff left to rebuild the company. We tendered for new jobs and we completed and serviced the old contracts. We won a contract to build a section of the M1 in Rotherham. I was posted there for a time but I afterwards spent most of my time working in the head office at Queen Anne's Gate as part of the team tendering for new contracts and preparing claims associated with old contracts. This also enabled me to continue attending Westminster Technical College where I completed my Higher National Certificate in civil engineering.

One of the agents I worked with had left Cubitts to become a contracts manager for a company called Ford & Walton. He encouraged me to join his team as a sub-agent on one of his contracts, a multi-storey block of flats in Chingford. The salary was appealing so I joined Ford & Walton. I left Cubitts for the first time. My duties there involved site management but of a different nature to that of my previous civil engineering jobs. The programming and planning and co-ordinating of the different trades in the construction of a multi-storey block of flats proved to be a different type of experience for me. It widened my scope in the construction industry, because building work is quite different to civil engineering. In building work you deal with trades like plastering. You deal with the first and second fixing, like fixing doors and domestic electrical units and you don't have that in civil engineering. So I became quite keen on this type of construction because, if I was going to return to the West Indies, I would need to have a much wider scope of engineering to be of better service to the Caribbean. So that was useful experience for me. When that contract was completed I was offered another post with a new company J.L. Kier. This was back into civil engineering again. I was a section engineer on the Wandsworth Bypass and later on the construction of a water treatment works at Hanningfield.

I then received a telegram from my previous contracts manager. He had left Cubitts also but he was brought back to Holland, Hannen & Cubitts to build a team for the biggest contract of its time. That was the £30 million Thamesmead housing project. In those days they were all £3 million and £4 million projects. Suddenly there was this housing project at Thamesmead and there was £30 million allocated to it. The first stage was £5 million. The contracts manager, Mr Frank Turner, returned to Cubitts and won that contract. He was made a director of Holland, Hannen & Cubitts and he was asked to build a team for the project. He sent me a telegram inviting me to join his team, we discussed it, the money was good, I liked Cubitts so I rejoined the firm. It was there I experienced, funny enough, a bitter taste of what is now referred to as unwitting racism.

I was made engineer-in-charge of all the site engineers until the foundation and infrastructure were in place to commence the superstructure of the houses. We laid out all the piles for the foundations of the houses and multi-storey blocks. We constructed the roads and the pump station for the sewerage. All the infrastructure was in place. Once the foundations were constructed we could start building the houses and handing them over. The director decided then that he wanted a contracts manager for civils, a contracts manager for building and a co-ordinating agent. He appointed a new contract manager for civils and for building and he appointed another gentleman, whom I knew well, for he was a contract supervisor when I was on the Southbourne contract for Holland, Hannen & Cubitts. That gentleman was appointed the co-ordinating agent to co-ordinate the work between the two senior contract managers. The director then left for a three-week holiday. I was told by them that he instructed each of them to appoint a deputy. They called me in first and I discussed the matter with them. They all wanted me to be their deputy but, fortunately for me, because of the experience I had on the multi-storey block of flats that I built in Chingford, my knowledge gave me the intimate components of both the civil and the building work. They knew of my experience in civil engineering and they now knew of my experience in building. So I was appointed deputy co-ordinating agent. They advertised and they found two new engineers to fill the other posts – the deputy civil engineering and building contracts manager.

The director came back from his holidays. He called his two contract managers and co-ordinating agent to a meeting to find out who they had chosen for their assistants. When he was informed that I was appointed deputy co-ordinating agent and in effect in senior management, he shouted in rage. I happened to be stationed in the office adjacent to his and there was just the four inch thin walls separating us. I heard the rage and the foul language and the manner in which he treated his three senior managers. He said, 'I don't care how good he is and I know how good he is but I do not want a coloured man working in this position' and that I should be put back to work on site. David Carpenter, the appointed co-odinating agent, was furious. There was a furious argument over this. Turner would not give in. After the argument the co-ordinating agent came over to my office and he said, 'Alex, I guess you heard what went on. He will not have you in this position. I'm sorry and I will resign.' He did so shortly afterwards.

I thought about it, and at the time I'd never really had to apply for a job – everybody knew everyone in the construction industry and even when Frank Turner left Cubitts the first time, he took a file of everybody he wanted with him and whenever the jobs came up they headhunted whoever they wanted and tried to bring them along. So the good and diligent guys were always headhunted. I was always asked by the chief engineer Robert Barlow, who was responsible for the design office, and who got a brown envelope when Cubitts made staff redundant, to join his new team. He became a chief design engineer for Sir Lindsay Parkinson. Several

240

times since then he had phoned me and asked me to come and work with him. But I wasn't ready to sit in an office and do designs at the time. The work I was doing was much more exciting. But I sat in my office the day after that earlier incident and I picked up the phone and I called Bob Barlow and I asked him if that job was still open. He said, 'How much do you want?' and we agreed a salary and I gave my resignation in and that's how I left Cubitts for the last time.

My work with Sir Lindsay Parkinson was wide and interesting. I carried out temporary work designs from the head office for projects I never even visited. Projects in Mombasa, Kenya, and Cookstown in Ireland. We employed a new technique there for planning which is the critical path method. That method enabled us to pinpoint the critical activities on the job and programme the job much more effectively. It is still used quite a lot today and has proved to be a revolutionary method of programming and planning.

At this time our eldest son was about ten years old and attending the local primary school at Woodend, Greenford. I attended the parents/teachers discussion which is normally about progress and assessment of your children. I was informed by the white teacher that there was a difference between the black and white students and that there was little hope of the black students making any academic achievements. Therefore I should not expect too much from them. I informed her that I came to discuss positive ways of helping my son and to identify any area which needed developing. I was not prepared to listen to her racist and biased views. She began weeping and in a short time the headmaster appeared and asked what was the matter. I explained to him what had happened. He apologised and said that she was young and inexperienced. When I got home that night I informed Curl what had happened and we immediately decided to send both our children to a private school for their education. Today my eldest son has obtained a Master's Degree in Hospital Business Administration and is the head of a department in one of New York's hospitals. Adrian, our second son obtained a diploma in Interior Design.

To continue with my work experience, I was introduced to Higgs

& Hill by the late Oswald Gibbs, High Commissioner for Grenada. Higgs & Hill were trying to build a Caribbean division and appointed me as their senior planning engineer but the Caribbean projects never materialised. In the end I accepted a more challenging post as senior planning engineer for the London area from George Wimpey & Company. My duties were to prepare programmes, monitor and report progress of contracts, provide method statements, ensure adequate safety devices were used on site, select the appropriate plant and tower cranes for the construction of several multi-storey office blocks. I did the planning and programming for several other blocks of flats and medical institutions, like the Raine Institute.

I wanted to start my own business. So I carried out private work, programming and planning for several small contractors, designing extensions and flat conversions and did a little property development for myself. By 1979 I'd won a £24,000 contract and resigned from Wimpey's to see it through. I obtained work for my company mainly from housing associations and hospitals. The tenders from housing associations were mainly issued to my company through the influence of black development officers working in these organisations. Usually the tenders would cease after black development officers left the organisation. Work from hospitals and other organisations, even private extensions, were awarded to my company through my golfing associates.

This takes me to my hobbies. One of which is obviously golf and, for the first time in my life, I'm a true fan of someone, Mr Tiger Woods, the most talented and the number one golfer in the world today. Golf has a special fascination for me. It's a game that depicts, to me, a similarity to life. The ball is always at rest before it is struck and therefore goes only where it is directed by you. That's similar to each decision one makes in life, where the ball comes to rest after what could be in accordance with your wishes. But if it's not or in trouble, one's main concern is to get out of trouble and not to focus on one's ultimate goal, the hole on the green. This compares to sickness or other severe difficulties in life, when one ceases to focus one one's ambitions in order to concentrate on overcoming the most pressing problem. The little tap in putt which requires no skill is equivalent to the long difficult stroke which requires enormous skill. This equates in life to the people who must work hard to achieve whilst others achieve by inheritance or luck. This is why I think golf has a great similarity to life.

Recently, though, I was involved in the development of a project known as the Caribbean Heritage Centre 2000. The concept and vision of this project is of Alex Pascall OBE, Joyce Rennie Pascall, his wife, and Keith Yeomans. If this project comes to fruition in accordance with its vision, it will offer a unique opportunity to develop a national focus for the contribution made to the United Kingdom and the world by black people and, in particular, people from the Caribbean. The Centre will consist of a multi-media facility featuring a web-based record of diverse Caribbean materials, an archive related to the Caribbean, a lecture theatre and many other activities promoting the very best of the Caribbean contribution to British life. This Centre will help to dispel the unwelcome, stereotype image of black people in Britain and focus on the positive achievements which will be an inspiration to future generations of black citizens.

I would not be a West Indian and not love cricket. So sometimes I do a little umpiring for the local team in Brent. I have to tell you about the first match I umpired. I read up all the rules and prepared myself. I stood behind the stumps and signalled to the bowler to commence his first over. When he bowled the fourth ball and it rapped the batsman on his pad, myself and the whole fielding team appealed with hands up in the air, 'How's that umpire?!' [audience laughter].

I thank you for your kind attention. Now I don't know if anybody wants to ask anything.

John La Rose: I want to thank Alexis or Gentle for his very interesting talk. It's about an aspect of life in Britain that we have not heard much about. I think we also have to involve the architects and the engineers and the scientists in our further talks. I remember being introduced by a friend, Margaret Busby and her father, George Busby, now dead, she said, 'You must meet this Trinidadian.' I said, 'Who is he?' They said, 'His name is Amoroso. Don't you know Amoroso?'

I knew an Amoroso, a family from Trinidad from the area called San Raphael. That is the cocoa-bearing area of Trinidad. But they said, he was one of the leading embryologists. I had never heard of a leading embryologist who came from Trinidad whose name was Amoroso. Some people here may know, because he subsequently came to Trinidad and gave a lecture. We have to seek them out because, unlike the social scientists, the historians, writers, artists, we don't discover them that easily. They are at Cambridge – Amoroso was in Cambridge – or they are in some other institution. But we must discover them and bring them to our own attention. Their experiences are important to our understanding to our life with Britain and our life in Britain in the future. So I want to thank Alexis or Gentle. I would like you to ask him why he is called Gentle. Thank him very much for this contribution to the work of the George Padmore Institute. I think it is a very valuable contribution and we are very pleased that he was able to come and give us this lecture here this evening. We are now open for discussion, comments or whatever else you wish to say.

Roxy Harris: Yes, could you say a little bit more about your life as a boy in Grenada?

Alexis Rennie: As a boy in Grenada? Well, I think I'd better let Joyce tell you about that. No, but as a boy in Grenada, first of all I went to this private school in Grenville and I can remember sitting in class. I don't know, maybe I was a difficult guy, I was sitting in class and the teachers used to gather us around the board for lessons, teaching us the ABC and everything. I decided I wasn't going to stand up around the board, I was going to sit on the bench at the back. So I sat on the bench in my short pants and the head teacher, headmistress, suddenly appeared behind me. Nobody made any fuss, she saw me sitting there and came over my shoulder, she probably had the strap over her shoulder that's how she always carried it and I got two good smacks on my legs. I looked down and all I could see was that my legs were swollen and she told me, 'Get up to the front' (laughter).

Response to member of audience

Alexis Rennie: Miss Douglas, and I think she was the best thing, one of the nicest things that happened to me. Miss Douglas had a private school in the little living room of her house. There was a big box in the middle and we used to sit on this box and she used to teach us more or less individually. I really began to make strides and did well there and after I left that school I then went to the Wesleyan School, and I think I stayed in the Wesleyan School until I went to Presentation College. But you know, I can tell you all the incidents, I had a lot of fun but I was always very, very, very difficult and awkward.

I was the one who had to go and do the shopping for my mother. We didn't say 'Do the shopping' in those days, we said, 'Make message' and I mean you can really understand the significance of 'Making message'. I didn't do any shopping. When you shop, you make the choice of what you want to buy. I mean, when you get a list of the messages that you have to make, you just go and buy them and you are a messenger. So one can understand why the term 'Make message' was better used and more appropriate than 'going shopping'. But you couldn't rely on me to come back with the message for dinner or anything like that. I remember one evening coming in late after making message and I really expected to get a good thrashing. Because I used to put the message basket down with all the containers and just play football, then I would soon forget all about anything else. When the moonlight comes and nobody else wants to play, then I would remember that I got to make some message. That night it was very late I went to the rum shop and knock up Mr. Tobias whose shop was closed, because everything closed at 9.00 pm. But the lights were on and the chaps were in there knocking the rum back. After knocking on the door for Mr. Tobias, I said, 'Please could I have this?' and 'Could I have that?' And it was very pitiful. Anyway I got home a lot later than I really expected. I was very fearful and I really expected to get a good thrashing. So when I got behind the kitchen I decided to kneel down and pray (laughter). I said a little three 'Hail Marys' and I knelt there. When I eventually showed my face inside they were so pleased to see me, that they just welcomed me. So I thought that these prayers must really work (laughter). Another night I decided to try it again, and just as I was doing some prayers behind the kitchen Raydon, my eldest brother, was leaving the house and he passed behind the kitchen and there was I kneeling. And he said, 'What you doing? Praying?', and he went back inside and exclaimed, 'Mother, there he is, praying.' I got the most terrible whipping that night (laughter). So prayers never worked after that. There have been a whole lot of stories like that, until I started attending secondary school in St Georges. It was then I became a different guy. But I could tell you lots more stories, and they're all in the same sort of vein. That's why Joyce would be so pleased to relate them to you.

Brian Alleyne: I wonder if I could press you on the question of education and recruitment as regards your own profession. I was wondering if you might be able to share a few thoughts with us on the possibilities for recruiting, given the structural problems that face black people in British education, particularly young black males. I wonder what your views might be on somehow securing a supply of new recruits to a profession such as your own.

Alexis Rennie: I was particularly lucky, and in those days it might even have been even better than it is today. Because today the institutions are controlling the racism, whereas before we had prejudice, we had concerns and lack of knowledge of people of different colours and race; today it is scientific. It's done scientifically. Institutions take you in under the guise of equal opportunities, but to them an equal opportunity is having a black face at the reception, having black faces at certain levels. But if one goes further up the management structure, there are less black employees or there are, in fact, none at all at board level. Black people are mainly featured in the government institutions that have special funds allocated to address that cause. But to get into the real nuts and bolts of these professions, like I did, to get into the nuts and bolts of the construction industry and the bigger companies, and not just get into areas where we are patronised, it is still a very difficult thing. I really don't know the answer. I really do not know the answer how we can break the barriers. It is left completely with our own resolve. Day by day, we have a stereotype thinking in this country and almost everything that happens, everything that's addressed with regards to black people makes it more difficult for us, in my opinion. For instance when the statement was made by Mr. Condon that 80 per cent of the muggers in London are black, it matters not whether the statistics mean eight out of ten are black. By making the statement alone leaves the feeling that 80 per cent of black people are muggers, and that automatically sets you back a long, long way to achieving and to being recognised in the manner that we should be recognised. And these are the kinds of obstacles we face, because confidence is lost, confidence is eroded and we have to build again after all the things we've done. So I believe the first thing we have to do is get rid of the stereotype thinking and that is the reason why projects like the Caribbean Heritage 2000 are paramount. Because it focuses on the positive contribution and it can help to break down that sort of stereotype thinking.

Having said all that, young engineers can always get in on the ground floor. You can always get in once you have the qualifications. Once you have the degrees, you can get in on the sites and work, and try to work your way up. But what might be better is once you've got the experience, you can do like I did to a certain extent and create your own business or be a consultant, if you can find and you can convince a bank with courage to back you, to develop in that manner. As needs change the demands in the industry change e.g. ordinary construction contracts are now changed to 'design and build' contracts, rather than just build contracts. If you are going to design and build you're going to need much bigger working capital and therefore you need a bigger banking facility. You need a bank to support you. In order to address that problem people of similar interests need to put resources together. The Indians have that off pat, and we should take a leaf from the Indian culture. To try and work together, put our resources together to enhance our position, to acquire the working capital to be able to develop the business and to be able to compete in the industry. I think that is the way we have to go.

John Weiss: I had been going to ask you a question earlier which was stimulated by Mr. Alleyne's question. We do have to face the English habit of stereotyping, but it's a serious mistake to restrict our vision just to black stereotypes. I fought for many years to help get established women's position in the construction industry. Now, I wonder how many women you encounter of whatever colour in your part of the building industry? And, if we are to do any encouraging, if we are to try to reduce the stereotyping, we certainly shouldn't just be talking about black males. We should be talking about black females as well, should they want to go into civil engineering and construction.

Alexis Rennie: I know a lot of black women in civil engineering and in the construction industry. Perhaps you will forgive me. When I talk of man, I mean women and men, and perhaps one should get out of the habit of talking about man. But when I talk man I mean woman too.

John Weiss: I guessed so. Could I ask a much more light-hearted question, please? Which was my original one. Deans Brook viaduct was part of my playground when I was little – and your story of staying out late and playing late – well, I used to play out late underneath Deans Brook viaduct, but I do recall that I was tremendously excited by the grandeur, that's to say of the railway viaduct, which was really one of the earliest in Britain. I think it was partly that, that led me into architecture, it was a very exciting place. Now, in laying out all these works before they were built, you must have faced quite a lot of dangers. There must have been lots of very difficult terrain for you to lay out your lines across. Was there anything especially exciting in your experiences?

Alexis Rennie: Well I will tell you how I did that. This is a very interesting question, because there was a little bit of a mystery about it. When I was sent there it was all, as you say, it was forest. The only part that was clear was the railway line. The railway was going straight through all the bushes. Normally, to ensure that the points I had to establish were correct, I had to do a complete traverse, a closed survey to make sure that my points were in the right place. In order to do that I have to go through all the bushes and everything else. Not like in Grenada where you have cutlass men to clear the whole thing for you. The guys here were just not interested in that. So I had to think of a different way of doing that. So from the very beginning I studied the information that I had for the layout of the motorway, and I realised that, to a certain extent, a long line was reasonably parallel to the railway track. I took an offset from the parapet of Deans Brook viaduct and dropped it down on to the railway track and I used the railway track itself as my line of measurement. I actually measured along the railway track and then offset the whole thing back into the bushes at the other end. So I got rid of all the difficulties and all the troubles by measuring along the railway track.

John Weiss: And you had to have the timetable in your hand to avoid that particular danger?

Alexis Rennie: Well, I didn't, but we had a few guys watching out for us, that's all (laughter). The interesting thing about that was we started from the middle of Deans Brook viaduct down to Scratchwood bridge. When I got to the point that I had to establish – the actual centre point of Scratchwood bridge – there was a stick concreted right next to the one that I was establishing. As a matter of fact it was in the way, but I looked at it and I thought it looks a bit interesting. So I thought somebody might have had this there for some other reason, I better not knock it away. I actually kept it in position, it was ten inches away from the one I established. I later learned that it was one of the points of the consultants who had to check my work. They had one point at Mill Hill station – the beginning – and another point at the end – the centre of Scratchwood Bridge – to check my work and that was the point they established. If I landed on that point then everything was OK. I was ten inches away and when they came and they saw my point, they knocked theirs away and kept mine. So that's how we overcame all the difficulties and the difficult terrain in that area. But it was good, it was great fun working there.

Member of the audience: What scope is there for young people to get that sort of practical experience, which took you right through your career? I think you had more practical experience in Grenada than any exams and that brought you here. What scope is there for young people here to have that sort of experience, given that when you go to university here you do a degree but you don't get that good experience like that? You come out and then you go into these firms.

Alexis Rennie: Well, that was the whole problem and that is why, when I was made section engineer looking after the Deans Brook viaduct and the Scratchwood bridge, I was given those two specifically to build and then I was the engineer in charge of that. I had about four chaps from university, you know green guys who just came straight from university, who I was actually told to take under my wing and help them. So this is the point I'm making. The only thing one can do is, once you come out of university, you have to just grin and bear it, and be prepared to work for small salaries, a pittance, to be able to get your experience. And today of course the instruments are all different, you can do a lot of computerised work with theodolites and the geodeometers and all these instruments. I wouldn't have half the problems today as I had then, if I had had those instruments. Because I would get all those distances electronically. So the fun really is taken out of it and it's all done from the computerised set-up. The practical experience is basically you have to know what you are doing and the risk is also reduced. So you probably don't need the extent of practical experience today as I had at the time. Except of course your concept, your knowledge and your approach to solving the problems is fundamental and that never changes.

Akua Rugg: I work in Lambeth College, a further education college in Brixton and one of our sites, our campuses, is called the Vauxhall College of Building, which I understand has an international reputation for training people for building works. Now, just recently there have been a number of cuts and not just on the arts side, but I understand they have just sacked all the really technically skilled people, like they used to have, say, a lot of carpenters. So they decided that these people are too expensive and so they've now all been got rid of.

Now, I was just wondering, for example, if there are young people and, of course, because of the area in which it's in there are young black people working in the construction business – and you said you didn't want to go much into the philosophical side – so on the practical experience side, would you as head of your company be willing to have a sort of scheme where, say, young people might come and shadow people in your company, or get work experience? And it might not be technical people, it might be someone who wants to work in an office. And I think that for a lot of black people we have to work on an abstract basis, if we want to imagine we could be something. Whereas for a lot of young white people, they don't actually have to imagine that, because they can see, if you like, a living architect or a living doctor or whatever. And I think that it's very difficult for people to work in this abstract way. And if they see people actually going about their business, then it's much easier. I mean, I'm an arts person but I remember at school I hated maths, because the maths teacher and the science teacher were so frightening, but you are a genial, accessible sort of human person. I'm sure that, you know, if my introduction to science had been with somebody like you – a sort of human person – I might have been more inspired to go into some kind of scientific business. And what I'm always telling young people these days, as Linton Kwesi Johnson, one of the people who works with us, says, 'This is the age of science and technology,' and he was an arts person. I always say to people, you know, you must be OK for the 21st century, you must get onto a scientific basis. And I just wondered if black people who have got businesses and that kind of thing, would be willing to assist in an educational way, with the lack of colleges?

Alexis Rennie: Well, I have no doubt at all that this is the case, but this is part of our problem. Now the difference is that most of black businesses are relatively small businesses. And the large businesses, the corporations, they can afford anything that they want to do. The burden that the black businesses have because they are small is that there is an awful lot of involvement from government, for instance, health and safety on sites, especially in the construction industry. That is a complete overhead, you get nothing for it, but it is a lot of money that has to be laid out to address health and safety. When I came to England and I was working on the projects, I was actually trained in first aid as engineer on site, to administer first aid and that was the beginning and end of the health and safety aspects at the time. On one of the jobs we actually had a fatality. A chap, driving a tractor on the dew in the morning, braked, but he didn't stop and he went over the cliff and he died. Now these days this would never happen because the health and safety legislation, you know, is so onerous, but so costly, that only the large companies can really cope with it. Now, if you are a small company and you are trying to survive and you have the added problems of bank problems and overdraft problems and cash flow problems and everything else, as much as you would like to help, the more people you bring into your organisation the greater the risks, and you are faced with the same onerous problems. So though the will is there and the assistance is there it's very, very limited and very, very controlled. So you could only go so far as your pocket would allow you, because you have to meet all the stringent legislation to stay in business or you will be completely out of it, or you will be faced with some serious liabilities. So this is the difference between the white corporation, which has the capital, and all the facilities in order to deal with that. Whereas we are working very, very hard and we have a lot more people that depend on us to help them without the capital. So that is what you have to always look at when there is a black company that's trying to survive or surviving or apparently doing reasonably well. Don't give it too much of a burden. Because we have so many to help that we probably will never make any progress if we try to be too benevolent to everyone around us.

Allister Bain: I'd like to say congratulations, I didn't know all the history, but I got it right. A friend of mine once said, 'Ability first, luck second and staying power, right?' You've proven that you have the staying power, now you've gone on to the Caribbean Heritage building. I know a lot of work has gone into this particular project. I know a little about it, but how many of us here know what's happening and how many of us would want that building? Is it possible to give in two or three sentences what it is all about, and what we have to gain by having a Caribbean Heritage building in this country? Because I know a lot of hard work is done by a few, but the many should give energy, either money – wise or help – wise. Could you just give us a brief outline?

Alexis Rennie: Thank you for the concern about the Caribbean Heritage Centre but, as you know, the Caribbean Heritage Centre is a vision which is being developed and all I can say about that is more or less what I've already said. If that project is developed in accordance with the vision, it will be a beacon to the black people in this country, and in particular Caribbean people. It is envisaged that the centre will contain all the things I mentioned and lots more. And if that comes to fruition every one of us will be inspired by it and in particular the younger black citizens. Basically that's all I can say about the Caribbean Heritage Centre until it's developed further.

Harry Goulbourne: Given your experience and the longevity of that experience, I was wondering what your reflections on that would be. What is there that enables us to blaze the trail, to achieve, but it remains largely at an individual level? In terms of your work, your own application, I just wonder how many others like you are there, either of your generation or of subsequent generations?

Alexis Rennie: I think I know what you mean. I always think the short answer I can give to that is that the reason why whatever achievement is kept to an individual level is purely a matter of finance. We are concerned in the same way as three generations back when my grandfather was born just at the end of slavery, when the most important thing for him to do was to try to survive and take advantage of the new-found freedom. And the fact that he was still being exploited, the fact that he was still working for nothing and he had to create his own income from the work he did and the estate owners got their estate developed because of it. Now, he had to take from that something which he can develop and which he can bring forward and have a legacy for his own children to develop from. In the same way we are very much in the same sort of situation. We haven't got the resources so we've got to take just what we have and make the best of that. Whatever we achieve is never big enough to make it an institution that other people can join in. Unless, as I said before, we can put it all together and create an institution and create something which would then make that bigger. Then it will have an impact. Unless we start thinking of sort of a co-operative action, unless we start thinking commercially in that sense, it's not going to be easy for us to have that sort of legacy to leave for those who come later. And I think, as I said before, we've seen it done in the Jewish community. They put everything they have together to build and to create a legacy for their children. We've seen it happening in the Asian community and I think we have got to put all the little things we have together to make it stronger. And unless we start thinking in that way, start moving in that sort of co-operative movement forward, I don't think we will be ready and have a lot. We will still be just individuals because we are individuals and that's first and foremost, but we as individuals have to do much more, put our resources together, not only our minds.

Nicole Moore: An easier question. Is there anyone in your family – you mention your two sons, I see in your biography that you have three children – would you have any nieces or nephews that have gone into the engineering profession? Are you thinking, now that when you are ready to just take off full time, if the business will go on, if the name will go on in the hands of a family member?

Alexis Rennie: It probably will, but I am working towards sort of changing the business to a certain extent. I am working to change to a development company rather than a contracting company, which it is at the moment. As I identified, I do need to find somebody who I can merge with to be able to take on the volume of contracts and the size of contracts that really are available these days. You know, whereas previously my company was involved in converting houses into three, four flats, you know, £250,000 contracts, now it's 'design and build' and one contract is £2 million, £3 million, and you need the working capital to do it, and the only way you can do that is to again merge, to be able to cope. But, I have not in my experience met many other people that I can merge with, to try and make the company that bigger – which, as you can see, is happening all over the world. So what I've decided to do is to go back to the old traditional thing and do property development, and basically I would prefer to do that in Grenada, rather than England. I mean I've done it here, but I would prefer to concentrate and develop it back there.

Member of the audience: The points you are talking about as a contracting company and the problems you face in having to look at 'design and build' if you want to take advantage of the jobs that are available. Now I understand that because, as a Development Officer working for a provider council, my responsibility is to co-ordinate the activities of diverse specialists, architects, engineers and so forth, for example on major regeneration contracts. And also to make an input in the continuing process that local councils have. And it's very much a closed shop, very difficult for a small company like yours to break through. Have you considered the possibility of, as you mentioned, servicing other companies with your skills as a consultant engineer, whereby a job is offered to a firm of architects, for example, where specialist engineering skills are required for a project, and they would bring you in as part of the team to do this work, because it's one of the things that I come across? For example, we have a company working on a £60 million regeneration project. One of the companies has to take on more than one architect, and they have to make use of a diverse range of skills, engineers – apart from civil they have structural engineers – and they bring these people on as part of the team. So it takes away the need for you to go to the bank, to get large sums of money from the bank to work on your own, so to speak, because you are not taking the financial responsibility. You are responsible to this first line of contract architects and you just bring your specialist knowledge to bear on the project. Can you not do that?

Alexis Rennie: Yeah, I am willing to discuss it, if you think the opportunities exist. What I have done is offer a project manager's skills to various companies and that way you act mainly as a consultant. But I'd be quite happy to talk to you about that and to see how that can evolve, to bring others on board, to increase the working population in our community.

John La Rose: One of the things I know from my own prior experience in the Caribbean, because I was a top executive in one of the biggest companies, in the Caribbean, Colonial Life Insurance Company, for about seven years. I worked directly with the founder of the company. One of the things I knew was that the question of commercial law and the implications of commercial law are important and there are very few lawyers in England who are black, who are not criminal lawyers. Most are criminal lawyers and therefore not commercial lawyers. And therefore if a small business of £2 million or £3 million for that matter, needs legal advice, they

256

don't turn to that kind of person or that kind of accountant for that matter, because they don't have that kind of experience, or they don't commit themselves to that kind of experience. I want to hear from the young solicitors here like Yvonne Brown of Yvonne Brown Associates, tell us something about that.

Yvonne Brown: I mean, there are solicitors who are going into commercial companies now. I think it's about where the opportunities are, once you have gained your qualification. You have to go where the work is. And that is why you tend to find solicitors moving into social welfare law, because that is where they can earn their living. You can, and there are many black lawyers working in the West End, and I've worked in the West End. But if you want to progress and to extend your wings, you may not be able to do that whilst you remain in the City or the West End. And that's why people may then move back or move out into those other areas. But there are a number of black solicitors now who are doing that work, who are setting up those firms, but they don't make themselves known perhaps in the way that they should. I mean, there's a new directory out called UK Black Links and there are a number of black firms in there who advertise. One should always, as people have done in the past, go on recommendations, and that is always the best way. But there are a number of them out there and they just have to be sought out, in the same way that people like Mr. Rennie have to be sought out.

Mr Lascalles: I have a couple of observations and also questions. I'm quite interested to know why you've actually decided to change your business strategy. I've been involved in a number of management consultancy practices in the past and there are echoes in terms of what you say, in terms of getting work at the mercy of black officers or people who can actually empathise with where you are actually coming from. Now is it that you reached a point in terms of business growth where, in order to get more contracts, you haven't got the linkage capacity within the kind of contracting firms of contracting companies? Or is it more that you've decided that, in order to take your company where you want to go, you have to go outside first in order to come in? Let me give you an example of that. I've recently moved into semi-retirement. Now in developing my consultancy company here, I reached a point where I could get a £200,000 contract. That was fine, but if I wanted to get a £500,000 or a £1.3 million contract, you know, there were problems. So what I had to do was to go into other countries, Russia, Eastern Europe as well as Africa. Specifically for example, we were responsible for putting together the first commercial television station business plan and equity structure for South Africa. We took on the Murdochs, Kerry Packers of this world and won. Now within the UK context, there is no way that the broadcasting institutions would look at us as a company. But it was only then in terms of already taking that piece of work and coming back here that, picking up the phone, the BBC would phone through and say, 'Listen if you do this' or NTL would phone through and say 'Listen, you know, we're looking at some new transmitters etc., etc. could you be a partner with us in that?' So specifically my question is why did you arrive at the business strategy you seem to be advocating at the moment? Is it a question of giving up, because you can't reach any further or is it the kind of early growth of wider business initiatives?

Alexis Rennie: No. Frankly it's personal. I spent the first 20 years of my life in Grenada and I was educated in Grenada. And I've been here since 1961 and at different stages of my life I had certain things that I wanted to do. And really my calling and my concerns are to make some other contribution to Grenada, rather than England. And that is the reason why I am more inclined to divert my attention to the development of Grenada, before it's too late. That's basically the reason. That's the way I feel, that I will get better satisfaction.

John La Rose: I want to take up the point you've just made. It's absolutely important because all business, really, in effect is international. People don't conceive it that way. But, for example, we started New Beacon Books, which is downstairs at this place here. We started as a company which related to books being sold anywhere in the world as Caribbean specialists. And we did a catalogue, which at that time was absolutely unheard of, because nobody yet had done it, in English, French, Spanish – I didn't know Dutch, and that's why it wasn't in Dutch. Because those are the four languages of the Caribbean. Now it meant that people all over the world were interested in what we were doing. They ordered, they came, they visited, they spoke to us, we spoke to them. We were absolutely thrilled by all of this that's happening. And I understand what you have just said, the idea that you have to stick to Britain is really a very parochial and narrow-minded idea.

I give you another example of that. There was a youngster came from Tobago. His father's name was Phillips, it's a well-known Tobago name. He came and stayed with us at my house in London. He was very bright. He had been to secondary school in Trinidad, he had done the usual school certificate, O levels and so on, and he wanted to go to university. So he was doing his A levels here with the intention of going to university, because in those days you didn't have to pay to go to university in England. So that's what he was doing. So he got his A levels but couldn't get admission for what he wanted to study in any of the English universities. So I turned to him one day and I said, 'Listen, why are you continuing to worry about British universities? There are other universities in Europe, try the Sorbonne.' Yes I told him that. I said, 'Try the Sorbonne, I know the situation in France fairly well, I know how it works, try the Sorbonne.' And he wrote to the Sorbonne and he was admitted and did his usual course of Civilisation Francaise, he had to do about six months of that first. And then he did his degree in philosophy and so on and he became a philosopher, and taught at universities in Africa and the United States.

But the whole point is the parochial, narrow-mindedness should be broken. Take a person like Althea McNish, who we had before. Althea started at the Royal College of Art (RCA), but she's everywhere in the world. She's an international figure and her work is accepted everywhere in the world. Especially now that we are in the European Union, that should be our idea. This idea, you have to learn only English, because English is what the world knows and they don't speak German or Dutch or French or Spanish, that's nonsense. We've got to break out of that and break out of the shackles of that. And at the same time too, I go along with what you said. You know, it is a fact that other people accepting you from outside of Britain means that other people inside of Britain will accept you. Also in the Caribbean. New Beacon Books could not have developed in the Caribbean, in spite of all the connections I said I had. It could not have been developed in the Caribbean. Take that as a clear assertion. You talk about globalisation. We have been in globalisation since the plantation economy and before that. So this question that you are bound to be in one place, that is a nonsense. So we must get rid of those ideas. All the opportunities everywhere, wherever they present themselves, we must use those opportunities.

Member of the audience: You spoke about the Caribbean Heritage Project and your vision. Sorry I haven't heard anything about it, what sort of vision are you talking about?

John La Rose: OK. I would like to introduce Joyce Rennie Pascall. She is one of the founders of the project, along with Alex Pascall and Keith Yeomans.

Joyce Rennie Pascall: This is a project that we have, myself, Alex and Keith and a few others. Keith is an English producer who worked with Alex for years and he also had this idea about setting up a centre for Caribbean people. This project is, we call it Caribbean Heritage and it is not only for, it is about the Caribbean. It is all the Caribbean people because we are a multiplicity of races in the Caribbean. So it is about the white, the black, the Indian and it is truly Caribbean. But it is about the Caribbean here and life experiences of Caribbeans here in Britain. We put a bid into the Millennium Commission and it is a £20 million project. We have to raise matching funds. They like the idea and have given us an unconditional offer for £8.75 million. They will ratify that if we get the funds. We should start building this project in the year 2000. We lay the cornerstone and it should be finished just in the year 2001/2002. It is a five-storey building, with everything that you could imagine in it. But what it is, it's about the art, the heritage. We want it to be something that black people, Caribbean and Africans, could see as something that they could go to and find out about their heritage. They can work there, they can have art, archives. Alex has one of the biggest black archives in this country, because of his radio programme, and it is about 50 years of the black, African and Caribbean presence in Britain. And that is one of the centrepieces of this project. So we have research library facilities, archives, innovations, inventions. We want to have workshops to provide spaces for young people. It's on Wednesday that the Millennium will make up their minds about whether they will give us this £8.75 million. But if they don't our project will still go ahead, because it has to happen.

John La Rose: It is good to see a black development officer here. I remember one of the things that Alexis said was that they got fare from black develpoment officers in the councils. That has happened with lots of other professions besides building. And the fact that the councils now have people that are black development officers is itself a tremendous step forward, compared with the past. Because, when I came to England, there wasn't anything like that in councils. And it's true we fought lots of battles and I think one of the essential big differences was the government's decision in 1981, the Conservative Party, when the New Cross Massacre occurred as well as the Black People's Day of Action on 2nd March 1981, with 20,000 people in the street for eight hours, forced certain kinds of settlements and changes which weren't there before. And that has made a lot of difference, but it can't make the only difference. What you've got to say is that people like Dr. David Pitt made a very important contribution. He was the first black head of the British Medical Association (BMA). That's historic, but there aren't many black surgeries with several doctors. That's the point that you are making. That's the point that Harry Goulbourne was making. And there aren't many institutions of that kind. You have to build institutions.

Institutions means co-operative effort and commitment and also disappointments. Because I have known several attempts to build black and Caribbean banks in London, all of which failed even though there are lots of people who committed themselves to it, and money was lost by people who wanted to see black banks in Britain, but they did not develop. But OK, that's part of building. Failures is part of building. We learn from failures as we've learned from successes and, in my view, if you don't build investment institutions of the kind you are talking about this evening, it means that the capacity to do some of the things we are talking about is not there for it to be done. So building investment institutions which can provide capital, which can provide investment innovations with capital. Bill Gates went to Harvard. Harvard is capital. It's billions of pounds and therefore it is research institutions like Harvard and MIT which went into the new computer world. But the point about all of that is that, if those institutions are not built, we do not have the necessary kinds of developments and it is important to attempt to do it. You won't always succeed, but you must have the idea and the vision that it can be done that you'll make the effort and the commitment to do it.

I welcome what Mr. Lascalles said because it is important that those discussions continue to take place as part of the process of change. 'Changing Britannia', so far as we are concerned, means our interventions in the changes which are significant and vital and crucial for ourselves and for the society as a whole. This is what the George Padmore Institute, as an institution with the various people who are here and who have helped to build and are helping to build it, will be attempting to do in the years to come. We are very grateful for all the co-operative commitment we have got, without which we could not have been here this evening. And, last of all, a special round of applause to Alexis Rennie, the man who has given us this special contribution tonight.

Alexis Rennie

Alexis Rennie is an experienced building contractor and civil engineer, who has worked on a large number of major projects. He is currently the managing director of his own company, Rennie Building Contracts Ltd.

Alexis Rennie was born in Grenada in 1939. He went to school there, attending Presentation Boys College. He wanted to become a civil engineer but at that time there were no colleges in Grenada which taught that subject. He had to follow a correspondence course in cadastral surveying and mapping while at the same time gaining practical experience working with a surveyor.

In 1955 there had been a heavy storm in Grenada which had demolished the pier in St George's, the island's capital. Three years later in 1958 Holland Hannen & Cubitts, an English construction company, were contracted to rebuild that pier. Rennie's passion for civil engineering led him to seek employment with them. He succeeded in getting a job and worked as an assistant site engineer, where he was responsible for setting out the works. This included reclaiming lands, steel sheet piling, erection of structural steelwork transit and banana sheds and other port services buildings and infrastructure. At the end of that contract Holland Hannen & Cubitts encouraged him to come to England to pursue his studies in civil engineering and they offered him employment in the UK.

Alexis Rennie took up the offer and moved to London in 1961. His skills in surveying and mapping were invaluable on construction sites on which he was employed, being able to set out sea defence walls, roads, bridges, water treatment works etc. In 1963 he was given the responsibility for establishing the base lines of the bridges that brought the Ml into London – the Scratchwood Bridge, Deansbrook Viaduct, the Edgware Road, Mill Hill and Salvage Lane Bridges. He was afterwards employed as site engineer on that contract for its duration. At the same time he attended day release courses at Westminster Technical College where he obtained his Higher National Certificate in Civil Engineering.

Alexis Rennie later played a major role in the construction of the £30 million Thamesmead housing development project, one of the largest of its kind in the country at the time. There he had to supervise and co-ordinate the work of the site engineers and to plan and co-ordinate the work carried out by the building and civil engineering departments.

In order to broaden his experience, between 1969 and 1979 he worked as a senior planning engineer with a number of major construction companies, including Lindsay Parkinson, Higgs & Hill and Wimpey, on a variety of projects such as multi-storey office blocks, flats and motorway construction.

In 1979 Alexis Rennie set up his own company – Rennie Building Contracts Ltd – of which he is the chairman and managing director. His company specialises in modifications and alterations to hospitals, commercial and residential properties and listed buildings and also carries out general building construction in the Greater London area. In particular they have worked on refurbishing large and small Victorian houses in the London area including flat conversions for a number of housing trusts. The responsibility of the company includes pricing tenders, liaising with clients and site managers throughout the life of the contracts, planning, programming, method statements, managing and organising the handover of sites, employing and supervising subcontractors, service engineers, labour, roofers and so on.

Alexis Rennie has a number of interests outside his engineering and building activities. He has assisted with a number of charitable trusts including the Lord Pitt Foundation and the Caribbean Heritage Centre 2000 Project. In 1998, as part of Black History Month celebrations, he lectured to year eleven pupils at the Cardinal Wiseman School in Greenford. His aim was to share his experiences and to help generate confidence in the school leavers and to assure them that they could achieve in their chosen occupation.

He is a keen golfer and is a full member of the Ealing Golf Club where he has served on two captains committees. He co-founded the Afro-Caribbean Golf Society in 1993 and is a member of several other golfing societies including being a committee member of the Westminster Clergy Golf Society.

Alexis Rennie is married with three grown up children.

Biographical notes

Adams, Geoffrey Former Director, Chartered Society of Designers. Consultant on design copyright.

Adams, Grantley (1898-1971) Leader of organised labour in Barbados (1940s and early 1950s). Founder of Barbados Labour Party. First and only Prime Minister of the West Indies Federation (1958-62). First Prime Minister of Barbados.

Aggrey, J.E.K. (Aggrey of Africa) (1875-1927) Born in Anamabu, Gold Coast (now Ghana). African intellectual, educator and missionary.

Albee, Edward b.1928. Award-winning American playwright.

Ali, Muhammed b.1942 as Cassius Marcellus Clay. World heavyweight champion boxer. Brought into the Nation of Islam by Malcolm X and given name Muhammed Ali. Ended career with 56 wins and five defeats.

Ali, Tariq b.1943 in Pakistan. Writer, journalist, political and cultural activist in Britain.

Alladin, M.P. (1919-80) Trinidadian painter.

Allen, Woody b.1935. American actor, director and comedian. One of the most prolific film directors of his generation.

Almandoz, Mildred American painter.

Althusser, Louis Pierre (1918-90) French Marxist philosopher born in Algeria who studied, lived and taught in Paris.

Amazulu Predominantly female ska band with a number of UK hit singles in the mid-1980s.

Amos, Valerie b.1954 in Guyana. Served in Tony Blair's Labour government as Leader of the House of Lords and in the Cabinet.

Andrew, Hewlette Born Dominica. Teacher and Methodist minister in London. Founder of the Queen Mother Moore Supplementary School.

Andrews, Maurice Born Jamaica. Lawyer in Birmingham, UK.

Annan, Kofi b.1938 in Kumasi, Ghana. Studied in Ghana and USA. Joined United Nations 1962 and was the seventh Secretary-General, serving from 1997-2007.

Aquinas, Saint Thomas (c.1225-74) Italian Roman Catholic philosopher and theologian.

Arnold, Elaine Born Trinidad. Social worker now residing in the UK.

Ascher, Zika (Zigmund) George (1910-92) Textile producer, Czechoslovakia and UK.

Atteck, Sybil (1911-75) Trinidadian painter.

Augustine, Saint (354-430) One of the most important figures in the development of Western Christianity. Born in Africa, educated and baptised in Italy. His *The Confessions* is often called the first Western autobiography.

Bain, Allister b.1932 in Grenada. Came to Britain 1958. Actor. Student of Caribbean folk dance. Founder of Grenada's first professional dance troupe, the Bee Wee Ballet. Partly responsible for dance sequences in the film *Island in the Sun*.

Biographical Notes

Bajan, Janet Ghanaian student at Rose Bruford Drama School alongside Yvonne Brewster.

Bakewell, Joan b.1933 in Stockport, Cheshire, UK. British broadcast journalist.

Baldwin, James (1924-87) Born in Harlem, New York, USA. Writer whose work always reflected his experience as a black man in white America. Famous works include *Go Tell It On the Mountain* (1953), *Notes of a Native Son* (1955) and *The Fire Next Time* (1963).

Bananarama All-girl British pop group founded 1981who scored a number of chart-topping hits.

Barrow, Errol Walton (1920-87) Born in St Lucy, Barbados. First entered Barbados House of Assembly 1951. Took island to independence from UK in 1966 and became first Prime Minister of the newly idependent nation.

Barrow, Jocelyn b.1929 in Trinidad. Came to England 1959. Educationalist. Has served with many national and local organisations including as a governor of the BBC. Made a Dame of the British Empire in 1992.

Bartley, Janet Actress who starred in classic Jamaican film *The Harder They Come*.

Batista, Fulgencio (1901-73) Head of State in pre-revolutionary Cuba.

Beatles, The English pop group formed in Liverpool in 1960 featuring John Lennon, Paul McCartney, George Harrison and Ringo Starr. Hugely successful commercially and artistically. Groundbreaking role in history of popular music.

Beaton, Norman (1934-94) Born in Guyana. Leading black actor in Britain. Worked on stage, including at National Theatre, and on TV. Became well known through such sitcoms as *Empire Road* and *Desmonds*.

Bennett, Louise (1919-2006) Outstanding Jamaican poet, writer, performer, folklorist and broadcaster. Known particularly for her pioneering writing and performance in Jamaican creole language.

Best, Winston Born Barbados. Former teacher and currently an educational consultant in the UK. Leading member of the North London West Indian Association in its earlier years in the 1960s and 1970s.

Bindman, Geoffrey b.1933. UK solicitor and civil liberties advocate, practising since 1960. Founder of Bindman & Partners 1974. Legal adviser to Race Relations Board (1966-76) and Commission for Racial Equality (1976-83).

Binns, Graham Chief Executive Officer of Radio Jamaica in 1960s. Husband of Gillian Binns.

Birkett, Lord b.1929. Former Director of Recreation and Arts for the Greater London Council.

Blair, Tony b.1953 in Edinburgh, Scotland. Barrister by profession. British Labour Party Prime Minister 1997-2007.

Boateng, Paul Born in Ghana. Came to Britain as a child in 1966 after fall of Nkrumah. Barrister. Labour MP 1987-2005. Currently UK High

266

Biographical Notes

Commissioner to South Africa.

'Bob and Marcia' – Bob Andy and Marcia Griffiths Well known Jamaican reggae vocalists. Famous for their hit recording in 1970 of the civil rights anthem 'Young, Gifted and Black', written by Nina Simone. Marcia Griffiths went on to become one of Bob Marley's backing vocalists the I-Threes.

Booker T. and the MGs US group of two black and two white musicians. Featuring Booker T. Jones (keyboards), along with Donald 'Duck' Dunn, Steve Cropper and Al Jackson. Came to prominence in 1960s on Stax record label. Recorded the international smash hit instrumental 'Green Onions' (1962). Also known for the 'Memphis Sound' and their work with artists like Otis Redding.

Boomtown Rats, The Irish Punk rock/New Wave band. Recorded a number of hits 1975-86. Led by Bob Geldof.

Boothe, Ken b.1948 in Kingston, Jamaica. Well-known reggae singer since 1963. Best known record 'Everything I Own' topped UK chart 1974.

Bowie, David b.1947 as David Robert Jones in Brixton, London, UK. International musician, performer and songwriter since 1960s.

Bowlby, Bishop Ronnie b.1926. Bishop of Southwark 1981-91.

Branson, Richard b.1950. Entrepreneur. Founder of Virgin record shop (1970) and Virgin music record label (1973). Awarded knighthood (1999).

Brathwaite, Kamau (Eddie) b.1930 in Barbados. Distinguished Caribbean poet, literary critic and historian. Worked at University of the West Indies in Jamaica (1970s-80s). Currently a Professor at the City University, New York. Co-founder of the Caribbean Artists Movement in 1966.

Brodber, Erna b.1940 in Jamaica. Historical sociologist and writer. Works include acclaimed novels *Jane and Louisa Will Soon Come Home*, *Myal*, *Louisiana*, *The Rainmaker's Mistake*; and the essay collection *The Continent of Black Consciousness*. Runs own research and study project 'Black Space' in home village of Woodside, Jamaica.

Brown, Bini Born in Jamaica. Birmingham based community activist.

Brown Sugar South London lovers rock trio. Included Caron Wheeler, who went on to sing with Soul II Soul.

Bruford, Rose (1904-83). Set up own drama school in 1950 based in Kent, UK.

Bullins, Ed b.1935. African American playwright. Active in Britain in 1960s when his play *The Electronic Nigger* was performed at London's first lunchtime theatre venue, the Ambience in Queensway. Returned to the USA and became part of the Lafayette Theatre movement with Leroi Jones (now Amiri Baraka).

Burke, Revd Eddie (1909-2000) Father of psychiatrist and George Padmore Institute trustee Aggrey Burke. Worked on community development for the United Nations in Ethiopia and Zambia. Author of *Water in the Gourd and other Jamaican Folktales* and *Newsy Waps*, a series of six books on Jamaican folklore.

Biographical Notes

Burning Spear b.1948 as Winston Rodney in Jamaica. Reggae singer since 1969. Known for his 'conscious lyrics' focusing on black culture and history, Garveyism and rasta beliefs.

Busby, George (1899-1980) Father of writer and publisher Margaret Busby. Born Barbados, grew up in Trinidad. Qualified as a doctor in Dublin, Ireland. Moved to Ghana in 1929 and worked there as a doctor.

Busby, Margaret Born in Ghana of African-Caribbean parents. Publisher, editor, writer, poet and painter. Co-founder of the publishing house Allison & Busby (1966). Compiled the major anthology *Daughters of Africa* (1992). Awarded OBE in 2006.

Cadogan, Susan b.1950s as Alison Anne Cadogan in Kingston, Jamaica. Reggae singer.

Callaghan, James (1912-2005). Born in Portsmouth, UK. Labour Prime Minister (1976-79). Became Baron Callaghan of Cardiff upon retirement.

Camara, Helda Brazilian Archbishop and liberation theologian.

Carey, Peter Manager of Camden Arts Centre, London (1966-70) then Arts Officer for Camden Council.

Carr, Andrew Trinidadian artist, educator, historian.

Cassandra UK lovers rock singer. Had hit with song 'I'll Never Let You Out of My Life' in late 1970s.

Cats, The Band formed by John Kpiaye in 1967. First UK reggae band to have a top 50 entry in the UK singles charts with their reggae/rock steady version of 'Swan Lake'.

Chalice Jamaican reggae group particularly prominent in the 1980s.

Chang, Carlisle (1921-2001) Trinidadian painter.

Chopin, Frederick (1810-49) Classical piano musician and composer. Born Warsaw, moved to Paris 1831. Seen as innovator and influential on music of many composers including Liszt, Wagner.

Clark, Elizabeth Barbadian actress and academic.

Clarke, Johnny Well known Jamican reggae singer backed by Matumbi on first UK tour in 1970s.

Cleage, Pearl b.1948 in Massachusetts, USA. Playwright, journalist, poet and novelist.

Cochrane, Kelso Born in Antigua. First recorded post-war racist murder victim in UK. Died in Notting Hill in 1959 after being attacked by six white youths. Caused huge racial tension. No one ever arrested for murder.

Cocker, Joe b.1944 in Sheffield, UK. Renowned blues/rock singer whose career dating from 1961 features numerous global hit records.

Cole, Nat King (1919-65) Born in Montgomery, Alabama, USA. Christened Nat 'King' Cole by a Los Angeles club owner (1937). Reached international acclaim as both a jazz pianist and singer of popular songs in 1950s and 1960s. Died of lung cancer.

Collins, Canon John (1905-82). Priest and political campaigner. Canon of St Paul's Cathedral, London, UK for 33 years. Activist against racial prejudice

Biographical Notes

and racial tyranny, helping to raise funds to support African National Congress in South Africa from 1950s.

Condon, Paul UK. Commissioner of London Metropolitan Police 1993-2000. Knighted 1994.

Cone, James b.1939 in Fordyce, Arkansas, USA. Influential theologian, writer, preacher and teacher, pioneer of Black Liberation Theology.

Connor-Mogotsi, Pearl (1924-2005). Born in Trinidad and came to London in 1948. First black woman to run arts/ theatre agency in the UK, representing black actors, musicians, dancers and bands. Best known for her pioneering work in the arts generally.

Cook, Captain James (1728-79) b. in North Yorkshire, UK. Explorer, navigator and cartographer who made three voyages to Pacific Ocean, accurately charting many islands and coastlines on European maps for first time, including the British 'discovery' of Australia.

Cousins, Frank b.1940. Jamaican actor and director. Started the pioneering Dark and Light Theatre company in Brixton in 1970s.

Coward, Wilfred Ruthan Proprietor, Boston (later Elite) Bus Company; Barbadian MP (1961-66).

Craig, Karl Jerry Jamaican painter and educator. Member of Caribbean Artists Movement in London in late 1960s. Former head of Jamaica School of Art.

Crawford, Jeff (1932-2003) Founding member of the West Indian Standing Conference and the North London West Indian Association.

Croll, Dona b.1959 Jamaica. Lived in London since 1964. TV, film and stage actress.

Cumper, Pat Jamaican-born playwright, novelist and writer. Author of *One Bright Child* (1998), based on the story of mother, Gloria Cumper.

Davis, Angela b.1944 in Birmingham, Alabama, USA. African American academic and political activist. Wrongfully imprisoned in 1960s because of her support for the black liberation struggle. Currently Professor at University of California, USA.

Davis Junior, Sammy (1925-90) African American singer, dancer and movie star, part of famous 'Rat Pack' with Frank Sinatra and Dean Martin.

Dekker, Desmond (1942-2006) Born in Jamaica as Desmond Dacres. Recording artist. Became internationally famous in 1960s for tongue-in-cheek stage presentation of Jamaican rude boy street style in his ska and rock steady music. Particularly known for major hit records '007 (Shanty Town)', 'The Israelites' and 'It Mek'.

Dickens, Charles (1812-70) UK. Famous English writer who achieved both popular and critical respect. His works portray social life in Victorian England, much of it derived from own experience.

Donnelly, Revd Lewis Supporter of racial equality in the UK in 1960s.

Drummond, Don (1943-1969) Admired Jamaican trombonist and black nationalist. Outstanding student at Alpha Boys' School. Was committed to Bellevue Mental Hospital after killing his common law wife in 1965.

Biographical Notes

Drummond Junior, Don b.1949. Nickname of veteran Jamaican trombonist Vin Gordon. Has accompanied most reggae stars including Bob Marley.

(Dennis Bovell) Dub Band formed by Dennis Bovell in 1980s to accompany Linton Kwesi Johnson.

Dummett, Ann UK. Campaigner for racial justice, and on matters of immigration and community relations especially in 1960s. At one time Liaisons Officer, Oxford Committee for Racial Integration. Wife of philosopher Michael Dummett.

Dummett, Michael b.1925 UK. Professor of Logic at Oxford University.Racial and social justice campaigner. Husband of Ann Dummett. Knighted 1999.

Dunbar, Sly b.1952 as Lowell Dunbar in Kingston, Jamaica. Started reggae recording career playing drums (1969). Best known for musical and production partnership with Robbie Shakespeare.

Dunkley, Errol b.1951 in Kingston, Jamaica. Reggae artist with hits in Jamaica and UK.

Durie, Sally English wife of wealthy Jamaican business man; writer of play *Lippo the New Noah*.

Dylan, Bob b.1941 as Robert Allen Zimmerman in Duluth, Minnesota, USA. Singer-songwriter, musician and poet incorporating politics, social commentary, philosophy and literary influences into work. Regarded as a landmark worldwide artist since 1960s.

Eagleton, Terry b.1943. UK. Writer, critic, academic. Professor of Cultural Theory at Manchester University.

Edwards, Herman (1925-98) Born in Antigua. Founded the Harambee organisation which worked with homeless black youth in Britain (1970s-80s). Popularly known as Brother Herman.

Ennals, David (1922-1995) Former UK Labour Government Minister.

Ernst, Cornelius Writer on theology, especially Roman Catholicism in Britain.

Evans, Deborah Singer with 1980s British pop group The Flying Lizards.

Eyre, Richard b.1943 UK. Former Artistic Director at Royal National Theatre. Knighted 1997.

Fagan, Bevin Lead singer with UK reggae band, Matumbi, in 1970s. Old school friend of Dennis Bovell. Died 2008.

Family Man (Aston Francis Barrett) b.1946 Jamaica. Bass player. One of the famous Barrett brothers in rhythm section of Bob Marley's backing band The Wailers from early 1970s.

Fanon, Frantz (1925-61). Born in Martinique. Psychiatrist. Pre-eminent 20th century thinker on the issue of decolonisation and the psychopathology of colonisation. His works including *The Wretched of the Earth* have inspired anti-colonial liberation movements for decades.

Fat Man Leader of one of the pioneering sound systems based in Tottenham area of North London. Opened record shop. Helped to found pirate radio

Biographical Notes

station RJR.

Feather, Vic (1908-76) Former British trade union leader. General Secretary of the Trades Union Congress of Great Britain 1969-73.

Fitzgerald, Ella (1917-96) Born in Newport News, Virginia, USA. African American jazz singer also known as 'Lady Ella', the 'First Lady of Song'. Gifted with three-octave vocal range, especially noted for her scat singing. Winner of 13 Grammy Awards.

Flying Lizards The UK experimental rock group of late 1970s.

Foley, Maurice (1925-2002) Former British Labour Party politician and Government Minister in Home Office responsible for immigration and race relations in 1960s.

Freddie Notes and The Rudies Reggae band of 1970s whose song 'Montego Bay' was a big hit.

French, Stanley Born St Lucia. Civil engineer and playwright.

Gad, Tony Bass player in British reggae band Aswad.

Gairy, Eric (1922-97) Born Grenada. Former union activist. First Prime Minister of Grenada. Overthrown by Maurice Bishop's New Jewel Movement in 1979.

Garvey, Marcus (1887-1940) National Hero of Jamaica. Active in Caribbean and USA. Founded the Universal Negro Improvement Association (1914) which asserted the principle of negro and African equality and due respect for the African past. His black pride and self help ideas have become influential again over the past few decades.

Gates, Bill b.1955, USA; computer scientist and businessman, founder of Microsoft computer systems.

Gaye, Angus (Drummie Zeb) b.1959. Drummer and vocalist in chart-topping British reggae band, Aswad since band started in 1975 in Westbourne Grove area of London.

Gaye, Marvin (1939-84). Born Marvin Pentz Gay Jr in Washington D.C., USA. Soul, R&B singer, arranger, multi-instrumentalist, songwriter and record producer, gaining international fame in 1960s and 1970s on Motown label. Shot and killed by father.

Geldof, Bob b.1951 in Dun Laoghaire, County Dublin, Ireland. Pop singer, songwriter and front man of The Boomtown Rats. TV company owner; political activist. Especially famous for organising with Ultravox singer Midge Ure the Band Aid charity single (1984) and the Live Aid charity concert (1985). Was also prominent in the Make Poverty History campaign in 2005.

Gibbs, Lance Born Guyana. Off spin bowler who contributed greatly to West Indian cricketing successes between 1960-76. Set a slow bowlers' record of 309 wickets in 79 tests.

Gibbs, Oswald Moxley (1928-95) High Commissioner for Grenada.

Gordon Walker, Patrick (1907-80) British Labour politician who lost seat of Smethwick in 1964 election to Conservative candidate Peter Griffiths' racist campaign.

Biographical Notes

Goulbourne, Harry b.1948 in Clarendon, Jamaica. Came to London in 1959. Academic. Currently Professor of Sociology at South Bank University, London and Director and co-founder of Race & Ethnicity Research Unit there.

Graham, Billy b.1918 USA. Evangelical Christian preacher.

Grant, Eddy b.1948 as Edmond Montague Grant in Plaisance, Guyana. Reggae recording artist and producer with a number of UK hits. Has also developed a career as a highly successful music industry enterpreneur.

Greyhound Early reggae band. Formed in London, UK, in late 1960s. Had a number of international hits during 1970s.

Griffiths, Charlie b.1938 Barbados. Feared West Indies fast bowler of 1960s.

Griffiths, Peter b.1928. Previously unknown teacher who ousted senior Labour MP Patrick Gordon-Walker from safe seat of Smethwick in 1964 general election using racist slogans. 1964-66 MP for Smethwick; 1979-97 MP for Portsmouth North.

Grimond, Jo (1913-93) Scottish Liberal politician; leader of Liberal Party 1956-67.

Hall, Peter b.1930. UK theatre, film and opera director. Founded Royal Shakespeare Company. Former Director of Royal National Theatre. Knighted 1977.

Hall, Stuart b.1932 Jamaica. Director, Centre for Cultural Studies, University of Birmingham 1972-79; Professor of Sociology, Open University 1979-98. Author of numerous books and studies. Leading cultural theorist in UK

Hall, Wes b.1937 Barbados. Fast bowler who contributed greatly to the success of West Indian cricket in 1960s. Claimed 192 wickets in 48 tests. Later managed several teams and served as a selector for the West Indian Cricket Board and as a government minister in Barbados.

Hammond, Mona b. Jamaica. Prolific TV and film actress who came to England 1959. Founding member of Talawa Arts along with Yvonne Brewster. Awarded OBE in 2005.

Hancock, Herbie b.1940. American jazz pianist, band leader and composer.

Hansberry, Lorraine (1930-65) Celebrated African American playwright and activist artist. Author of *A Raisin in the Sun*, which opened to critical and popular acclaim in 1958 and brought black audiences to professional Broadway theatre.

Harewood, David b.1965. Leading black British RADA-trained actor of stage and screen.

Harris, Dennis Jamaican. Owner of record company DIP Records in Lewisham, London. One of the early organisers of coach parties of Caribbean people to UK seaside. Committed supporter of Jamaican music. Involved in pioneering of reggae's lovers rock genre.

Harris, Roxy b.1949 UK, of Sierra Leonean parents. Lecturer at Kings College, London. Writer, campaigner for racial and social justice and trustee of the George Padmore Institute.

Haslam, Revd David Methodist Minister. Former Secretary of the Churches

Biographical Notes

Commission on Racial Justice.

Headley, Samuel R. Barbados. Uncle of Dennis Bovell. Musician who played in Barbadian band Barbara and the Rhythmeers.

Hearne, John Jamaican novelist and journalist. Author of six novels including the prize-winning *Voices Under the Window* (1955). Died 1994.

Heidegger, Martin (1889-1976) Influential German philosopher. Also controversial for his alleged support of the nazis.

Hendrix, Jimi (1942-70) born as Johnny Allen Hendrix in Seattle, Washington, Virtuoso guitarist, songwriter and cultural icon.

Henzell, Perry (1936-2006) Jamaican writer and film director, best known for the film *The Harder They Come*.

Hibbert, 'Toots' Lead singer and founder member from early 1960s with Jamaican reggae band the Maytals.

Hicks, Trevor UK. Father whose two daughters died in the Hillsborough football stadium tragedy in 1989.

Higman, Barry Historian. Author of numerous studies including *Slave Populations of the British Caribbean 1807-34* and *Slave Society in the Danish West Indies*.

Hill, Robert Academic. Son of impresario Stephen Hill.

Holder, Geoffrey b.1930. Trinidadian painter, dancer, singer and actor.

Holland, Endesha Ida Mae b.1944. African American playwright.

Holland, Merlin Grandson of writer Oscar Wilde.

Hot Chocolate UK pop band formed in 1969 in Brixton, London, led by Errol Brown. Had a huge number of chart hits, and became popular again when their tune 'You Sexy Thing' was used in the film *The Full Monty* in 1997.

Howe, Darcus b.1943 in Trinidad. Active in radical black politics in UK from 1960s. Member of Black Panther Movement, Race Today Collective (RTC) and the Alliance of the RTC with the Black Parents Movement and Black Youth Movement. Moved into mainstream media journalism in mid-1980s.

Huddleston, Bishop Trevor (1913-98) UK. English Anglican missionary, served in Tanzania and South Africa. Opponent of apartheid. Chairman of Anti-Apartheid Movement 1981-94, Chairman of the International Defence and Aid Fund for South Africa 1983-98.

Humphry, Derek b.1930 UK. Former journalist and writer. Co-author with Gus John of *Because They are Black* (1971) and *Police Power and Black People* (1972).

Hunte, Joe Wrote pamphlet entitled 'Nigger-hunting in London'(1966) about police harassment and mistreatment of black people in 1960s. Member of the West Indian Standing Conference.

In Brackets Popular UK reggae band of 1970s who played on club circuit and backed most of the live reggae performers playing in Britain.

I-Roy b.Jamaica 1949 as Roy Reid. One of the pioneering storytelling reggae DJs of 1970s.

James, C.L.R. (1901-1989) Trinidadian born writer, lecturer and influential

273

independent Marxist intellectual. Author of *The Black Jacobins, Beyond A Boundary, Minty Alley* and many other titles on history, politics and culture.

Jeffrey, Pansy Born in Guyana, moved to London. Co-founder of Berbice Co-operative Housing Association in London in 1960s.

John, Clement Born Grenada. Brother of Gus John. Youth worker, Deputy Director of Youth and Sport, Government of Grenada.

Johnson, Linton Kwesi b.1952 in Chapelton, Jamaica. Lived in UK since 1963. Reggae poet and recording artist, published first book 1974; released first album in 1977. Formed own record label, LKJ Records, in 1981.

Jones, Brian (1942-1969) UK. Guitar player and founder-member of rock band the Rolling Stones.

Jones, Claudia (1915-64) Born in Trinidad. Journalist. Active in left wing politics in USA and after expulsion from there came to Britain in 1950s. Founded pioneering *West Indian Gazette* (1958). Was a founding organiser of the Notting Hill Carnival.

Jones, Quincy b.1933. Major African American musician, arranger, record producer, composer and television executive. Well-known for his work with Michael Jackson, Frank Sinatra, Ray Charles, Johnny Mathis and other legends.

Jung, Carl (1875-1961). Influential Swiss psychiatrist and founder of analytical psychology.

Kanhai, Rohan b.1935 Guyana. Outstanding West Indies Test cricket batsman from mid 1950s -mid 1970s. Scored 28,774 runs including 83 centuries in 416 first class matches.

Kapo (1911-1989) born in Jamaica as Mallica Reynolds. Self-taught artist and sculptor whose art was heavily influenced by religious spirituality.

Kasavubu, Joseph (1917-69).Congolese nationalist who became first President of Democratic Republic of Congo (1960-65). Was involved in power struggle with Patrice Lumumba, the then premier of Congo, who was eventually assassinated.

Kay, Janet b.1958 as Janet Kay Bogle in London, UK. Lovers rock singer and actress. Biggest hit 'Silly Games' reached number two in UK charts (1979).

Keats, John (1795-1821) Born in London, UK. One of principal poets of English Romantic movement.

Kelly, Pat b.1949 Jamaica. Reggae singer – made name in the rock steady era (late 1960s), regarded as one of the great Jamaican soul voices.

Kelly, 'Tabby Cat' Roots reggae artist from Birmingham. Particularly known for his classic track 'Don't call us immigrants' (1977).

Kent, Nick b.1945 UK. Artistic director of Tricycle Theatre in London, which has staged many plays by, with and for black people.

Kerr, Fergus Born UK. Dominican friar, theologian.

Kierkegaard, Soren (1813-55) Danish philosopoher and theologian generally recognised as a key existentialist thinker.

King, Audvil b.1943 in Jamaica. Cultural activist and early dub poet. One of

274

the contributors to the *One Love* poetry collection published by Bogle L'Ouverture Publications in 1971. Emigrated to North America.

King, Ben E. b.1938. African American soul singer, front man for the Drifters. Best known for solo hit song 'Stand By Me'.

King, Martin Luther (1929-68) Historically important and iconic African American civil rights leader and Southern Baptist minister.

King Tubby (1941-1989) Brilliant sound mixing engineer who helped popularise dub from early 1970s in Kingston, Jamaica. Often worked with Lee 'Scratch' Perry amongst others.

Kirby, Alex Curate, Isle of Dogs; later Newham Liaison Officer, editor of *Race Today* 1970-73.

Kissoon, Jeffrey Trinidad-born TV and film actor who came to Brtian as a child. Has also worked with some of the major British theatre directors.

Kpiaye, John b.1948 in UK of Nigerian/ English parentage. Major producer of British lovers rock and guitarist with the Dennis Bovell Dub Band, as well as having hit with own solo album *Red Gold and Blues*.

Kuti, Fela (1938-97) Nigerian musician, singer and political critic. Created Afrobeat, a mixture of funk and jazz with traditional Yoruba music, and used it to criticise Nigerian government.

Lambert, John UK sociologist.

Lamming, George b.1927 in Barbados. Well known novelist and essayist. Lived and worked in London in 1950s and 1960s. Presently moves between the Caribbean and USA. Best known work is novel *In the Castle of my Skin*.

La Rose, John (1927-2006) Born in Trinidad. Influential political and cultural figure, active in both Trinidad and Britain, where he settled in the early 1960s. Co-founder of the Caribbean Artists Movement (1966); founder of New Beacon Books (1966); founding chairman of the George Padmore Institute.

La Rose, Keith b.1957, Trinidad. Came to UK as a child. Youth worker and cultural activist. Founder member of Peoples War Sound System and ran Peoples Music for many years.

La Rose, Michael b.1956 Trinidad. Came to UK as a child. Health and Safety Inspector. Leading cultural activist at forefront of movement to develop West Indian carnival in Britain. Founder member of Peoples War Sound System and Peoples War Carnival Band.

Laswell, Bill American musician and producer. Has worked as a producer with many important figures including Herbie Hancock.

Lawrence, Doreen Jamaican-born mother of Stephen Lawrence who was killed in infamous racist attack in London (1993). Campaigner and activist.

Lawrence, Neville Jamaican-born father of Stephen Lawrence who was killed in infamous racist attack in London (1993); campaigner and activist.

Lawrence, Stephen (1974-93) Young black student, born of Jamaican parents in London; killed in a racist attack in South London. His parents have waged a long and principled campaign ever since to bring his killers to justice.

Lee, Bunny b.1941 as Edward O'Sullivan Lee in Jamaica. Started working in record production from 1966. Changed face of Jamaican music in 1970s, breaking dominance of big producers like Clement Dodd, by using opportunities offered by new technology.

Lester, Anthony b.1936, UK. Barrister. Former trustee of Runnymede Trust. Became Baron Lester of Herne Hill (1993).

Lewis, Rupert Reader at the Department of Government, University of the West Indies, Jamaica. Authority on the Garvey Movement and also wrote an intellectual and political biography of Walter Rodney.

Lindo, George Jamaican-born factory worker living in Bradford who was wrongfully imprisoned for armed robbery in 1970s. Won a successful campaign to clear his name – he received record damages in compensation.

Livingstone, Dandy b.1944 in Kingston, Jamaica as Robert Livingstone Thompson. Responsible for many of the UK's reggae and rock steady hits in 1960s.

Livingstone, Ken b.1945 UK. Labour politician. Former leader of Greater London Council. Subsequently Mayor of London (2000-2008).

Lloyd, Clive b.1944 in Guyana. Outstanding cricketer who recorded over 7,500 runs at Test level and captained the most successful ever West Indies team 1974-85.

Lloyd, Errol b.1943 Jamaica. Artist, sculptor, writer and children's book illustrator who has lived in London since 1960s.

Lorca, Federico Garcia (1898-1936) b. Granada, Spain. Poet, dramatist, also a painter, pianist and composer.

Lord Kitchener (1922-2000). Born as Aldwyn Roberts in Arima, Trinidad. Started calypso career at age 16 and became known as one of the most famous calypsonians of 20th century. Lived in England 1947-63.

Los Bravos Spanish pop group of 1960s who sang mainly in English and who had an international hit with their song 'Black is Black'.

Lubbock, Eric b.1928 UK. Former Liberal Party MP and trustee of Runnymede Trust. Became Lord Avebury (1971).

Lumumba, Patrice (1925-61) Congolese nationalist politician. Helped form the *Mouvement National Congolais* in 1958 to challenge Belgian rule and was made first Prime Minister when Congo became independent in 1960. Murdered mysteriously with some alleging Belgian Government involvement.

Macdonald, Gary UK actor of Jamaican parentage.

Mackenzie, Fred Printer, former lecturer, London College of Printing and Graphic Arts (now part of London University of the Arts). One of the inventors of Letraset lettering system.

Macmillan, Harold (1894-1986) UK. Former Conservative Party Prime Minister (1957-63).

Macpherson, Sir William b.1927 UK. Retired High Court Judge. Well known for producing the Macpherson Report (1999) after inquiry into murder of Stephen Lawrence and subsequent mishandled police investigation.

Major, John b.1943 UK. Former Conservative Prime Minister of Britain

Biographical Notes

1990-97. Succeeded Margaret Thatcher.

Mandela, Nelson b.1918 South Africa. Former head of African National Congress and political prisoner of South African apartheid regime. Freed in 1990 and became first black President of South Africa in 1994. Retired 1999.

Mandeville, Gay Lisle Griffith Bishop in Barbados in 1950s.

Manley, Beverley Anderson Wife of former Jamaican Prime Minister Michael Manley.

Manley, Michael (1924-97) Jamaican barrister, politician, trade union leader and writer. Son of Norman Manley. Leader of Peoples National Party (PNP) from 1969, and served as Jamaican Prime Minister 1972-80, 1989-92, when he resigned due to ill health.

Manley, Norman (1893-1969) Jamaican barrister, politician and trade union leader. Founder of the Peoples National Party (PNP) 1938. Chief Minister in Jamaica, 1955; Premier of Jamaica 1957-62.

Manley, Rachel Writer and poet. Daughter of Michael and Beverley Manley.

Mantero, Riccardo Silk printer in Milan, Italy.

Mark, Louisa b.1960 UK. Singer. Kick-started UK lovers rock phase of reggae with classic hit 'Caught You in a Lie' (1975) when she was 15 years old.

Marley, Bob (1945-81) Outstanding Jamaican reggae artist. Key figure in global popularisation of reggae and Rastafarianism after his album *Natty Dread* was released in 1975.

Marryshow, T. Albert (1885-1958) Grenadian politician and journalist. Elected to the Legislative Council (1925). Campaigned for constitutional change. Advocate of Caribbean unity and opponent of repression in the colonies.

Martin, George b.1926 UK. Musician, arranger and legendary producer of almost all of the Beatles' records. Knighted (1996).

Marvin, Hank b.1941 UK. Influential guitarist with the Shadows, a highly successful instrumental group who also acted as Cliff Richard's backing band from late 1950s.

Marx, Karl (1818-83). Immensely influential German philosopher, political economist and socialist revolutionary who, along with Frederick Engels, had a huge influence on 20th century politics in terms of class struggle. Most famous works are *Communist Manifesto* and *Das Kapital*.

Masefield, John (1876-1967) English poet and novelist.

Mason, Philip (1906-1999) UK. Director of Institute of Race Relations in 1960s.

Matisse, Henri (1869-1954) Influential French painter.

Matumbi Leading UK reggae band in the 1970s. Included Dennis Bovell on bass guitar. Huge hit 'After Tonight' was biggest selling UK reggae single of 1976.

Maxwell, Ken Comic actor and sketch writer; commentator on Jamaican affairs.

Maxwell, Neville Born in Barbados. Lawyer and legal tutor at Holborn

College of Law and Commerce in London in 1960s. Co-founder of the West Indian Legal Panel and member of the West Indian Standing Conference.

McCabe, Herbert UK. Theologian. OP, *Ordinis Praedicatorum* (of the Order of Preachers, or Dominicans).

McCartney, Paul b.1942 in Liverpool, UK. Singer, songwriter and musician. Became globally famous as part of the Beatles from early 1960s. Knighted (1997).

McKay, Claude (1890-1948) Jamaican writer, novelist and poet. Works include *Banana Bottom, Home to Harlem* and the famous sonnet 'If We Must Die' urging blacks to fight for their freedom and dignity, and quoted by Churchill in World War Two.

McNee, David b.1927. Former Commissioner of London Metropolitan Police 1977-82.

Mighty Sparrow b.1935 in Grenada as Francisco Slinger. Family migrated to Trinidad when he was 18 months old. Leading calypsonian from mid-1950s. Crowned calypso king numerous times.

Miller, Glenn (1904-44) American trombonist and band leader of 1930s and 1940s.

Milner, Roger English playwright prominent in 1960s. Best known for *Beyond A Joke*, a play based on P. G. Wodehouse and his Nazi connections.

Minshall, Jean Trinidadian writer and journalist.

Minshall, Peter b.1941. Leading Trinidadian artist and Carnival Mas designer.

Mitchell, Keith b.1946 in St Georges, Grenada. Became an MP for the New National Party in Grenada in 1984, was elected Prime Minister in 1995.

Mittelholzer, Edgar (1909-65) Pioneering Guyanese born novelist. Well known for his *Kaywana Trilogy*.

Moloney, Patricia Wrote MA dissertation entitled *The Brush is my Language* on Althea McNish (1998).

Monet, Claude (1840-1926) Renowned French impressionist painter.

Moody, Ronald (1900-84) Jamaican sculptor. Moved to London 1923 and studied dentistry at King's College. Taught himself wood carving and had first success in Paris exhibitions in 1930s, followed by success in USA and UK. Was a regular exhibitor in the London art scene of 1950s and 1960s, joined Caribbean Artists Movement in 1960s. Brother of Harold Moody, who founded the League of Coloured Peoples in London to fight racial discrimination.

Morgan, Derrick b.1940 in Stewarton, Jamaica. Pioneering figure in Jamaican recording industry. Recorded in ska and rock steady styles especially in 1960s and 1970s.

Morris, Bill b.1938 Jamaica. Came to Birmingham, UK in 1954. 1958 joined Transport and General Workers Union (TGWU). 1991-2003 served as General Secretary of TGWU. Received Order of Jamaica 2002, knighted 2003, April 2006 gained seat in the House of Lords.

Morris, Mervyn Distinguished Jamaican poet, literary critic; lecturer at

Biographical Notes

University of the West Indies Mona Campus, Jamaica. Books include *The Pond* and *Making West Indian Literature*.

Moses, Pablo b. Pablo Henry in 1953 in Jamaica. Internationally known reggae artist.

Mugabe, Robert b.1924 in Rhodesia, now Zimbabwe. 1962 co-founded and became Secretary General of Zimbabwe African Peoples Union (ZANU) political movement. Detained 1964-74. Escaped to Mozambique. Led armed struggle 1975-79. Prime Minister of Zimbabwe 1980-87, President since 1988.

Munroe, Carmen b.1932 in Guyana. One of Britain's most successful black actresses in theatre and TV. Particularly well known for part as Desmond's wife in the TV sitcom of that name. Founder member of Talawa Arts.

Murdoch, Rupert b.1931. Publisher and owner of News International plc (UK), Times Newspapers, Fox News and British Sky Broadcasting.

Musa Suso, Foday Gambian-born kora player and griot.

Naipaul, Vidiadhar Surajprasad b.1932 in Chaguanas, Trinidad. Novelist and writer whose works include *A House for Mr Biswas* and *Miguel Street*. Knighted in 1990, won Nobel Prize for Literature in 2001. Lives in UK.

Nandy, Dipak b.1936 India. Academic and former Director, Runnymede Trust.

Narayan, Rudy (1938-98) Guyanese born barrister. Worked closely with legal advice centres in London. Became prominent in fighting some of well-known cases involving black people (1970s-80s).

Newman, Kenneth b.1926 UK. Commissioner of London Metropolitan Police 1982-87.

Newton, Huey P. (1941-89) African American black power activist. Founder member of the Black Panther party.

Nkomo, Joshua (1917-99) Born in Rhodesia, now Zimbabwe. Labour organiser and nationalist leader. Founder of the Zimbabwe African Peoples Union (ZANU) together with Ndabaningi Sithole (1961). Defeated by Robert Mugabe in the post-liberation elections in Zimbabwe.

Opel, Jackie (1938-1970) Gifted Bajan singer and songwriter who spent time in Jamaica where he made a major impact singing with the Skatalites.

Orange Juice Post-punk Scottish band led by Edwyn Collins from late 1970s, best known for song 'Rip It Up' (1983).

Orton, Joe (1933-67) English playwright. Known for his highly successful plays such as *Entertaining Mr Sloane* and *Loot*.

Ouseley, Herman b.1945, Guyana. Chief Executive of the Inner London Education Authority 1988-90, Chief Executive of London Borough of Lambeth 1990-93, Chairman of Commission for Racial Equality 1993-2000. Became Baron Ouseley of Peckham Rye in 2001.

Pablo, Augustus (1954-1999) Born as Horace Swaby in St Andrew, Jamaica. Reggae artist and producer paricularly known for his distinctive use of the melodica in dub recordings..

Packer, Kerry (1937-2005) Australia media tycoon who pioneered the

279

commercialisation of test cricket.

Padmore, George (1902-59) Born as Malcom Nurse in Trinidad. One of the major figures working for global black liberation in the 20th century. Brought an independent marxist perspective to these struggles in the USA, Soviet Union, continental Europe, the UK and Africa. Key adviser to Nkrumah in the campaign for Ghanaian independence and for colonial freedom more generally.

Pamberi Steel Orchestra World-renowned steel band originating in Trinidad and Tobago in 1980, based in San Juan, Port of Spain.

Pang, Amy Leong (1908-89) Trinidadian painter, founding member of the Society of Trinidad Independents who met to discuss ideas and themes to paint in early 1930s.

Pascall, Alex b.1936 Grenada, came to London 1959. Singer, drummer community and cultural activist, journalist and broadcaster. Presented first daily black radio programme in British history, *Black Londoners* (1974-88). Awarded OBE.

Perry, Lee 'Scratch' b.1936 as Rainford Hugh Perry in Hanover, Jamaica. Songwriter, producer and reggae artist with international reputation. Seen as one of the leading innovators in Jamaican music.

Persuasions, The A cappella singing group formed in New York, USA in 1962. Had a number of hits in 1970s.

Picasso, Pablo (1881-1973) Spanish artist, dominant figure of early 20th century art and a pioneer of Cubism.

Pioneers, The Band formed in Jamaica in 1967 – one of the most successful vocal groups in Jamaican history.

Pitt, David (1913-94) Born Grenada. Medical doctor. President of the West Indian National Party in Trinidad. Practised as a doctor in Britain from 1946. Active in Labour Party politics. Former Chairman of Campaign Against Racial Discrimination. Failed to become an MP but made a life peer in 1970s.

Plato (c.427-347 BC) Immensely influential Greek philosopher. Widely regarded as a major architect of Western thought and culture.

Poitier, Sidney b.1927 of Bahamian parentage. Leading African American theatre actor and Oscar-winning film star. Well known for acting in dramas of racial conflict such as *In the Heat of the Night*, *Guess Who's Coming to Dinner* and *To Sir With Love*.

Poulantzas, Nicos (1936-79) Greek marxist political sociologist who lived and became prominent in France.

Powell, Enoch (1912-98) British Conservative politician and scholar who derailed his mainstream political career by attacking the presence of black and Asian migrants in Britain. Famous for racist 'Rivers of Blood' speech made in 1968.

Powell, Wesley Jamaican educationalist. Prime mover in adult education movement.

Prince Miller Reggae musician and entertainer.

Biographical Notes

Ramphal, Shridath b.1928, Guyana. Commonwealth lawyer, politician and diplomat. Secretary General of the Commonwealth 1975-90.

Rampton, Anthony UK; entrepreneur, founder of the Hilden Charitable Trust, trustee of Runnymede Trust. Chair of the Rampton Committee that reported in 1981 on racial inequalities in British education.

Randall, Paulette Black British theatre director of Jamaican parentage. One of the leading female theatre directors. Former Artistic Director of Talawa Theatre Company.

Redding, Otis (1941-67) African American soul singer. Died in plane crash. Although he died young he has since been recognised as one of the most influential soul singers.

Reid, Duke (1915-74) Born in Jamaica. Reggae producer – seen as one of the biggest influences on reggae music along with Sir Coxsone Dodd.

Rhone, Trevor b.1940. Jamaican playwright whose plays include *Smile Orange* which later appeared as a film (1974). Co-authored the script of the film *The Harder They Come* and wrote numerous pantomimes. Directed the Barn Theatre with Yvonne Brewster.

Richard, Cliff b.1940 in India as Harry Webb. British pop singer. Came to prominence along with his backing group The Shadows from the late 1950s. Remarkable for having chart hits in every decade since the 1950s. Knighted in 1995.

Robeson, Paul (1898-1976) World famous African American singer and actor. Supported fight against racism and backed working class and independence movements around the world in the face of direct hostility and obstruction from the US government and its agencies.

Rodney, Walter (1942-80) Guyanese born historian, intellectual and political activist. Author of the influential works *Groundings with my Brothers* and *How Europe Underdeveloped Africa*. Assassinated in Guyana.

Rohlehr, Gordon b.1942 Guyana. Studied at University of West Indies and University of Birmingham, UK in 1960s. Professor of Literature at University of the West Indies in Trinidad. Has written many essays and books on subjects including Carnival and Caribbean culture.

Rolling Stones, The Internationally famous British rock band who rose to prominence in 1960s, led by Mick Jagger. Influenced by electric blues and rock. Hugely successful and still undertaking global concert tours well into the 2000s.

Romero, Archbishop (1917-80) El Salvador. Roman Catholic prelate and Nobel Prize winner. Spoke out against political violence and repression of the poor. Murdered while preaching.

Rosso, Franco British film director and leading film editor of Italian parentage. Worked with John La Rose on *Mangrove Nine* film (1973). Produced a film, *Dread, Beat and Blood* on Linton Kwesi Johnson (1979). And directed pioneering Black Britsh film *Babylon* (1980). Has also worked with Horace Ove.

Biographical Notes

Sakamoto, Ryuichi b.1952 in Nakano, Japan. Internationally acclaimed musician, composer, producer and actor.

Salkey, Andrew (1928-95) Jamaican born novelist, children's story writer, essayist, journalist, broadcaster and academic. Lived in London (1950s-70s). Co-founder of the Caribbean Artists Movement (1966). Taught in Amherst, USA, for last 20 years of his life.

Samuels, Oliver b.1948 in St Mary, Jamaica. Renowned comedian and stage and screen actor.

Sartre, Jean Paul (1905-80) Born in Paris, France. Existentialist philosopher, dramatist, novelist, critic and political activist. Life-long companion to pioneering feminist writer Simone de Beauvoir.

Schwegler, Markus Germany. Son of sculptor Gudrun Kruger.

Scott, Dennis (1939-91) Distinguished Jamaican poet, playwright, actor and dancer. Principal of the Jamaica School of Drama. Appeared on American TV programme *The Cosby Show*.

Scott, Elizabeth UK. former management committee chair, Cryptic One Youth Club. Runnymede trustee.

Scott, Nicholas (1933-2005) UK. Former British Conservative Party government minister.

Sealy, Clinton Ran supplementary school in St Thomas Hall, Shepherd's Bush, London in 1960s, founded by the Shepherd's Bush Social and Welfare Association of which Wilfred Wood was part.

Sekka, Johnny (1934-2006) Born in Dakar, Senegal. African film and television star, first appearing in British films in 1960s before moving to USA and becoming a regular on American film and TV.

Shadows, The British instrumental popular music band active from 1958-2004. Originally formed as a backing band for Cliff Richard.

Shakespeare, Robbie b.1953 in Kingston, Jamaica. Bass player renowned for musical partnership ('Sly & Robbie') with drummer Sly Dunbar. Also runs own record label, Taxi.

Shakespeare, William (1564-1616) UK. Enduringly famous and globally respected English playwright, poet and actor.

Shange, Ntozake b.1948 as Paulette Williams in New Jersey, USA. African American playwright and poet. Author of *For Colored Girls Who Have Considered Suicide/When the Rainbow is Enuf* (1975).

Shannon, Sharon Irish accordionist, fiddler and singer from County Clare. Founded the traditional band Arcady and through the 1990s worked with some of the top names in Irish music.

Simpson, O.J. b.1947 African American football player and actor. Achieved notoriety after the fatal stabbing of his former wife and her friend in 1994 and the subsequent televised trial, at which he was controversially acquitted of the offence.

Skatalites, The Jamaican music group which popularised ska from early 1960s onwards. Best known for tunes like 'Guns of Navarone'. Split up in

Biographical Notes

1965 but a re-formed band has been playing together since 1983.

Slits, The All-female punk rock band formed in London, UK. Band played together from 1976-81, and re-formed in 2006.

Smart, Leroy Born Jamaica. Reggae vocalist who started recording in 1970s.

Smith, David (1906-65) American abstract expressionist sculptor.

Smith, Ian (1919-2007) Former Prime Minister of Rhodesia, now Zimbabwe. An open racist who was eventually forced into a transfer of power to the African majority in 1980 after a sustained armed struggle against his regime led by Robert Mugabe, Joshua Nkomo and others.

Smith, Lloyd Barbadian MP (1942-74); father of Ina Wood, the wife of Wilfred Wood.

Smith, Michael (1954-83) Leading Jamaican performance and dub poet who took Europe by storm after appearing at first International Book Fair of Radical Black and Third World Books (1982). Stoned to death in Jamaica.

Sobers, Garfield b.1936 in Barbados. Famous West Indian cricketer. Widely regarded as one of the greatest all-round players in the history of the game. Knighted in 1975.

Soledad Brothers George Jackson and two other young black men who were incarcerated in the maximum security cellblock in Soledad Prison in California, USA when charged with killing a guard in retaliation for the murder of three black activists at the prison in January 1970. George Jackson wrote two best-selling books and was killed in San Quentin Prison in 1971 in an alleged escape attempt, and was buried as a Field Commander of the Black Panther Party.

Soul To Soul Highly successful 1980s British music collective specialising in black music styles, beats and fashions. Best known for songs 'Back to Life' and 'Keep on Moving', and led by 'Jazzie B'(b.1963 as Beresford Romeo in London).

Soyinka, Wole b.1934. Nigerian poet, playwright, novelist, essayist and academic. Winner of the 1986 Nobel Prize for Literature. Long term campaigner for democracy in Nigeria.

Spence, Basil (1907-76) Scottish architect most notably associated with Coventry Cathedral.

Stacey, Tom Defeated Conservative candidate in North Hammersmith constituency of London who wrote inflammatory racist article for *Sunday Times* (1964).

Stewart-Liberty, Arthur Former chairman of Liberty's textile producers, London.

Straw, Jack b.1946. British Labour politician and Cabinet Minister from late 1990s onwards. Home Secretary responsible for setting up Stephen Lawrence public inquiry.

Strindberg, August (1849-1912) Swedish dramatist and novelist, regarded as one of Sweden's greatest modern writers.

Sufferer Hi Fi North London sound system in 1970s.

Biographical Notes

Syal, Meera b.1964. British Asian actress and novelist, best known for comedy series *Goodness Gracious Me.*

Sylvester, Roger Black British man killed while in police custody in North London in January 1999. Subject of ongoing campaign for justice.

Sylvester, Sheila Mother of Roger Sylvester.

Tebbit, Norman b.1931, UK. Former Conservative Cabinet Minister in Margaret Thatcher's government..

Telfer, Junior Trinidadian entrepreneur of 1960s and 1970s. Ran London's first lunchtime theatre venue, the Ambience in Queensway.

Tenyue Brothers Henry and Patrick – musical brothers who have played on albums by Linton Kwesi Johnson and UB40 among others.

Thatcher, Margaret b.1925 in Grantham, Lincolnshire, UK. Conservative Prime Minister of the UK from 1979-90 – the longest serving British Prime Minister of 20th century. One of the most significant British politicians in recent political history, loved and loathed in equal measure.

Thomas, Clive Guyanese economist. Director of the Institute of Development Studies at the University of Guyana. Member of the New World Group.

Thomas, Nicky (1949-1990) Jamaican born reggae recording artist who moved to Britain and became best known for his major hit 'Love of the Common People' in 1970.

Thompson, Errol 'ET' – Sound engineer working in Kingston, Jamaica in 1970s. Part of dub movement.

Thomson, Hollins (later Thomson, Tootal) Worked in conjunction with ICI and Althea McNish to design for newly-developed manmade material that could take strong colours.

Thompson Twins UK pop group of the 1980s who had a number of chart hits.

Thucydides (c.460 BC to c.400 BC) Ancient Greek historian and author of *History of Peloponnesian War.*

Tilby, Douglas Member, Society of Friends; Secretary, Community and Race Relations Unit of British Council of Churches.

Tshombe, Moise (1919-69) Congolese politician. Declared the copper-rich province of Katanga independent in 1960, triggering crisis that led to the murder of Patrice Lumumba.

Van Gogh, Vincent (1853-90) Dutch post-Impressionism painter, one of the pioneers of Expressionism.

Visconti, Tony Record producer and musician, b.1944 in Brooklyn, New York. Lived in London from 1968 for around 30 years. Famed for his production work with many well-known pop music artists including David Bowie.

Wailers, The Originally a ska, rock steady and reggae group formed in Kingston, Jamaica in 1963 comprising Junior Braithwaite, Beverley Kelso, Bunny Livingston, Bob Marley, Peter McIntosh and Cherry Smith. Name subsequently used for Bob Marley's backing band.

Waithe-Smith, Cicely Early Jamaican playwright, author of *The Creatures, Africa Sling-shot* and *Uncle Robert.*

Biographical Notes

Walcott, Derek b.1930 in St Lucia. Renowned poet, playwright and academic. Winner of the 1992 Nobel Prize for Literature.

Walker, Junior (1931-95) Saxophonist. Born Autry DeWalt in Arkansas, USA. Formed Junior Walker and the All Stars in late 1950s, had string of major and enduring hits from mid-1960s onwards with Motown record label.

Walters, Sam British theatre director and founder of Orange Tree Theatre Company. With his wife helped to establish a theatre company and drama school in Jamaica before returning to UK in 1971.

Washington, Booker T. (1856-1915) Famous African American educationalist. Author of *Up From Slavery*.

wa Thiong'o, Ngugi b.1938 as James Ngugi in Kiambi District of Kenya. 1964 first novel *Weep Not, Child* published. 1977-78 detained for his political beliefs in Kenya's maximum security Kamiti Prison. 1982 left Kenya for self-imposed exile in London. 1992 moved to the USA. Currently Distinguished Professor of English and Comparative Literature at the University of California.

Weiss, John Architect, silversmith, historian and former lecturer. Author of *Free Black American Settlers in Trinidad 1815-16*. Husband of Althea McNish.

Wet Wet Wet Scottish pop group formed in 1987, best known for spending 15 weeks at number one in the UK charts in 1994 with song 'Love is All Around', featured in hit film *Four Weddings and a Funeral*.

Wheeler, Caron Jamaican connected London-born singer who started with reggae band Brown Sugar before moving into soul and R'n'B. Had smash hit with Soul II Soul song 'Back to Life' in late 1980s.

White, Sarah b.1941 UK. Scientific historian, publisher, cultural activist. Co-founder of New Beacon Books and trustee of the George Padmore Institute. Business and personal partner of John La Rose for over 40 years.

White, Willard b.1946 in Jamaica. One of the world's greatest bass opera singers who made his debut with the New York Opera in 1974.

Whylie, Dwight (1936-2002). Jamaican-born broadcaster. First black radio announcer in the BBC's domestic service in 1961, and once head of Jamaica Broadcasting Corporation.

Whylie, Marjorie Highly respected Jamaican musicologist, musician and teacher.

Wilde, Oscar (1854-1900) Irish playwright, poet, essayist and novelist, renowned for his wit.

Williams, Aubrey (1926-90) Guyanese painter who lived in London from 1954. Studied at St Martin's College of Art. Founder member of the Caribbean Artists Movement. Key figure in British postwar painting, drawing visual influences and cultural perspectives from diverse sources such as ornithology, classical music and pre-Columbian iconology among others.

Williams, Eric (1911-81) Founder and political leader of Peoples National Movement in Trinidad and Tobago. First Chief Minister (1956); first Prime

Biographical Notes

Minister of independent Trinidad (1962 until his death). Outstanding historian and author of *Capitalism and Slavery*.

Wilson, August (1945-2005) African American playwright. Twice awarded the Pulitzer Prize. Wrote a cycle of plays chronicling the lives of African Americans in the 20th century, in which each play focuses on a different decade.

Wilson, Harold (1916-95) Former British Labour Prime Minister 1964-70, 1974-76. Amongst other things, introduced the 1968 Race Relations Act, the Race Relations Board and the Community Relations Commission.

Wonder, Stevie b.1950. Renowned African-American singer, composer, musician and producer.

Woods, Tiger b.1976. Part African American, leading golfer in the world from late 1990s onwards.

Worrell, Frank (1924-1967). Barbadian born legendary West Indies test cricketer. Known as one of the famous Three Ws, along with his team mates Clyde Walcott and Everton Weekes. First black captain of West Indies cricket team. Knighted in 1964.

Worsley, Peter b.1924 in Merseyside, UK. Eminent sociologist and anthropologist and defender of minority rights.

Wynter-Carew, Sylvia b.1928. Jamaican Professor of Literature and playwright, scripted films such as *The Big Pride* (1961) shown on UK television.

X, Malcolm (1925-65) Leading African American black nationalist leader of the 1960s. His ideas have remained influential since his assassination.

Yeomans, Keith Executive producer of *Black Londoners* and formerly Head of Educational Programmes for BBC Radio London.

Index

Index

Index

Index

Index